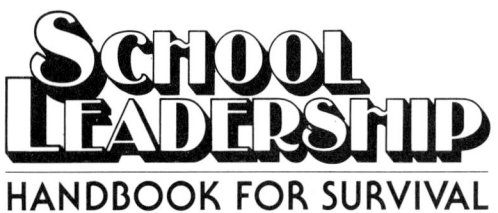

SCHOOL LEADERSHIP
HANDBOOK FOR SURVIVAL

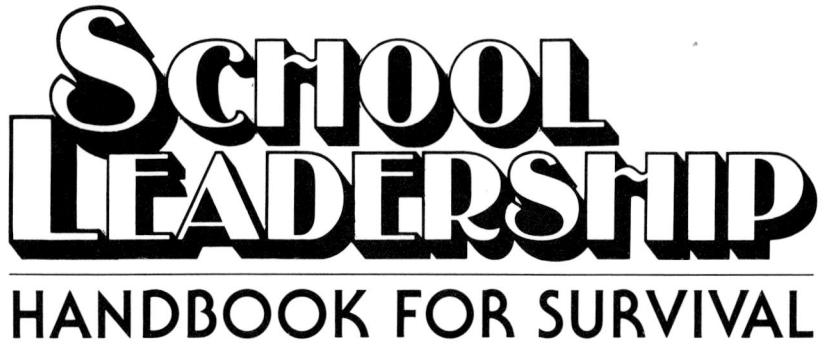

SCHOOL LEADERSHIP
HANDBOOK FOR SURVIVAL

Edited by
STUART C. SMITH
JO ANN MAZZARELLA
PHILIP K. PIELE

Clearinghouse on Educational Management
University of Oregon
Eugene, Oregon 1981

International Standard Book Number: 0-86552-078-X
Library of Congress Catalog Card Number: 81-82931

Printed in the United States of America
ERIC Clearinghouse on Educational Management
University of Oregon, Eugene, Oregon 97403

Second Printing, January 1983
Third Printing, February 1985

This publication was prepared with funding from the National Institute of Education, U.S. Department of Education under contract no. 400-78-0007. The opinions expressed in this report do not necessarily reflect the positions or policies of NIE or the Department of Education.

ABOUT ERIC

The Educational Resources Information Center (ERIC) is a national information system operated by the National Institute of Education. ERIC serves the educational community by disseminating educational research results and other resource information that can be used in developing more effective educational programs.

The ERIC Clearinghouse on Educational Management, one of several clearinghouses in the system, was established at the University of Oregon in 1966. The Clearinghouse and its companion units process research reports and journal articles for announcement in ERIC's index and abstract bulletins.

Research reports are announced in *Resources in Education (RIE),* available in many libraries and by subscription for $42.70 a year from the United States Government Printing Office, Washington, D.C. 20402. Most of the documents listed in *RIE* can be purchased through the ERIC Document Reproduction Service, operated by Computer Microfilm International Corporation.

Journal articles are announced in *Current Index to Journals in Education*. *CIJE* is also available in many libraries and can be ordered for $90 a year from Oryx Press, 2214 North Central at Encanto, Phoenix, Arizona 85004. Semiannual cumulations can be ordered separately.

Besides processing documents and journal articles, the Clearinghouse has another major function—information analysis and synthesis. The Clearinghouse prepares bibliographies, literature reviews, state-of-the-knowledge papers, and other interpretive research studies on topics in its educational area.

CONTENTS

PREFACE — xiii

FOREWORD — xvii

INTRODUCTION — 1
    Powerlessness and Frustration — 2
    What Is Leadership? — 4
    Leading to What? — 6
    Leadership and Effective Schools — 7
    How This Book Was Written — 9
    Overview — 10

PART 1 — THE PERSON — 13
    Introduction to Part 1 — 15

CHAPTER 1 — PORTRAIT OF A LEADER — 17

Nature and Nurture — 19
IQ — 20 . . . Birth Order — 21 . . . Childrearing Variables — 22 . . . Socioeconomic Variables — 23 . . . Implications for Administrator Selection — 24

Person to Person — 24
Social Participation — 25 . . . Communication — 27 . . . Listening — 27 . . . Implications for Selection, Evaluation, and Training — 28

Character Qualities — 29
Goals — 30 . . . Security — 31 . . . Proactivity — 32 . . . Implications for Selection, Evaluation, and Training — 33

Conclusion — 35

CHAPTER 2 — TWO SPECIAL CASES: WOMEN AND BLACKS — 37

Introduction — 37
Quality Education and Effective Leadership — 37 . . . To Leaders and Aspiring Leaders — 39 . . . What about Other Racial Minorities? — 39

The Woman Administrator — 40
Where Is She? — 40 . . . A Woman's Place — 42

Can a Woman Succeed? — 44
The Obstacle of Negative Attitudes — 46 . . . Some Practical Problems — 47

The Black Administrator: Still Segregated — 48
Disappearance of the Black Leader — 49 . . . Persistent Discrimination — 51

A Program for Change — 53

Conclusion — 56

CHAPTER 3 — LEADERSHIP STYLES   58

Introduction — 58
History of Style Theory — 59 . . . Practical Applications — 59

What Is It? — 60
Components of Style — 60 . . . People or Work — 63

The Ideal Style — 64
Risk Taking — 65 . . . What Is the Situation? — 66 . . . Situation and Personality — 69

Can You Change Your Style? — 70
Identifying Your Style — 70 . . . Style Flex — 71 . . . Synthesizing the Theories — 74

So What? — 75
Becoming a Better Leader — 78 . . . Training Programs — 82 . . . Leader Selection — 85

Conclusion — 85

PART 2 — THE STRUCTURE   89

Introduction to Part 2 — 91

CHAPTER 4 — SCHOOL-BASED MANAGEMENT   94

The Rationale — 95
Autonomy and Control through History — 95 . . . The Deficiencies of Centralization — 97 . . . The Efficiency of Decentralization — 98

Examples of Implementation to Date — 99
Florida — 100 . . . California — 107 . . . Lansing, Michigan — 111 . . . Edmonton, Alberta — 113 . . . Cherry Creek School District, Colorado — 114

The Transfer of Authority — 116
The School Board — 116 . . . The Central Office: Facilitator — 117 . . . The Principal: School Leader — 119

Three Critical Control Areas — 121
Curriculum — 122 . . . Personnel — 122 . . . Budget — 123

Shared Decision-Making — 124
Staff Involvement — 125 . . . Community Involvement — 126

Conclusion — 128

CHAPTER 5 — TEAM MANAGEMENT   130

Organizational Considerations — 132
Power and Trust — 133 . . . The Board-Administrator Agreement — 134 . . . Membership and Organization — 136 . . . Decision-Making — 138

Examples of Successful Teams — 139
Yakima, Washington — 140 . . . Rio Linda, California — 142 . . . Attleboro, Massachusetts — 145

Conclusion — 148

CHAPTER 6 — PARTICIPATIVE DECISION-MAKING   150

Advantages of Participation — 153
Quality of Decisions — 154 . . . Organizational Effectiveness — 155 . . . Teacher Satisfaction — 156

Guidelines for Implementation — 159
Varying Decision-Making Style — 159 . . . Who Should Be Involved — 161 . . . Extent of Involvement — 162 . . . Areas of Involvement — 162 . . . Forms of Involvement — 163 . . . Moving to PDM — 163

Approaches to Involvement — 165

Conclusion — 167

CHAPTER 7 — SCHOOL CLIMATE   169

Measuring School Climate — 171

The Importance of School Climate — 175

Improving School Climate — 178
The Stability of Climate — 179 . . . The Process of Change — 180 . . . Practical Suggestions — 183

Conclusion — 186

PART 3 — THE SKILLS   189

Introduction to Part 3 — 191

SCHOOL LEADERSHIP: HANDBOOK FOR SURVIVAL

CHAPTER 8 — COMMUNICATING 194

Learning to Communicate — 194
How the Process Works — 195 . . . Communication Skills — 196 . . . Exercises for Improvement — 200 . . . The Principal's Responsibility — 202 . . . Communicating in Small Groups — 203

Reaching the Public — 205
Public Relations Strategies — 206 . . . Parents — 207 . . . Key Communicators — 208 . . . Citizen Groups — 209 . . . The Media — 211 . . . Surveys — 213 . . . A Time-Saving Suggestion — 213

Conclusion — 214

CHAPTER 9 — LEADING MEETINGS 215

Choosing a Leadership Pattern — 216

Goals and Values of Meetings — 219
Meetings with Purpose — 219 . . . Is a Meeting Necessary? — 223 . . . Hidden Values of Meetings — 224

Basics of Meeting Planning — 224
The Agenda and Time Considerations — 225 . . . Who Shall Attend? — 229 . . . Seating Arrangements — 231 . . . The Meeting Room — 232

The Art of Leading the Meeting — 233
The What and How of Meeting Management — 234 . . . Task Functions — 235 . . . Maintenance Functions — 237 . . . You as a Participant — 239 . . . Utilizing Minutes — 240 . . . The Interaction Method — 242

Tools for Evaluating and Improving Meetings — 243

Conclusion — 245

CHAPTER 10 — MANAGING TIME AND STRESS 247

Blocks to Time/Stress Management — 248

Boosts to Time/Stress Management — 249
Self-Control — 250 . . . Job-Control — 250

Time Management Strategies — 251
Goal-Setting and Prioritizing — 252 . . . The Daily Time Log — 253 . . . Managing Time Wasters — 255

Stress Management — 263
Daily Stress Log — 266 . . . Managing Controllable Stressors — 269 . . . Managing Uncontrollable Stressors — 272

Conclusion — 273

CHAPTER 11 — MANAGING CONFLICT   275

The Value of Conflict — 275

Understanding Conflict — 276
Types of Conflict — 277 . . . Sources of Conflict — 279 . . . Stages of Conflict — 281

Techniques for Managing Conflict — 282
Avoiding Conflict — 284 . . . Superordinate Goals — 286 . . . Creative Problem-Solving — 286 . . . Compromise and Use of a Third Party — 288 . . . Authoritative Command — 288 . . . Altering Organizational Structure — 289 . . . Preparing for Conflict Management — 291 . . . Some Final Advice — 292

Conclusion — 292

CHAPTER 12 — SOLVING PROBLEMS   294

Understanding a Situation: Force-Field Analysis — 296

Finding Solutions: The Nominal Group Technique — 299
An Alternative to Brainstorming — 301 . . . The Nominal Group as an Intervention Technique — 303 . . . Planning New Programs — 303

Achieving Consensus: The Delphi Technique — 305
History and Assumptions of Delphi — 306 . . . The New Forms of Delphi — 307 . . . Sample Applications — 308 . . . Using the Delphi — 313 . . . The Consensus Phenomenon — 315 . . . A Comparison of Nominal Group and Delphi — 316

Conclusion — 317

BIBLIOGRAPHY   319

INTERVIEWS   342

PREFACE

School leadership has long been a priority topic for publications of the ERIC Clearinghouse on Educational Management. Our interest in leadership has been born out of a dual motivation. Convinced by overwhelming research evidence proving that good leadership—especially at the school site—does improve the quality of schooling, we have prepared numerous publications with the purpose of helping administrators be more effective leaders of their schools.

Reinforcing this purpose is the Clearinghouse's mandate, as part of a federally funded information center, to respond to the expressed needs of its clientele. With a frequency that has increased dramatically in recent years, individual principals, superintendents, other administrators, and officials of the major national and regional associations representing them have communicated to us their need for practical materials on leadership effectiveness.

This book was conceived when we took stock of the variety of our publications aimed at school leaders and decided the materials would better fulfill our purposes if compiled into a single volume. Titles out of print would be brought up to date. As the book's contents were outlined, it also became clear that a lot of new materials would have to be written. This resulting handbook is offered as a practical resource for school leaders as they confront the unique problems of schools in the eighties.

One regret we have in publishing this volume is that we could not include thirty or forty chapters instead of twelve. Leadership's many dimensions and requirements extend well beyond the outline of topics presented in these pages. Rather than write generally about many topics, however, we decided to deal expansively with a few. Our intent has been to expound each topic with sufficient detail to suggest specific directions for school practitioners. Space limitations forced us to exclude a substantial amount of materials earlier prepared by the Clearinghouse on topics related to management of resources (personnel, pupils, facilities), community relations, and instructional leadership. These materials have been reserved for possible compilation into subsequent volumes.

Work on the book actually began in 1974. That was the year the Clearinghouse teamed with the National Association of Elementary School Principals to launch a series of publications called the School Leadership Digest. As the Digest's foreword explained, the purpose of the series was to provide "school administrators with concise, readable analyses of the most important trends in schools today," as well as point up "the practical implications of major research findings."

Only two of the twenty-five issues of the School Leadership Digest have made their way, following substantial revision, into this book. The series' contribution to this volume is significant nonetheless, consisting not so much in content as in methodology. The School Leadership Digest summarized educational literature—especially *research* literature—so that its readers, chiefly school principals, might better grasp and apply knowledge useful for the operation of the schools. Research findings were surveyed, synthesized, and interpreted with a view to pointing out their relevance for educational practice.

Over the years the Clearinghouse has continued to apply and refine this method of information analysis. Although the School Leadership Digest ceased in 1976, the format was reborn the following year in the School Management Digest, this time with the Association of California School Administrators as the Clearinghouse's partner. Of the twenty-one issues in this more recent series, four are reprinted here, having undergone varying degrees of revision.

Of the other six chapters, half are entirely original and the other half substantially so. The Clearinghouse has written extensively about school leadership in yet another publication format—the Research Action Brief series. Portions of five issues of this series—originally distributed by the National Association of Secondary School Principals and the American Association of School Administrators—have been incorporated into three different chapters.

The chapters' authors are research analysts and writers with a special interest in education who were commissioned by the Clearinghouse. When an older piece was updated by another author, both authors' names appear. Appreciation is due all the authors for their skill in organizing and bringing clarity to the volumes of information that attended their topics.

We owe special gratitude to Thomas Sergiovanni for his insightful and prompt critique of each chapter. Seldom does a reviewer read so thoroughly or respond so helpfully. Because of Professor Sergiovanni's contribution, the concept of leadership expressed in these pages is broader and better articulated than it would have been otherwise.

We also thank Linda Wisner for the book's attractive design, Mary Russell for her tireless supervision of production, Susan Davie for her painstaking proofreading, and Ellen Rice for her unequalled expertise in mechanical editing and in preparing the bibliography.

FOREWORD

In recent years the educational community has adopted a public policy orientation. More and more, we have looked to state and federal levels for answers to our school problems. This has resulted in a shift away from giving attention to local schools and local school leadership. Forays into management science, accountability systems, teacher-proof curricula, competency testing, and other technologies in search of easy answers have further distracted us from attention on local school leadership. But the dust is settling and once again attention is being focused on the principalship and the local school site.

This book, *School Leadership: Handbook for Survival,* is thus timely as well as effective. It is clear that no single person is more key to school effectiveness than the principal and that the deciding factor in determining this effectiveness is the leadership he or she brings to the school. The survival metaphor included in the book title suggests that the going is tough and indeed that the principalship is under attack. Despite the relative accuracy of this portrayal, a welcome feature of this book is that it interprets survival more broadly. The struggle for existence must continue at *two* levels — competency and excellence. It is obvious that school excellence is beyond the reach of the incompetent principal or school. But the quality stakes for American education are too high to assume that routine competence is in itself all that is needed for school survival. *Competence and more* is the slogan needed in the decade ahead. The survival stakes have been elevated to new heights in this book, and this characteristic itself is worth celebrating.

Embedded in the book's chapters is a comprehensive framework for quality leadership that I will conveniently summarize as five P's: Prerequisites, Purpose, Passion, People, and Principle.

Prerequisites refers to the management and information skills so necessary in developing a competent and effective school. Lest we deceive ourselves, management basics and knowledge of technical skills provide the critical base upon which to build excellence. Routine leadership competence is, therefore, a prerequisite to school excellence.

Leadership without *purpose* is a contradiction. Effective leaders have a keen sense of what they hope to accomplish and are able to communicate this sense in a meaningful way to others with whom they work. Although I would not want to choose between the two, what the leader stands for and believes in is more important than what the leader actually does or how he or she behaves with respect to leadership style.

Passion refers to the strength of leader beliefs and the ability to stir the loyalty and commitment of others to these beliefs. Knowing what is important and being personally committed is not enough. These ideas and ideals need to be shared and convincingly accepted by others. Highly effective work groups, for example, are characterized by loyalty and commitment of members to each other, to a common purpose, and to the organization of which they are a part. It is important to remember that leadership has an emotional quality to it, and human responses to leadership share this characteristic.

Of course, others too must have a stake in what is going on; indeed, a close correspondence exists between the quality of their feelings and this stake. Sensitivity to *people* — to their needs, preferences, beliefs, and ways of doing things — competes favorably with the other P's for top billing. Principals are dependent upon the cooperation and good will of others to get things done. Obtaining this cooperation and good will is an art cultivated by attention to motivation theory, shared decision-making, group process techniques, school climate concepts, leadership styles, and other topics included in this book.

Important to quality leadership are the *principles* that form the basis for the principal's leadership. The leader's sense of well-being, self-esteem, integrity, and conviction are key here. Effective leaders are known quantities to followers. No mysteries exist with regard to what they stand for and believe in. Members know and understand what the leader is about and the principles upon which he or she stands. They consider the leader as a highly principled person in such dimensions as integrity, honesty, fairness, sensitivity, and forthrightness. They are confident, as well, that the leader is primarily motivated by the welfare of the work group and of the school and not by self-interests or self-aggrandizement.

The leadership prerequisites are mastered by training. The other four P's are informed by training but are developed by growth in maturity, perspective, and experience. All five are accessible in this book, for it indeed has its training components; but more importantly this is a book to live with, to read and reread, and to grow with. The array of offerings in the book is varied, and the range of topics is large. But I liken the book's contents and arrangements more to Hemingway's moveable feast than I do to a smorgasbord. Unlike many edited books, things hang together; a certain coherence limits the book's contents into a sensible whole, and more importantly, the feast is uplifting. Demonstrating that the principalship is important and that skills can be learned is only part of the book's story. Capturing some of the more qualitative aspects of leadership is the other part.

I have had the rare opportunity of reading sections of the book as they were being developed and was even invited to comment on the material from time to time. With this special advantage, I can state with confidence that this forward-looking book measures up to the standards of quality and usefulness professionals have a right to expect.

Thomas J. Sergiovanni
Professor and Chairperson
Department of Administration,
Higher, and Continuing Education
College of Education
University of Illinois at
Urbana-Champaign

INTRODUCTION
LEADERSHIP FOR SURVIVAL

> Administrators today are engaged in mortal combat. They are worried about survival — this volume does not appear to address that issue.
>> An Assistant Superintendent interviewed during the early stages of this volume.

Survival. A catchword that is quickly becoming a meaningless, or rather, too meaningful cliché. Everybody talks about it, many are attempting to do something about it, but everybody means something different by it and is doing something different to survive.

Survival for school administrators does not mean enduring without a food supply, nor does it mean fending off physical attack. Rather, for school administrators, the fight for survival is fought on two levels. On one level, administrators are simply concerned with a fight to keep their jobs. As enrollment declines, so do jobs for educators; as schools are closed, the number of principalships declines. In 1979, E. Mark Hanson wrote in his textbook for school administrators, "As many school superintendents would admit, the toughest part of this job is keeping it." This quote becomes more and more true every day. One hears a lot these days about "top heavy" organizations. Many administrators are being classified as superfluous, especially at the central office level. Who will be the next to go?

On another level, administrators fight for survival of their peace of mind. As some administrators fight tooth and claw for their positions, others, whose positions were secure, are quietly turning in their resignations. They are "burned-out." They can't take it any more. Managing schools is no longer worth the trouble.

What does the fight for survival have to do with this book? In a sense, the assistant superintendent quoted above was right — there are no chapters here on keeping your job or keeping your sanity. So why talk about survival? Because the purpose of this book is to help school administrators be the

1

best leaders they possibly can be. Because excellent leaders lose their jobs and their sanity a lot less often than poor ones do. Because leadership means both influence and ability to get things done, and both are necessary to survive in schools today. And finally, because an understanding of the ideas and methods and skills presented here is absolutely essential for those who are going to succeed in school management in the eighties.

POWERLESSNESS AND FRUSTRATION

In 1978, Richard Gorton and Kenneth McIntyre, under the auspices of the National Association of Secondary School Principals, surveyed a carefully selected national sample of sixty effective principals. The authors found that a majority of the respondents, some of the nation's most outstanding principals, did not intend to remain in the principalship. They did not want to be principals any more.

One reason for such attitudes may be that administrators are feeling powerless. These feelings were expressed by one principal interviewed in a study by Arthur Blumberg and William Greenfield — a principal who had been identified as an unusually effective leader.

> I think a good deal of my discontent is over loss of power. I mean a loss of power in the sense that I don't have anywhere to fight. The population's changing, the neighborhood's changing, and the school system's changing and I have no control over any of it. What I have to do now is try and eke out enough supplies for the kids. That's not very exciting.

There are good reasons for the feeling of loss of power. Donald Myers has noted that reasons for school administrators' loss of power may be

- increased power of citizens
- control of the school by the local school board
- increased independence of teachers
- increased power of students
- growth of teacher organizations and collective bargaining

He might well have added declining resources and the loss of confidence and negative public image the schools are now suffering.

The realization that power has been lost is not a lament for the good old days when "administrators were administrators" and were obeyed unquestioningly. The changes Myers listed have been, on the whole, very good for schools. Yet a loss of formal power can be traumatic no matter how good the reason, especially if there is nothing to take its place. When power is replaced only by feelings of powerlessness, then frustration and "burn out" begin.

Coupled with this loss of power, paradoxically enough, is an increase in responsibility. Roland Barth has aptly described this situation as it relates specifically to his perspective — that of the principal.

> The principal is ultimately responsible for almost everything that happens in school and out. We are responsible for personnel — making sure that employees are physically present and working to the best of their ability. We are in charge of program — making sure that teachers are teaching what they are supposed to and that children are learning it. We are accountable to parents — making sure that each is given an opportunity to express problems and that those problems are addressed and resolved. We are expected to protect the physical safety of children — making sure that the several hundred lively organisms who leave each morning return, equally lively, in the afternoon.
>
> Over the years principals have assumed one small additional responsibility after another — responsibility for the safe passage of children from home to school, responsibility for making sure the sidewalks are plowed of snow in winter, responsibility for health education, sex education, moral education, responsibility for teaching children to evacuate school buses and to ride their bikes safely. We have taken on lunch programs, then breakfast programs; responsibility for the physical condition of the furnace, the wiring, the playground equipment. We are now accountable for children's achievement of minimum standards at each grade level, for the growth of children with special needs, of the gifted, and of those who are neither. The principal has become a provider of social services,

food services, health care, recreation programs, and transportation — with a solid skills education worked in somehow.

Blumberg and Greenfield believe the situation is similar for superintendents. As evidence they point to the 1977 Suburban Superintendents Conference (organized by the American Association of School Administrators), where a featured highlight was an all-day program entitled "Learning to Deal with Stress: How to Cope."

Along with loss of power and increased responsibility, school administrators today are suffering from a sense of isolation. Blumberg and Greenfield, from interview data and observations of principals at work, determined that "their position is one of relative isolation, particularly with regard to work relationships with other principals." They note that

> For some, the singular fact of being isolated from meaningful work relations with peers may create an emotional drain for which they must somehow compensate. This lack of integrated work relationships among principals may additionally result in their being deprived of personal and professional stimulation and learning experiences, which may be important both to their own private sense of themselves and to the enthusiasm and skill with which they perform their jobs.

A return to an era (if indeed it ever existed) when the job was simple, when school administrators ruled with an iron hand, and when principals felt more connected with their staffs and communities is of course impossible, even if desired. But neither should school leaders resign themselves to feelings of powerlessness and overwork and isolation as all that remain. Administrators in many places are finding that good leaders do not have to be isolated, that they can reach out and get some help from colleagues and staff, and that something new can replace formal power — something called "influence." And influence is what leadership — and this book — are all about.

WHAT IS LEADERSHIP?

Probably more has been written and less is known

about leadership than any other topic in the behavioral sciences.
   Warren Bennis

Literally hundreds of definitions of leadership have been offered. Some emphasize change or moving forward (implicit in the verb "to lead"), such as James Lipham's definition of leadership as "that behavior of an individual which initiates a new structure in interaction within a social system."

Other definitions see the leader as a facilitator or helper, such as this from Charles Bird: "Ideally, leadership is a form of mutual cooperation through which the superior skill of a person enables the led to attain ends or to satisfy motives." Other definitions differentiate between management and leadership as Carl Welte does. Welte defined management as the "mental and physical effort to coordinate diverse activities to achieve desired results" and included in this process "planning, organizing, staffing, directing, and controlling." In contrast, he saw leadership as "natural and learned ability, skill, and personal characteristics to conduct interpersonal relations which influence people to take desired actions."

This emphasis on personal relations occurs in many definitions of leadership. Fred Fiedler, Martin Chemers, and Linda Mahar have noted that leadership includes "the ability to counsel, manage conflict, inspire loyalty, and imbue subordinates with a desire to remain on the job."

One of the best definitions of leadership was suggested by George Terry, who called it "the activity of influencing people to strive willingly for group goals." This is the definition of leadership on which this book is based. The goal of the book is to suggest the knowledge, structure, and skills necessary to increase administrator influence.

Another, simpler and yet somehow more elegant way of putting the same definition was offered by Scott Thomson, executive director of the National Association of Secondary School Principals: "Leadership is best defined as 'getting the job done through people.' " This definition means that two things are necessary for effective leadership: accomplishment (getting the job done) and influencing others (through people). These two are intertwined. An ability to get things done makes leaders more influential.

A study by James Balderson revealed that teachers were influenced most by principals who had "expert power," a term that simply means competence. These teachers were not influenced by the principal's power to punish, by his or her status or position, or even by the power to reward. They were influenced by their perception that the principal was an expert, was competent, could get the job done. The goal of this book is to give school administrators more "expert power" by helping them become more competent at what they do.

LEADING TO WHAT?

At this point we must ask some important questions: Influence for what? Leadership to what? Survival for what? As terrifying as loss of job or sanity may be, there are other more important motivators of school administrators. Those who are concerned only about the monthly paycheck or even personal job satisfaction are not true educational leaders because they have lost sight of the true goals of education. Thomas Sergiovanni reminds us of this when he says, "Leadership skills are important, but they cannot bring genuine leadership if the leader does not have a sense of purpose and direction." Of course, those who want only money or a "fun job" do not become educational leaders. Those who do become educational leaders care about something else — educational excellence, which is the "purpose and direction" of which Sergiovanni speaks.

Yet there is a great deal of disagreement about what "educational excellence" is. The goals of education have been debated since ancient times and will continue to be debated by every generation to come. It is not the purpose of this book to address what those goals ought to be; rather, we are here concerned with leadership as one of the key means to achieve them. Lest we become ensnared by utilitarianism, however, we do well to heed Sergiovanni's warning that such goals must not be forgotten. Those who lead must not lose sight of where they are going.

Speaking in more general terms, James MacGregor Burns has been led by his extensive study of leadership to express similar concerns.

Above all, the absorption with short-run, specifiable goals may dilute attention to the likely final outcome of a long and complex process of leadership-followership interaction. Attention may continue to center in the predictable, visible matters of technique and process and personality rather than in the prospects and nature of fundamental, substantive alterations in people's lives and welfare and opportunities — of "real change." Political leadership, however, can be defined only in terms of, and to the extent of the realization of, purposeful, substantive change in the conditions of people's lives.

LEADERSHIP AND EFFECTIVE SCHOOLS

Another way to express the goal of educational leadership is "effective schools." Like educational excellence, this term can be defined in many ways; but no matter how it is defined, research has revealed that good leadership is important to achieve it. In response to those who see principals and superintendents as mere functionaries or facilitators has come research to show that school leaders have great effects on schools, that it very much matters what school leaders do, who they are, and how they operate.

Gilbert Austin, after reviewing studies of school effectiveness in New York, Pennsylvania, Delaware, and Maryland, summarized the factors that distinguish effective schools from others. The first four factors in his list reveal the importance of the role of principal.

- Strong principal leadership (for example, schools "being run" for a purpose rather than "running" from force of habit);
- Strong principal participation in the classroom instructional program and in actual teaching;
- Higher expectations on the part of the principal for student and teacher performance advancement;
- Principals felt that they had more control over the functioning of the school, the curriculum and program, and their staff.

This evidence suggests that principals can and do have

influence over what happens in schools and that this influence has real and measurable effects. Again, we point out that this kind of influence is precisely what we mean by leadership in this book.

James Lipham and John Daresh reviewed a number of studies done on individually guided elementary (IGE) schools and discovered principles that can be extended not only to other innovative schools but to all types of schools. One study found that "instrumental, supportive, and participative leadership" on the part of the principal was related to an effective instructional program. Another found that the leadership behavior of the principal (in particular "work facilitation, support interaction facilitation, and goal emphasis") increased job satisfaction in the school. Clearly, the principal's behavior does make a difference.

Ronald Edmonds too reviewed studies done on effective schools and found leadership to be a key factor. In his summary of the "indispensable characteristics" of effective schools, he listed as first "strong administrative leadership without which the disparate elements of good schooling can be neither brought together nor kept together." He saw leadership as not only important, but the most important factor in school effectiveness.

This emphasis on the importance of the role of the school administrator is not new. In 1971, Keith Goldhammer and his colleagues looked at the differences between outstanding schools (called "beacons of brilliance") and extremely poor schools (called "potholes of pestilence").

> In the "beacons of brilliance," the principals are charismatic leaders; they seem to instill enthusiasm in their teachers. The teaching staffs seem to be working as teams because their morale was high, their services extend beyond normal expectations. Teachers and principals, along with parents, constantly appraise the effectiveness of the schools in an attempt to devise new programs and strategies to overcome deficiencies. Programs of study are adaptable and emphasis in the instructional program is placed on children's needs. Principals are confident they can provide relevant, purposive learning without having to lean on traditional crutches.

The "potholes of pestilence" were just the opposite, and

these authors maintain, the result of weak leadership and official neglect.

Perhaps this report from the 1972 Senate Select Committee on Equal Educational Opportunity says it best:

> In many ways the school principal is the most important and influential individual in any school. He is the person responsible for all of the activities that occur in and around the school building. It is his leadership that sets the tone of the school, the climate for learning, the level of professionalism and morale of teachers and the degree of concern for what students may or may not become. He is the main link between the school and the community and the way he performs in that capacity largely determines the attitudes of students and parents about the school. If a school is a vibrant, innovative, child-centered place; if it has a reputation for excellence in teaching; if students are performing to the best of their ability one can almost always point to the principal's leadership as the key to success.

HOW THIS BOOK WAS WRITTEN

The purpose of this book is not to present new views or the authors' views of leadership. The authors of these chapters have attempted instead to summarize and explain a large body of literature with which educational leaders want and need to be familiar. Although readers are encouraged to refer to the original sources cited in the bibliographies, a perusal of them makes it apparent that no busy administrator or student has time to read all these books and articles. Nevertheless, the sources are important and contain many ideas useful to administrators. To make these important works easily accessible, we have tried to present the best ideas briefly and succinctly. This technique of distilling the most useful and important ideas is called "information analysis."

The authors of this book are more than mere "translators" of information and ideas. As well as analyzing information, they also attempt to synthesize information, to show how theories and ideas are connected, to resolve conflicting views.

Perhaps the most important kind of information synthesis in this book is the integration of theory and practice. Many books have been written on leadership theories and almost as many concern the "how to" of leadership practice. Practitioners complain that the theoretical writing is not useful in their everyday work, and researchers and theoreticians look askance at "practical" works whose ideas and suggestions are not empirically validated. Practitioners perceive that researchers and theoreticians are too isolated from the real problems of schools, that theories validated in laboratory settings may disintegrate in actual classrooms. Researchers and theoreticians argue that recommendations that are validated by only the experience of one administrator or one school are much too subjective to be useful to others.

Few books try to integrate these two conflicting views. This book tries to present the most useful aspects of theory along with the most thoughtful recommendations for action. It is felt that a synthesis of the two, especially in areas where findings agree, can avoid many of the problems inherent in each single approach.

As well as presenting theories gleaned from educational literature and suggesting practices that might be derived from these theories, the book also contains ideas from practitioners in the field. These ideas are taken not only from written works but, in many chapters, from interviews with administrators who are struggling with actual problems in schools.

OVERVIEW

This book has many authors. Many of the chapters were written specifically at the request of leading organizations of educational administrators who wanted to supply their members with information overviews on the topics school administrators are most concerned about. In this volume, we have combined those publications (both previously published and unpublished) that are most helpful to administrators who want to be more effective leaders in their schools.

The volume looks at leadership from three perspectives: the person, the structure, and the skills. Chapters focusing on the person who holds a leadership position provide something of a theoretical background. These chapters answer the questions, Who is today's educational leader? What makes an effective leader different from a less effective leader? What are the particular problems faced by women and minority educational leaders or would-be leaders? What is a leadership style and what is the best one to use?

The part of the volume focusing on the structure takes a look at the systems or support structures that underlie school leadership. It examines the balance of authority between the central office and the school site, the team approach to management, the context for making wise decisions, and the components of school climate. These chapters concern structures and management systems that can make good educational leadership possible — or impossible.

The chapters on leadership skills highlight the abilities needed by administrators to be effective leaders in education today. This part of the volume looks at such knotty problems as how to communicate in today's more open, power-sharing organization, how to lead meetings more efficiently and effectively, how to manage time and avoid an overdose of stress, how to manage conflict, and how to attack and solve problems.

This book is called a handbook because it is designed to be used as a reference when particular problems and concerns arise as well as to be read straight through. Those concerned about communication or decision-making or the effects of leadership styles can turn immediately to the appropriate chapters for the information they are seeking without reading the previous chapters. It is a book to be sampled, to be digested slowly, and to be turned to again and again as leaders grow in their leadership skills and effectiveness. It is hoped that those charged with leading the nation's schools and those who aspire to this role will find the handbook useful as a source of encouragement and practical counsel.

PART 1
THE PERSON

PART 1: THE PERSON
INTRODUCTION

This part of the book deals with the people who are leaders in the schools, their identity, their characteristics, and their personal styles of leadership. More theoretical than the rest of the book, this part helps put the other chapters into perspective.

The first chapter looks at research findings concerning the characteristics of leaders. It begins with a discussion of traits that are inborn or acquired very early in life. The author looks at those characteristics that result from the intertwining of accidents of birth and early environmental influences and makes some generalizations about who the leader is. The next section focuses on leadership traits and skills in the area of human relations. The research cited concludes that leaders are better than average at interacting with others, they enjoy socializing, and they are good talkers and listeners.

The final section of chapter 1 concerns character qualities of a particular type of leader — the effective school leader. This section suggests that successful principals and other educational administrators have some traits that distinguish them from those who are less successful. These characteristics are a clear, unwavering vision of goals, enough security not to resist needed change, and an ability to be "proactive" — to initiate, to lead, to go out on a limb — rather than passively reacting to environmental stimuli.

Practical implications of these findings for the selection, evaluation, and training of educational leaders are interwoven throughout this chapter. Those in charge of hiring school administrators or planning training programs for them should find the chapter especially helpful.

Chapter 2 examines the ethnic background and sex of educational leaders and discovers that, even after decades of civil rights and feminist activities, nearly all are white and nearly all are male. This chapter has several audiences in mind. It should be helpful for those who are involved in hiring administrators and for those who work every day with women and blacks who are striving to become or who have become educational leaders. Women and minorities themselves should find the chapter especially helpful in understanding the current situation regarding the hiring of educational administrators, how it got that way, and what can and should be done about it.

The authors make a case for the value of diversity in educational leadership, then convincingly state some surprising findings: There are today fewer women and fewer minorities in educational administration than there were thirty years ago. The attitudes and practices that foster this situation are explored. Finally, the authors make practical and specific suggestions for remedying the situation.

The final chapter in part 1 looks at theories of leadership style. Leadership style is defined simply as "how the leader leads," and significant ideas about the important components and environmental determinants of leadership are presented and explained. After asking such questions as what the best style is and whether leaders can change their styles, the author then examines the many conflicting answers that have been offered to these questions. It is not a chapter for those searching for simple recipes for action or for easy answers, but is rather for those who want to examine and evaluate how they function as leaders and the theoretical reasons behind and implications of leaders' behaviors. Yet the chapter is more than mere theory; a lengthy section presents specific ways in which important aspects of each theory can be translated into action in schools.

Although containing implications and suggestions for action, this part of the book stresses leadership theory more than the other two parts of the book. It acquaints readers with some of the most important thought concerning leadership to emerge in the last half century. A prime function of this chapter is to set the stage for the more practical chapters to follow: those on structure and skills.

CHAPTER 1
PORTRAIT OF A LEADER
Jo Ann Mazzarella

What kind of people become leaders? Highly intelligent people or those of average intelligence? The rich or the poor? Gregarious people or strong, silent types?

And what kind of people make good leaders? Those who follow the rules to the letter or those who stretch them a little? Those who are clearly aware of their goals or those who rely on their instincts? Secure people or those who are secretly insecure?

In the early twentieth century, research on leadership concentrated almost solely on the personal traits of leaders. Early researchers studied the characteristics of Indian chiefs, football captains, or Girl Scout leaders and frequently came up with very different conclusions about leaders' characteristics.

They often then used these conclusions to make generalizations about all leaders. As each study about a different kind of leader uncovered new characteristics, the list of leader characteristics grew until it was too large to be capable of any real differentiation. Many critics used these widely varying characteristics to substantiate their claim that there are no (or very few) true leader traits.

After years of data collection, such trait theories were largely abandoned in favor of situational theories of leadership based on the belief that there are no inherent leadership traits, just leader styles or behaviors that may change radically depending on the situation. Situationists believe that a person who is a leader in one situation may be a follower in other situations. This means that traits useful in one situation may actually be disastrous in others. For such situationists, leaders are not born with any particular traits that determine leadership. Situationists have less interest in who the leader is than in what the leader does.

Although the situationists have added much of value to leadership theory, it is beginning to appear that throwing out all the trait research and theories is less than wise. Although it does not make much sense to use findings about particular leaders to make generalizations about all leaders, there are other ways trait research might be viewed. It does seem reasonable to look at large numbers of trait studies to see what characteristics of leaders appear repeatedly. That only one study shows leaders differentiated from the followers by intelligence does not mean much; if twenty studies show it, the findings are more convincing.

It also makes sense to use findings about a particular leader to make generalizations about this kind of leader alone. Each kind of leader has a number of unique characteristics. Studies about Girl Scout leaders are quite valuable to Girl Scout leaders—and those of school leaders most valuable to school leaders.

Now research is turning again to leader traits and characteristics—this time to the characteristics of effective leaders, to what makes good leaders different from poor leaders. To followers of what could be called the "new trait theory" it very much matters who the leader is. These researchers have concluded that regardless of the situation, there are some traits that are characteristic of many effective leaders—or, at least, of effective educational leaders.

This renewed interest in the characteristics of effective leaders suggests that it may be time to look again at the early trait research to see what is worth saving and what implications it has for present leaders. Explored in these pages are the most significant findings of previous trait research and the findings of more recent research on effective educational leaders in an attempt to paint a portrait of what an effective leader looks like.

It is important to remember that none of this research reveals any single characteristic that determines leadership. Rather it suggests that there are groups or "constellations" of qualities that appear to correlate with leadership. Not all leaders have all these traits, and not even all effective leaders have all of them. Many followers have many of them, and many more have a few of them. Yet people who have many of these characteristics do appear to have a better chance of being effective leaders than do those who have none of them.

These pages look at several kinds of leader characteristics: inherited traits and those that spring from early childhood experiences; attitudes toward and relationships with other people; and character qualities that differentiate effective from ineffective leaders.

Readers may want to accompany this chapter with an imaginary checklist to see how they compare to this portrait of an effective leader.

NATURE AND NURTURE

If leaders do have traits and characteristics that separate them from followers, these traits must be acquired somewhere. Some characteristics, like intelligence, are believed to be an as yet imperfectly understood combination of genetic endowment and early nurturing. Other characteristics, like ease in groups or cooperativeness, are believed to spring chiefly from parental influences. Endowments like socioeconomic status come solely from environmental factors, the family situation in which the leader was born.

Explored here are the characteristics leaders acquire early in life, those they are born with or acquire from their early interactions with their parents. Many such traits or endowments have been investigated, but only a few repeatedly show a significant relationship with leadership.

Those who reject the trait theory of leadership are fond of listing, with amusement, the large number of leadership traits that have been identified. If every study turns up a different trait, they reason, perhaps none of the traits is really significantly correlated with leadership. Jack Speiss has put it:

> Scholars duly noted that leaders are older, taller, heavier, more athletic, better appearing, and brighter than followers. Leaders can be considered superior to followers in scholarship, knowledge, insight, originality, adaptability, initiative, responsibility, persistence, self-confidence, emotional control, sociability, diplomacy, tact, popularity, prestige, and cooperativeness.

Although such critics have gone too far in dismissing all leadership traits, there is an important warning implicit in their observations; it is crucial not to base generalizations about all leaders on isolated studies. Rather, to find general leadership traits it is necessary to look at the body of the research as a whole to see what traits appear again and again in different kinds of studies of different kinds of leaders.

IQ

In 1940, Charles Bird reviewed twenty studies exploring the personal characteristics of leaders. He found that seventy-nine different traits had been examined, with only a few looked at by more than one researcher, which dampened his enthusiasm considerably for any "trait theory" of leadership. One characteristic, however, that appeared repeatedly in studies of leaders was intelligence. In at least ten studies reviewed, leaders were found to be, on the whole, more intelligent than their followers.

Bird warns, however, that the distinction is not absolute. He notes that there are many followers who are more intelligent than leaders and concludes that "intelligence, therefore, is a contributing factor to leadership, but taken by itself, without assistance from other traits, it does not account for leadership." It should also be remembered that such studies reveal statistical correlations only. That is, high intelligence and leadership appear to be often found together — more often than chance — but are not necessarily related as cause and effect.

Ralph Stogdill, looking at 124 studies of the characteristics of leadership, found 23 studies that showed leaders are usually brighter than followers. Although many of these studies were of child or student leaders, Stogdill felt that the results were applicable in other contexts. Yet Stogdill too warned that "there is considerable overlapping of intelligence test scores, indicating that superior intelligence is not an absolute requirement for leadership."

It might seem that the implications of these findings are that those with the highest IQs will always emerge as leaders. However, Bernard Bass has reviewed a number of studies that show things are not so simple. Bass found that leaders usually have higher intelligence than do followers, but not too much higher. He found that leaders' intelligence is often only slightly above average for their respective groups. For example, in a group of mean IQ of 100, someone with an IQ of 160 has very little chance to emerge as leader of that group. Instead, the leader will have an IQ between 115 and 130. Bass ventured several possible explanations of this finding: a "too superior" leader might not be concerned with the group's problems; he or she might not share "interests or goals" with a group; the very intelligent leader may not be able to communicate with the group; and finally, this sort of leader may exhibit ideas that are too radical to be acceptable to followers.

What Bass found to be true of leaders in general appears also to be true of leaders in education, according to Robert Wilson's study of effective Ohio superintendents. This study revealed that successful superintendents are intelligent and good students, but not "gifted."

BIRTH ORDER

Since intelligence appears to be correlated with leadership, it makes sense that researchers would look in turn at other correlates of intelligence in an attempt to link them too with leadership and leadership potential. Bass looked at several research reviews that indicated the intelligence of the firstborn is less than that of the youngest of the family. Herbert Yahraes, however, looking at a number of other studies, found that firstborns got higher scores on intelligence than did younger children and that scores on intelligence tests grew worse as the number of children increased. According to these findings, the firstborn, rather than a younger child, would be more likely to become an adult leader because he or she is more likely to have the highest intelligence of the siblings.

Since these findings appear to be irreconcilable, it is more useful to look at other effects of birth order. Bass cited additional studies that report the oldest child as more socially maladjusted, more conservative, less aggressive, less self-confident, more introverted, and less inclined toward leadership than other children. Elizabeth Hurlock, too, in her work on child development, found that the oldest child lacks self-confidence and leadership qualities.

Bass guessed that one reason firstborns suffer from so many problems that inhibit leadership is that parents of firstborns are inexperienced and less secure in their marriage and finances. Another reason is that older children have to adjust to decreased attention. Hurlock cited parental overprotectiveness and anxiety about sickness and nursing as additional causes for the firstborn's insecurity.

These findings appear to contradict the popular view that the firstborn child is more success-oriented and achievement-oriented than the children born later. Yet as we shall see in later sections, this desire for success or achievement may not be as important a component of leadership as other characteristics—such as ability to deal with people or to be a nonconformist when necessary.

We might conclude from all this, as did Bass, that "all other things being equal, we expect the younger siblings to attempt more leadership as an adult than the older siblings to some slight extent."

Here again, it is important to remember that birth order alone (or any single characteristic) does not in any way determine or guarantee leadership ability. This is merely one of a combination of attributes and traits that make leadership more likely. Those who are firstborn ought not be discouraged from attempting to realize their leadership capabilities. Firstborns who have many of the other characteristics described in this chapter have a good chance to be successful leaders.

CHILDREARING VARIABLES

Bass reviews a number of studies that uncovered childrearing techniques or styles that appear to be related to leadership. In one study, children who are allowed to participate in family decision-making are more resourceful, self-reliant, cooperative, and at ease in groups. Bass feels that such characteristics facilitate potential to be a successful leader.

Another study cited by Bass concluded that "sociability and cooperativeness" were greater when parents were clear and consistent, explained decisions to their children, offered opportunities for decision-making, had rapport with their children, and understood their children's problems. Bass believed that "sociability and cooperativeness" were important in the development of leadership potential.

SOCIOECONOMIC VARIABLES

Stogdill found fifteen early studies (1904-1947) and nineteen later studies (1948-1970) that suggested leaders came from a higher socioeconomic background than did followers. These studies were done with a wide variety of leaders and followers.

Bass found the same. In spite of the myth that great presidents are born in log cabins, Bass noted that few U.S. presidents have come from lower socioeconomic groups. He also mentioned a study that found that town leaders tend to be children of town leaders and that 70 percent of the fathers of businessmen are businessmen.

One indication that this correlation may apply to school administrators as well is found in the work of John Hemphill, Daniel Griffiths, and Norman Frederiksen. In their comparison of 232 elementary school principals to the population as a whole, these researchers found that disproportionately more were children of business or professional men and appreciably fewer were from laboring or farming families.

To summarize these studies of biographical factors, there is good evidence that leaders have a higher (but not much higher) IQ than do followers and that leaders generally come from higher socioeconomic groups. Evidence concerning parenting styles indicates that leaders may be the products of more "liberal" parents. Evidence concerning birth order is less clear, but firstborns seem less likely to be leaders than do their siblings.

None of these characteristics—neither high IQ, nor birth order, nor high status, nor liberal parents—is a guarantee of leadership ability. Nor are these the only qualities correlated with leadership. The most that can be said is that research shows that many — but not all — leaders have these qualities.

IMPLICATIONS FOR ADMINISTRATOR SELECTION

Because the characteristics discussed in this section are inherent or acquired at a very early age, the research discussed here has almost no applicability to administrator training or evaluation. Training programs cannot raise administrators' IQs, and evaluation procedures that give higher ratings to those who come from higher socioeconomic families would not (and should not) survive for long.

There is one finding here, however, that can be helpful in administrator selection. It does seem desirable that some minimal level of intelligence be demanded for admission into administrator jobs or training programs. Kenneth St. Clair and Kenneth McIntyre have suggested that the work of researchers like Stogdill lends "credence to our long-held notion that ignoramuses should be selected out of preparation programs." Although there are those who would argue the irrelevance of such tests as analogies tests or the Graduate Record Examination, St. Clair and McIntyre believe that the results coordinate closely enough with intelligence to be valid selectors of candidates for administrator training programs.

St. Clair and McIntyre do not worry that using such selection criteria might encourage the selection of administrators who are too intellectually superior to their subordinates to be effective. They believe that there have been "too few occasions to test this finding in educational settings to accept it as a cause for concern." And beyond this lack of evidence, one flinches at the prospect of rejecting applicants because they are *too* intelligent. Nevertheless, the suspicion remains that an overly intelligent administrator might be unsuccessful. Perhaps the solution to this problem is that intelligence be only one of a large number of selection criteria.

PERSON TO PERSON

One finding to emerge repeatedly in studies of leaders, including studies of educational leaders, is that leaders are people-oriented. They are outgoing and successful in dealing with people and they have good social and interpersonal skills. Such characteristics separate both leaders from non-leaders and effective from ineffective leaders.

A number of outstanding principals were interviewed by Arthur Blumberg and William Greenfield for a study to be described in more detail later in this chapter. That successful leaders put a high importance on dealing with people is well illustrated by a statement made by the outstanding principal identified by Blumberg and Greenfield only as "John":

> If you want to cultivate kids you really have to care about them and convey that caring to them. You've got to be seen as more than just the guy who suspends kids from school. I try to talk to them in the halls, at ball games, in the cafeteria, in classrooms. I try to get to know as many of them by name as I can. In a large school that's tough, but a principal should know four or five hundred kids by name, even in a school of fifteen hundred.

SOCIAL PARTICIPATION

Richard Gorton and Kenneth McIntyre in their national study of the principalship found that effective principals have as their strongest asset "an ability to work with different kinds of people having various needs, interests, and expectations." The researchers added:

> They seem to understand people, know how to motivate them, and how to deal effectively with their problems. It is primarily this factor, rather than a technical expertise, that caused the "significant others" to perceive these principals as accessible and effective administrators.

Keith Goldhammer and his colleagues in a much earlier, but similar, study, identified principals of outstanding schools (institutions they labeled "beacons of brilliance"). These researchers found that principals of these good schools "had an ability to work effectively with people and to secure their cooperation." They also found that the principals "used group processes effectively and appeared to have intuitive skill and empathy for their associates."

The effectiveness of such an approach is illustrated by a statement from another of Blumberg and Greenfield's effective principals who spoke about his efforts to work with teachers.

> The first year my expectations were that we would meet, talk about instruction, and get to know each other. It was just an opportunity to sit down and let each other know how we felt, the things that bugged us, and so forth. It was really something. For the first time they started to talk about caring what was going on in the school, not just in their own classroom.

What about successful superintendents? Sitting in the central office, are they too removed from students, teachers, and parents to profit from good social skills and abilities? Apparently not. Robert Wilson, in a study of successful Ohio superintendents, found that the successful superintendent "is a very personable and friendly individual who believes in the importance of human relations skills and demonstrates them daily." Outstanding Ohio superintendents also participate widely in the community—in church, PTA, and civic, social, and hobby clubs—because they depend heavily on face-to-face contact for building rapport with citizens. According to Wilson, the results of these public relations efforts are evident in the success these superintendents have with school bond elections, at the bargaining table, and in their relations with media representatives and school boards.

This kind of interest in people is also uncovered in studies of other types of leaders. Charles Bird, in the research review mentioned earlier, found several studies in which leaders were found to be more extroverted than were followers. Bird defined an extrovert as "a person who prefers to engage overtly in social activities, to manipulate the external world, to mix with people, to make decisions without regard for fine distinctions, to delight in action, or to show indifference to criticism."

Ralph Stogdill reviewed numerous early studies showing that leaders participate in more group activities than do followers. Many early studies, as well as the later studies he looked at (after 1948), also show strong correlations between leadership and sociability. Thirty-five of these later studies uncovered positive findings regarding what he called "social characteristics"; he concluded that leaders are active participants in social activities. According to Stogdill, the studies suggested that leaders interact easily with a wide range of personalities and that their interaction is valued by others.

If sociability is correlated with leadership, children's future leadership ability may be influenced by their parents' social participation. Bernard Bass reports a study showing that if parents participate in social activities, children do also.

COMMUNICATION

As well as being sociable or people-oriented, leaders appear to have aptitudes and skills that help them in social situations. They are born with verbal abilities and they have picked up the skills they need to interact well with others; they know how to communicate.

Gordon and McIntyre, in their study of the principalship, found that "significant others" (those knowledgeable about the principals' performance) see effective principals as strong in oral communication. Apparently, not only leaders in general, but effective school leaders in particular, are good at communicating. It appears possible that leaders are born with a natural facility for language. Verbal ability also correlates with leadership. Bass cites a number of studies supporting "the proposition that successful leaders are apt verbally."

Blumberg and Greenfield, in their indepth study of eight outstanding principals, found, in spite of great diversity, five characteristics held in common by these effective principals. One of these characteristics was "extremely well-developed expressive abilities."

> All of these principals had very well-developed interpersonal skills and were able to communicate effectively in face-to-face interaction with a diverse range of individuals and groups.

Here again it appears that ability to communicate may be an important component of leadership.

LISTENING

The outstanding principal known as John (interviewed by Blumberg and Greenfield) had this to say about listening:

> Teachers have to see you as caring, as listening to their problems. And after listening, you have to follow through so that teachers know you cared enough to do something and then communicate back to them. You may not follow through the way the teacher thought you should, but at least you did something. You heard the problem and you dealt with it in a way that you saw fit.

Blumberg and Greenfield noted that the ability to listen was common to the effective principals they studied. These effective leaders were very sensitive to what was going on around them. They were not only good at communicating ideas, they were good at absorbing ideas too.

Goldhammer and his colleagues found that principals of outstanding schools "listened well to parents, teachers, and pupils." And Gorton and McIntyre as well found that effective principals listen to students, community, and staff.

All this interrelated research points toward the same thing. One quality that makes leaders different from followers and good leaders different from poor leaders is the way they relate to people. Specifically most true leaders enjoy social participation and do a lot of it, have an ability to communicate and well-developed communication skills, and are good listeners.

IMPLICATIONS FOR SELECTION, EVALUATION, AND TRAINING

Like the characteristics discussed earlier, the characteristics discussed here are only one facet of leadership. Not every effective leader is necessarily a good communicator, and this is not the only quality that makes a good leader.

Yet it still seems likely that knowing the importance of certain characteristics can help in the selection, evaluation, and training of administrators.

Since *some* criteria must be used in choosing and evaluating administrators, it seems logical that *one* criterion (but not the only one) should be their skills and abilities in working with people. Measuring such skills is tricky, but there are some fairly good indicators. Prospective administrators can be given paper and pencil tests that measure verbal ability and extroversion. The personal interview would appear to be especially helpful in gauging how well job candidates or current administrators communicate and listen. Superiors, subordinates, and peers might give administrators or applicants for administration programs evaluations on how well they get along with and understand the problems of different kinds of people. Although this smacks a little of a popularity contest, the research reviewed here strongly suggests that administrators who have trouble dealing with people are going to have a much harder time being effective leaders.

These findings also have apparent implications for administrator training. Training programs might do well to put strong emphasis on improving communication skills, both listening and verbal expression. Training programs also ought to accentuate the importance of being a good communicator; they can emphasize that time spent merely communicating is never lost and pays off in leadership effectiveness.

CHARACTER QUALITIES

Some research studies have suggested that effective educational leaders have particular character qualities that make them different from less effective leaders. These studies suggest that effective leaders (as well as having the good human relations skills described in the previous section) are goal-oriented, energetic, secure, proactive, and well aware of the dynamics of power.

Two things make this more recent research on leadership traits even more valuable to school people than was the earlier trait research. The first is that current researchers are focusing on educational leaders only and looking for leadership characteristics that are unique to this group.

The second reason is that recent research looks at the characteristics that separate effective from ineffective leaders. Rather than examining the traits that identified good leaders, early researchers looked only at the traits that distinguish leaders from nonleaders. By lumping good leaders in with bad, these early researchers made it less likely that they would find any traits in common. Dorwin Cartwright and

Alvin Zander, among others, have suggested that studying instead the traits that distinguish effective from ineffective leaders may well have more valuable results.

One study that did just that has fascinating and useful implications for educators. This study, described in the volume *The Effective Principal: Perspectives on School Leadership,* looked at one kind of leader — the school principal — and used the findings to make pronouncements about this kind of leader alone. Equally important, the researchers, Arthur Blumberg and William Greenfield, looked only at effective principals and tried to discern what makes them different from other principals.

GOALS

Blumberg and Greenfield decided the best way to gather data about effective principals was to talk with them personally. They conducted lengthy indepth interviews with eight principals identified by teachers, parents, district administrators, and students as outstanding.

Following their detailed examination of these principals, Blumberg and Greenfield made several generalizations. One of these was that principals who are effective leaders seem to be "highly goal-oriented and to have a keen sense of goal clarity." The researchers noted that these effective principals "were continually alert for opportunities to make things happen, and if the opportunities didn't present themselves, they created them."

The effective principal whom Blumberg and Greenfield identified as "Paul" said it well:

> Once I took leadership, after that first year, I never relinquished the fact that I was their principal. I accepted the fact that I wasn't going to be their buddy. I accepted the idea that I was going to take some flack for things I had not done; I accepted the idea that if there were screw-ups I'd take the responsibility for them but that I would also take the role of making final decisions when necessary. And things changed from that point on.

In other words, effective principals have clear goals and

will work hard to try to achieve them. Blumberg and Greenfield felt that almost every school principal has a number of goals for the school; yet for most, the mere espousal of goals appears to be enough and substitutes for action.

Blumberg and Greenfield are not the first to discern the importance of strong goal orientation. When Ralph Stogdill reviewed 163 studies of leaders done between 1948 and 1970, one of the qualities that often appeared was "vigor and persistence in pursuit of goals." He discovered too that leaders in these studies had a "strong drive for task completion." On looking over all these studies, Stogdill observed that this characteristic "differentiates leaders from followers, effective from ineffective leaders, and higher echelon from lower echelon leaders."

Charles Bird too, after looking at twenty studies of leadership, found that one of the five leader character qualities that was mentioned with frequency was "initiative." It seems clear from all these studies that effective leaders are people of action. They get things done.

SECURITY

Blumberg and Greenfield also found that effective educational leaders are secure; that is, they are not threatened by new ideas or confrontations with others. Blumberg and Greenfield put it: "their sense of themselves as people and what it is they are about seems rather highly developed." The authors felt that this sort of security and sureness about themselves fosters a high tolerance for ambiguity. They can survive in a confusing situation where rules are ill-defined. They can live with uncertainty. This tolerance for ambiguity means effective leaders are not afraid of positive change.

There is great similarity between these findings and those of Keith Goldhammer and his colleagues, who made this comment about principals of effective schools:

> The ambiguities that surround them and their work were of less significance than the goals they felt were important to achieve. As a result, they found it possible to live with the ambiguities of their position.

Openness, security, and tolerance for ambiguity seem to make successful administrators unafraid of change when it is needed. This ability to change and to effect necessary change is so important to being a successful leader that some authorities, like James Lipham, see initiating change as a necessary and central part of the definition of leadership. Lipham defined leadership as "that behavior of an individual which initiates a new structure in interaction within a social system."

Although it is not clear that initiating change is the only activity that makes leaders leaders, such emphasis indicates that it is at least a very important part of leadership activities.

PROACTIVITY

One outstanding principal interviewed by Blumberg and Greenfield was faced with a seemingly unsolvable problem. His desire for student input into school committees was blocked by teachers who threatened to resign from committees that had student members. His solution?

> The answer to this situation was an end run. We formed a Parent-Teacher-Student Council, which was outside the formal organization of the school, but it wasn't a tea and cookies PTA. We met to discuss problems that involved parents, teachers, and students. Primarily, it was a sounding board for faculty meetings and department chairmen. It worked.

Blumberg and Greenfield noted that their effective principals do not merely accept all the rules and customs that make up "the way things are." They are "proactive," always testing the limits in an effort to change things that no one else believes can be changed.

Yet these principals do not take foolish risks and do take care to establish a power base, both inside and outside the school, on which successful change can be anchored. They are aware of the need to establish alliances to get things done. Blumberg and Greenfield emphasize that these principals are strongly aware of the dynamics of power.

Goldhammer and his research team too discovered that the most successful principals "found it difficult to live within the constraints of the bureaucracy; they frequently violated the chain of command, seeking relief for their problems from whatever sources that were potentially useful."

Nevertheless, they "expressed concern for the identification of the most appropriate procedures through which change could be secured."

These findings suggest that leaders who follow rules to the letter, who never make waves and never challenge authority are probably less effective than leaders who stretch the rules a little or fight to accomplish goals that are important to them. Blumberg and Greenfield further elaborate:

> A characteristic of principals who lead seems to be that they behave in ways that enable *them to be in charge of the job* and *not let the job be in charge of them.* They are not pawns of the system. They seem to be adept at playing the games on which their survival depends, but they don't let the game playing consume too much of their energy.

It is clear that even though these effective leaders stretch the rules, they are not rebels; they *do* play the game. Both studies agree that these leaders understand how power works and know how to survive.

IMPLICATIONS FOR SELECTION, EVALUATION, AND TRAINING

These findings about the characteristics of effective leaders are not simply and immediately applicable as selection and evaluation criteria and administrator training objectives. It is not easy to measure proactivity or security. It is difficult to teach initiative or tolerance for ambiguity.

Nevertheless, it is likely that we will never identify any characteristics required for being an effective leader that are easily measurable or teachable. As we learn more about leadership, it becomes clearer that there are no simple ways to identify it or foster it.

Furthermore, it is also beginning to be apparent that traditional methods of selection, evaluation, and training, though easy to implement, may not truly be relevant to the production of effective leaders. Blumberg and Greenfield found little to suggest that university graduate training had much direct or observable influence on any of the effective leaders they studied. They suggested a switch from "formal indices of competence" like years of teaching and administrative experience, number of advanced degrees, and grade point averages to more relevant measures of competence. Goldhammer and his colleagues likewise discovered that principals who were effective could not, on the basis of their formal preparation, be distinguished from those who were not.

These findings all suggest that even though the characteristics of effective leaders are difficult to measure or teach, we have to make some effort to use them in evaluation, selection, and training simply because they are better than the methods we are now using.

Some possible applications come to mind. In choosing teachers or administrators for promotion, superiors ought to look to those who need little supervision and who accomplish a lot. Too often, those who are promoted are those who do what they're told and always do everything by the book. Rather, those who are given positions of leadership ought to be those with initiative and minds of their own. They ought to be those who have clear goals, can articulate them, and have shown concrete evidence of progress at moving toward those goals. Training programs, though not likely to inculcate initiative in those who haven't got it, can encourage those who are naturally endowed with initiative not to be afraid to use it. Often, training programs, rather than fostering personal initiative, squelch it through an overabundance of rules, structures, and regulations that do not leave room for personal goal setting.

Although feelings of inner security are probably too complex to be measured during selection procedures, it seems more possible that attitudes toward change can be elicited and assessed, and actual changes initiated can be measured. Although training programs are not capable of instilling feelings of security, they can emphasize an openness toward change and the importance of the leader's role as change agent.

CONCLUSION

A small part of the portrait of an effective educational leader has been revealed by each of the research studies and research reviews mentioned here. Now, like the pieces of a jigsaw puzzle, all these fragments can be assembled to reveal a more coherent (though by no means complete) portrait of an effective educational leader. The earliest research surveyed here has supplied the outlines of a portrait of a typical leader. It has revealed not characteristics that separate effective from ineffective leaders, but characteristics that separate most leaders from followers.

According to this research, typical educational leaders are a little more intelligent (but not too much more) than nonleaders. As children they were probably not firstborn and were probably allowed at an early age to make many of their own decisions. It is likely that they came from a higher socioeconomic group than their followers.

The later research surveyed here fills in the outlines a bit and fleshes out a portrait of a more specific kind of leader—an effective educational leader. According to these findings, effective educational leaders are outgoing, good at working with people, and have good communication abilities and skills. They have initiative, are aware of their goals, and feel secure. As proactive people, they are not afraid to stretch the rules, but also understand the compromises that must be made to get things done.

More of a sketch than a portrait, this depiction of an educational leader leaves out a great deal. Even more important, the sketch itself is not of a real leader but only of an imaginary one. The leader whose characteristics are set down here is a pure "form," who in actuality does not exist. Like the typical voter or the typical consumer, this typical leader is only a composite of common characteristics. No real flesh and blood counterpart exists. The real effective leaders interviewed by Blumberg and Greenfield were more different than they were alike.

Then what is the point of an imaginary portrait of a nonexistent leader? Although we cannot hang it on the wall, this composite has several possible uses. One is to recognize potential leaders by determining if they have many (but not necessarily all) of these characteristics. Another is for evaluation. Those who evaluate administrators can use this portrait to help them formulate evaluation criteria. This imaginary portrait can also be used for self-evaluation. Those who are in leadership positions can compare themselves with more effective leaders to see how they measure up. Also, knowing the characteristics of an effective leader can be useful in planning administrator training programs, as a guide to which aspects of the job ought to be emphasized.

Finally, the most important use for this ideal portrait is to help leaders set priorities. When things get rough and they are tempted to lock themselves in their offices, such a vision can remind them that human relations and communication skills *are* important. When they are coasting along, day-by-day, not going anywhere in particular, it can remind them that being goal-oriented and that knowing where they are going *do* make a difference. When they are criticized by superiors for breaking unnecessary rules and cautioned not to make waves, it can give them the courage to continue doing things their own way—as long as that way has been successful in accomplishing their highest priorities. In short, the most important use for this portrait is the function performed by any ideal. It offers something to strive for.

CHAPTER 2
TWO SPECIAL CASES: WOMEN AND BLACKS
David Coursen and Jo Ann Mazzarella

INTRODUCTION

Educational leaders come in all ages, all shapes and sizes, and all temperaments. Studies of leadership have looked at many physical characteristics of leaders: height and weight, eye color, overall attractiveness. All these have been examined and none has been found to significantly differentiate leaders from others. Significant differences are found, however, when one looks at two particular physical characteristics of educational leaders: sex and race.

Almost anyone who remembers "school days" has two images of school officials. The favorite teacher, in fact nearly every teacher, was probably a woman. But the feared and revered final authority, the principal, especially in high school, is likely to have been a man. When the memory then turns to the race of the principal, the pattern of the white, male school administrator begins to emerge.

QUALITY EDUCATION AND EFFECTIVE LEADERSHIP

Today, the problems of women and blacks in public school leadership may seem a little passé. Surely these problems are dwarfed by our worries and fears about such major issues as school violence or shrinking resources. Surely the problems of women and minorities were solved long ago.

Yet such a judgment is not only superficial but inaccurate. The extent to which women and minorities participate in administering the schools is one measure of education's real commitment to the ideal of equal opportunity for all Americans, an ideal that is far from being realized.

It is easy to be lulled into the false assumption that women and minority representation in educational leadership now roughly reflects their representation in the general population. Yet, as this chapter will show, this is not the case. Not only are things not changing rapidly, things are not changing at all; in fact, in some areas, things are getting worse.

In addition, if sexual or racial characteristics are more important than ability in determining who is hired for positions of power and responsibility in the schools, the caliber of public education will suffer. The question then becomes one of quality education, and surely *that* is always important, is beyond political dispute, and is genuinely timely, never passé.

Staffing policies are as important to the educational process as curriculum. The best policy decisions will come from administrations that include a variety of points of view. Women or members of minority groups have unique perspectives on certain problems, perspectives that can broaden and enrich the decision-making process at every level. In fact, a diverse staff may even help shape more desirable curricula. For example, women have a special sensitivity to sexism in study materials, just as nonwhites are more sensitive to racism. Schools educate children not only by what is taught in the classroom, but also by what is shown about how the world operates. For this reason, too, the identity of administrators is important in determining how schools socialize their students. When there is someone in authority who has characteristics in common with a child, that person may become a role model, a figure for the child to admire and emulate. Thus school officials can teach children appropriate behavior and help shape their aspirations and attitudes.

Children may come to feel that it is normal for the kinds of people they see running the schools to fill all executive positions. Black children who see only whites in authority may conclude that blacks are excluded from power, that it is futile for them to strive for decision-making positions. Similarly, girls who see women only as teachers, taking orders from male principals, may become convinced that this is natural and inevitable, that the most they can hope for in life are positions subordinate to men. By thus teaching some children not to strive for their highest human potentials, the schools are encouraging the waste of human resources. Surely this is a perverse and destructive form of "education."

And here once again arises the pressing contemporary issue of "survival"—not only survival of female and minority administrators but survival of the public school system itself. For unless we choose tomorrow's educational leaders from among the most qualified and able prospects (regardless of sex or race), the quality of educational leadership will not be sufficient to extricate public education from the morass in which it finds itself. If, in the search for educational leaders, excellent educators are passed over in favor of less able candidates, public education may not have adequate leadership to survive into the 1990s.

And the issue of survival extends even further to the issue of the very survival of our society. If the schools are to attract members of all cultural and racial groups, they must have leadership that is representative of all these groups. All races and cultures must feel that their concerns are sincerely being addressed by those with power in the school. Otherwise the alienation that begins in a discriminatory school system may accompany these students into an adulthood in which they become a drain on an already badly depleted society.

TO LEADERS AND ASPIRING LEADERS

It is important for today's educational leaders to become aware of the true situation regarding women and minorities in education.

Those in charge of hiring and promotion especially must understand the situation, how it got that way, and how it can be changed. Other leaders need to become aware of the special problems faced by their female and minority colleagues so that they can offer support to those who have achieved leadership positions and to those who aspire to such positions. Finally, women and minority leaders and those seeking to become leaders need to understand more about the situation that exists outside their own subjective experience. If the path seems blocked, they need to know that there is some hope. If the path seems easy, they need to know that others still face obstacles.

WHAT ABOUT OTHER RACIAL MINORITIES?

In the literature on school administrators, "minority" is virtually synonymous with "black." This fact alone defines the status of Chicanos, Native Americans, and all other racial minority groups, who are denied even a token consideration.

This chapter reflects this situation, ignoring the status of all nonblack racial minorities in school administration, not because the subject does not demand attention, but because most writers tacitly assume, by their omissions, that it is simply not worth considering. There is an urgent need for studies that will correct this imbalance.

This chapter, then, will be largely limited to discussing blacks and women. It is tempting to think that, since both groups suffer from discrimination, being judged according to group roles rather than individual performances, they can be considered together. But discrimination is as complex and subtle as it is pervasive; what is true for blacks is not necessarily true for members of other racial minorities and may have nothing to do with women. For this reason, women and blacks will be discussed separately.

THE WOMAN ADMINISTRATOR

The successes of the women's movement seem to justify the "common sense" notion that discrimination against women in school administration is not serious and is rapidly disappearing. In fact, such optimism is false. The central facts about women administrators are that there aren't many of them, and that the women in the schools are not employed in executive capacities.

WHERE IS SHE?

The statistics provide compelling evidence for these assertions. A 1979 National Association of Elementary School Principals study reported by William Pharis and Sally Zakariya revealed that only 18 percent of elementary principals are women. In the large-scale study of the secondary principalship done by the National Association of Secondary School Principals in 1977, David Byrne, Susan Hines, and Lloyd McCleary found that at the secondary level only 7 percent of the principals are women.

The significance of these figures can be seen only by comparing the present with the past. In 1928, 55 percent of all school principals were women. In 1948, the percentage had dropped to 41, in 1958 it was 38, and by 1968 it was only 22.

In addition, Dorothy Johnson notes that women principals are older and more experienced than men. She also observes that, while the number of women principals declined by 16 percent between 1958 and 1968, the median age of women in that position rose from 52 to 56, while that of men stayed fairly constant at around 44. Finally, she remarks, "I heard over and over the report of many members that upon retirement as principals their vacancy had been filled by a young man, occasionally the winning high school coach!"

This pattern of discrimination extends to the prestige of the jobs women get. Byrne, Hines, and McCleary discovered that 75 percent of female principals work in schools of 745 students or less, whereas only 37 percent of male principals are employed in these smaller schools; also, 14 percent of male principals are assigned to schools of 2,000 or more, but only 1 percent of female principals are found in these larger schools.

It is not surprising to discover that women are most severely underrepresented at the top job, the superintendency. Barbara Pierce, writing about a 1980 conference for women superintendents organized by the American Association of School Administrators, reported that of more than 16,000 school districts in the country, only 153 are headed by a woman—less than 1 percent.

As Earl Funderburk notes, "Only when top public school positions are elective rather than appointive do women educators stand a chance to hold a high administrative job." In support of this claim, he notes that in 1950, six states had female school superintendents. As five of these jobs became appointive, each woman was replaced by a man.

In summary, these figures indicate that few women work as school administrators, that the jobs women get are the lowest ranking ones, that the women who get the jobs are older than men working at comparable levels, and that the situation is getting worse all the time. There seems to be an unwritten policy that women always be assigned "women's work" instead of executive responsibilities.

A WOMAN'S PLACE . . .

No single explanation can account for such widespread discrimination, but one important factor is the general acceptance of stereotypes about working women in general and women in administration in particular. At the heart of all such stereotypes is a single notion, that a woman's place is in the home, in the completely fulfilling full-time role of motherhood, the natural state of all women. It is thus appropriate for a woman to teach a small child, a "motherly" task, but to supervise teachers requires the executive skill that can come only with a "man's touch."

Anyone with such beliefs can find specific reasons for excluding women from virtually any job. Barbara Krohn describes how the process can work:

> Instead of looking at women administrators as individuals, the system draws the same conclusions about all women: that their home responsibilities keep them from doing well in administration, that they don't want demanding jobs, that they are too emotional, that they have to stop work to have babies (the reason actually given for denying a Catholic nun entrance to a college program).

Such attitudes seem to form very early in potential decision-makers. Ginny Mickish cites a 1966 study of the attitudes of graduate students in education toward the abilities of women as administrators. The students indicated an overwhelming preference for men as principals. Mickish quotes from the report's conclusion:

> Most of the students questioned described male principals as being more democratic, more sympathetic, more understanding, more pleasant, more congenial, more relaxed, and more personally interested in their teachers. They further claimed that the men are not as critical, allow more freedom to teachers, do not supervise as much, do not get excited as easily, and can be approached and influenced more easily. An equal number of students pictured women principals as being too autocratic, too demanding, too critical, too particular, too moody, too emotional, and too "nosy." Moreover, they criticized the women for giving too much concern to petty matters, for super-

vising too much and for being too deeply involved in their work.

These findings are particularly significant since the graduate students who shared these beliefs were, in effect, being trained to run school systems, and eventually many of them will be in positions to act on these beliefs, doubtless through hiring policies systematically favoring men.

Stereotypes about men too help explain the problem. Sari Biklen quotes a position paper prepared by the National Conference on Women in Educational Policy that maintains that the popularity of the view of the school as a business makes women less likely to be chosen for administrative positions. Biklen states, "As schooling becomes more of a business, those in administrative positions turn to their image of effective business managers: business men."

A number of authors have attempted to determine whether there is any factual basis for such attitudes. Regarding the claim that family responsibilities interfere with the work responsibilities of women administrators, Carol Truett cites the well-documented fact that women enter administration at a later age than men (usually not before forty). This means that their children will be grown or independent and their duties more manageable.

There also is evidence that women have some characteristics that make them preferable to men as administrators. Neal Gross and Anne Trask, in their landmark study of women in school management, found that the quality of pupil learning and the professional performance of teachers were higher, on the average, in schools administered by women. They also found that women exerted more influence over their teachers' professional activity than did men. This last seems most important when one remembers that influence over others is an integral component of leadership.

The last finding was confirmed by Patricia Schmuck in a 1981 publication presenting studies indicating that female principals were seen by teachers as having more power to influence school affairs.

Virtually every evaluation of the comparative performances of women and men as principals has shown the complete inaccuracy of negative stereotypes of women administrators. In 1956, Vynce Hines and Hulda Grobman reported on a survey in which women scored better than men in evaluations based on student morale, teacher morale, frequency with which teachers used desirable practices, and program development. Meskin, after surveying all the studies, concludes:

> When we highlight some of the specific findings concerning women administrators in these studies—their propensity toward democratic leadership, thoroughness of approach to problem solving, and bent toward instructional leadership, as well as the general effectiveness of their performance as rated by both teachers and superiors—we puzzle over the small number of women administrators employed by school districts.

It is interesting that several surveys found that men who had never worked under a woman principal were generally unfavorable to the idea. However, men who actually had such experience expressed a preference for women as principals.

It should also be noted that all the studies Meskin discusses were made before 1965. But the survey of graduate student attitudes Ginny Mickish describes was made in 1966. At the very least, this suggests that graduate schools are so indifferent to the abilities of women administrators that these findings were not considered significant enough to require that students be familiar with them. By this tacit rejection of compelling evidence that women make good principals, the graduate schools are clearly not doing their job, preparing their students to shape the best possible policies for the schools.

According to John Hoyle, women may make better principals than men because of their longer teaching experience as well as their greater potential empathy with other women who still fill most teaching jobs. Mickish concurs, saying that the higher ratings given women principals "can be explained by the fact that women are teachers for a longer period, have greater self-confidence in their ability to direct instruction, and are more deeply committed to their positions."

CAN A WOMAN SUCCEED?

What these facts actually indicate is that a woman must

be better qualified than a man if she hopes to become a successful school administrator. In view of the difficulties she will face, she *has* to be extraordinary. She is confronted with different expectations than a man faces, and her actions are judged by different standards. Betty Friedan and Anne West cite an attitude survey that solicits a response to the following statement, which suggests some of these differences:

> They may act exactly the same way, but they are called: *absent-minded* if they are men, *scatter-brained* if they are women; *intellectually curious* if they are men, *nosey* if they are women; *planners* if they are men, *schemers* if they are women; *sensitive* if they are men, *emotional* if they are women; *logical* if they are men, *intuitive* if they are women.

According to Charlene Dale, women in administration are treated differently than equally qualified men in comparable positions. Superiors hold certain tacit assumptions about women that make it difficult for them to advance. For example, it is simply assumed that a young woman will not be able to accept a new job if it means relocating her family. In a comparable situation, it would be assumed that a man would be free to move.

This is one way in which women are faced with performance expectations that become self-fulfilling prophecies. Professionals tend to be either job-oriented, finding satisfaction in careers, or place-oriented, finding satisfaction in friendships and activities in a specific location. If a professional woman is not offered promotions, if her job seems to be leading nowhere, she may become place-oriented relatively early in her career. Once this has happened, if a promotion finally *is* offered, it would be undesirable if it meant relocating. The woman professional might then refuse to move, "demonstrating" her "lack" of both mobility and ambition.

That such an attitude may be fairly common is suggested by the findings of a survey done by Stefan Krchniak, who queried Illinois female teachers certified as administrators. Only 16 percent were willing to move if it were necessary to get a job as an administrator. Less than 30 percent were willing even to commute more than twenty miles round trip.

THE OBSTACLE OF NEGATIVE ATTITUDES

Another important factor in job success is the attitude a male superior may have toward a new person working in his department. A supervisor naturally assumes that any man hired for a job is competent or he wouldn't have been hired at all. Even if he is unsuccessful, the results may be blamed, not on professional inadequacy, but on an "impossible situation." But if the same superior has misgivings about the ability of women, he will expect a new woman to fail and may even unconsciously look for signs of that failure. In addition, if his commitment to her success is minimal, he may deny her any significant support. In such circumstances, the woman's chances of at least a perceived failure are thus very great. Not surprisingly, this may eventually cause her to lose self-confidence, to become disoriented on the job, and, finally, to perform according to the expectations the superior has done so much, albeit unconsciously, to confirm.

In addition, in this society women are socialized to accept subordinate roles. Krchniak found that only 39 percent of the Illinois women certified to be school administrators were interested in an administrative position at the time of the survey, only 13 percent were extremely interested, and a mere 3 percent were "making an all-out effort." In 1975, Patricia Schmuck found that

> some of the most formidable barriers to women's entry and upward mobility into management positions in school organizations are their own lack of self-confidence, their self-deprecation, and their doubts about their ability as capable individuals to do a good job.

She found that many of the thirty Oregon female administrators she interviewed, when first presented with an opportunity to take on a position of influence, had betrayed their own lack of self-confidence by responding with the query, "Who, me?"

Schmuck in an undated article also describes some of the ways a teacher can be gradually prepared for an administrative position. A supervisor may delegate various responsibilities to the teacher, with the tacit understanding that promotion will eventually result if the duties are handled well. A supervisor who believes that men make better administrators than women will not be anxious to offer such promotional opportunities to women. Consequently, more men will be in positions to be promoted, and those who are promoted will be, by virtue of their informal training, more likely to succeed immediately in their new jobs.

There seem to be other, even more informal ways in which men, rather than women, are able to advance up the administrative ladder. One woman Schmuck interviewed in 1975 commented:

> I am upwardly mobile but here come the roadblocks. Men naturally flock together. They golf together and swim together so they get to know one another. Men who are in low positions striving upward golf and swim with the guys in power to decide. Those avenues are closed to me. These are the way roles get filled— even before they are advertised, someone suggests a bright young man. I won't be known in the district. No one will communicate to others that I am interested in a position and by the time announcements are made it may be too late.

Some supervisors also feel that a kind of locker-room camaraderie is essential to the proper functioning of an administrative "team." Whether or not this has any basis in fact, if a man *thinks* it is important, he will be reluctant to hire a woman who might not work well with "the boys."

It must have been such a feeling that led Phi Delta Kappa, the prestigious national educational fraternity, to exclude women from membership until 1974. This led to a supreme irony: an entire issue of *Phi Delta Kappan*, the journal of the organization, was devoted to women in education, while women were excluded from the organization itself. This, too, supports Schmuck's conclusion in her undated article that "women are denied access to the main avenues of socialization into the profession by the predominance of men as administrative role-models and by the informal friendships and connections between men in power."

SOME PRACTICAL PROBLEMS

Overt discrimination is not the only cause of the recent decline in the number of women in administration. The recent trend toward consolidation of schools has meant that fewer positions are available. According to a study cited in *Behavior Today*, consolidation has been responsible for the closing of nearly 60,000 schools, many of them small, rural, and headed by women.

Another problem for women has been the recent effort to attract more men into education, especially at the elementary level, supposedly to prevent the "feminization" of the schools. To attract men into the field, it was considered necessary to offer them the incentive of possible advancement. Men entering education thus compete with women for administrative positions; supposedly, the men *must* be promoted or they will leave the field, so their promotions often come at the expense of qualified women.

One result of this is that male principals have less specific teaching experience than do women and serve for a shorter period, because they are actually upwardly mobile. This situation is particularly unfortunate since it prevents women from becoming principals and substitutes less-committed men.

Thus in more than just a few principalships, we find a "bright young man" on the way up, who temporarily serves as principal. His primary concern is not to do the job well so much as to use it as an avenue for promotion. The seriousness of this problem is articulated by William Seawell and Robert Canady: "The elementary school principalship today demands those individuals who have a particular ability and natural talent for the principalship and who desire to make it their lifetime career."

If there are factors other than discrimination responsible for the exclusion of women from administrative positions, the basic problem is still the secondary role women are assigned in all parts of society. Why else should it be women who are displaced by the closing of small schools? Similarly, why else should the opportunity for promotion be essential to the male educator, even when it limits the opportunities for qualified women?

THE BLACK ADMINISTRATOR: STILL SEGREGATED

"Common sense" suggests that the apparent successes

of the civil rights movement should have significantly improved the position of blacks in educational administration. Blacks were once the victims of systematic patterns of discrimination. But now, more than twenty-five years after the Supreme Court's historic desegregation ruling in the case of *Brown v. Board of Education of Topeka*, individuals may still be prejudiced, but, in public institutions like school systems, the black educator is treated in the same way as everyone else.

This analysis is attractive because it is both plausible and optimistic. It implies that the situation is under control and that desirable changes are taking place. Unfortunately, such optimism can flourish only amidst ignorance. Since *Brown*, the number of black administrators has declined dramatically. This is most true of the decision-making positions, where the real power is increasingly in the hands of white males.

DISAPPEARANCE OF THE BLACK LEADER

Historically, the southern pattern of "separate but equal" school systems tended to help the black school leader. The logic of segregation dictates the complete separation of the races. This can be accomplished only if black school systems are entirely black—teachers, students, superintendents, and principals. In addition, in a society in which racism is an institutionalized value, a principalship of a black school or superintendency of a black system could not seem very desirable to most whites. This fact, too, would help blacks become administrators, if only by default. The motivation may not have been commendable, but the result was that, in dual school systems, there were countless opportunities for black administrators.

This situation did not change immediately after the Supreme Court outlawed "separate but equal" systems, but once it became clear to the states that the decision could not be circumvented, the dual school systems were gradually dismantled. This dramatically altered the status of the black administrator. Blacks supervising other blacks may have been acceptable in the South, but the possibility of black officials giving orders to white teachers and overseeing the education of white students was virtually unthinkable.

The disappearance of the black administrator, though

the Court could hardly have anticipated it, has clearly come about as the result of southern compliance with the *Brown* decision.

During the 1960s, as Gregory Coffin points out, "the number of black high school principals in 13 southern and border states dropped more than 90 percent .... If casualties among black elementary school principals were included, the result would be even worse," he states.

Thus people who were qualified by training and experience to administer the new unified school systems were prevented from doing so because of their race. Many of the dismissed blacks undoubtedly were replaced by people less qualified, except for the vital racial criterion, to run the schools. The loss of expertise and resulting decline in educational quality are incalculable.

By 1975 things were not much better. At that time, Samuel Ethridge calculated that to reach "equity and parity" (that is, for the percentage of black principals to equal the percentage of blacks in the total population) the nation would have to hire 5,368 more black principals. Almost half this number were needed in the seventeen southern and border states.

Even by 1977, the NASSP survey done by David Byrne, Susan Hines, and Lloyd McCleary found that in spite of "initiatives taken to educate and employ minorities for administrative positions," only 3 percent of high school principals were black.

More than quality education disappeared with the black principal. In the Old South, educational administration was one of the few vocations in which a black could achieve affluence, power, and middle-class respectability, and this opportunity vanished. In addition, a black principal was often the most prominent black citizen, a community leader. Finally, for black children, the black educator was often the only available role model that suggested it was possible for a black to exercise authority or leadership, and this, too, was lost.

This loss of administrative ability and community leadership was nearly absolute, since the talents of displaced blacks were almost always discarded by the school systems. According to J.C. James, a black principal might be transferred to the central office of a district as "the highly visible token of desegregation," or, worse, given "some other title completely foreign to all known educational terminology, a desk, a secretary, no specified responsibilities or authority, with a quiet prayer that he will somehow just go away." Doubtless any black administrator with ambition or self-respect would himself echo that quiet prayer.

PERSISTENT DISCRIMINATION

As the legal system of segregation has broken down, it has been replaced by urban segregation based on residential patterns. The white, male decision-makers in many of these systems have, like their southern predecessors, decided that these all-black schools are appropriate places for black administrators.

Thus the belief that blacks are capable of supervising only black districts remains as strong as ever. Charles Moody examined twenty-one major school systems with black superintendents, seventeen regular and four acting. In each of these systems, the majority of the students were black, and every permanent superintendent worked in a community where more than half the residents were black. In addition, most of the districts had black majorities on their school boards.

Moody discovered several other facts about these districts that may explain why they were considered suitable for black superintendents. Virtually all the superintendents he studied had taken over districts with serious financial problems. From the evidence, he concludes that "when blacks are appointed it is often just because the district is unattractive." In addition, "black superintendents are not appointed in districts which provide them with the time and resources to develop educational programs relevant to their school community."

Charles Townsel's experience as a black administrator confirms this practice. He put it:

> Blacks are often called upon to serve in difficult administrative positions located in school districts with financial difficulties, where personnel and/or students are in revolt, where discipline is nonexistent, where academic achievement levels are low, and where the community is divided.

51

Black officials at all levels share a number of problems: difficult schools, ambiguous roles, and the unrealistic expectations of others. Robert Chapman reported on a study that compared what others expected of black principals in an urban school system with what the principals expected of themselves. The evidence was that high administrators and most people in the black community expected the new principals to make a far greater difference in the schools than the principals themselves anticipated making. Thus the new black officials were placed in difficult situations to begin with and then confronted with the unreasonable expectations of others. In such a situation, someone is bound to be disappointed, and the principal's relative or "perceived" failure seems virtually inevitable.

The ambiguous role assigned to the black administrator is best illustrated by Robert Frelow's analysis of the plight of a typical black administrator below the rank of principal. The primary assignment for the new official was to serve as liaison to dissident black students in a school with a biracial enrollment and a primarily white staff. He was successful in this assignment but was not rewarded for his professional skill. Instead, it became clear that, by dealing with a specific group of students, he had provided his superiors with "a rationale for his exclusion from decisions that affect the whole system. He has, in effect, defined a peripheral involvement for himself." This kind of doublethink, which can turn success into failure, is typical of the way white supervisors treat black administrators.

This problem illustrates the need for blacks in the highest decision-making positions in school systems. Until blacks enter the real power positions, the role of all black administrators will remain peripheral. But the evidence that this has not yet happened is overwhelming. Frelow says, "only in a few instances have school districts chosen to employ blacks in decision-making, policy-influencing positions."

This situation prevails in spite of the fact studies have shown that minorities have strong qualifications for management positions. After studying more than one hundred white and minority managers, John Miner concluded that minorities in management have unusually strong motivation to become managers. And Edward Adams found that black managers were perceived by their subordinates as exhibiting more consideration behavior (behavior indicative of friendship, mutual trust, respect, and warmth) than did white managers.

Since the late seventies, it has been more and more difficult to find even the most basic data or information on blacks in educational administration. Literature is strangely silent on the topic. In the face of such frightening problems as declining enrollment and resources and public loss of confidence in the schools, interest in the problems of minorities has waned. Yet there is no reason to believe that the problem has been or is being solved. Although a few very visible blacks have achieved token administrative positions, the decline in the number of positions available makes it impossible for enough minority administrators to be hired to accomplish anything close to equity. And if the policy of "last hired, first fired" continues to be invoked in times of retrenchment, the situation will get even worse.

It seems that nothing has really changed. The location of the all-black school systems may have moved from the South to the cities, but these remain the only systems with room for black administrators. A black educator's chance of being appointed superintendent in a "white" district is probably not much greater now than it was when the Supreme Court issued its ruling in the case of *Brown*.

A PROGRAM FOR CHANGE

Although the only permanent solution to the problems of women and minorities in school leadership is their inclusion in the decision-making process, there should be other, more immediate ways of improving the situation. Gradually, as more women and members of minority groups work into leadership positions, their acceptability in such positions will increase. In addition, if they gain some "line" positions, jobs that ordinarily lead to promotions, they will enter the pool of potential decision-makers.

One obvious way of producing change is by adopting laws and regulations. Unfortunately, specific cases of discrimination are often difficult to detect and nearly impossible to prove. For example, there are at least three federal remedies available to protect women from discrimination in school administration — The Equal Pay Act, Title VII of the Civil Rights Act of 1964, and Executive Order 11246. Since these policies have been adopted, the status of women in education has substantially deteriorated. Clearly, then, laws alone will not bring about meaningful change.

What is needed is a comprehensive program, not merely to prohibit discrimination, but actively to promote equality of opportunity. A number of writers have attempted to devise such a program; it is clear that the following ideas are essential to any workable solution:

- establish the hiring of women and minority administrators as a definite priority
- eliminate all forms of discriminatory treatment, such as different pay for equal work and enforced maternity leaves
- work for the establishment of a clearinghouse where the names of qualified women and minority men will be available
- establish a policy of actively recruiting women and minority men for administrative jobs
- encourage schools of education to train more women and minority men for these jobs
- work to develop internship programs for potential administrators

The first two points are self-explanatory. The need for the third policy is equally great, since one of the most serious obstacles to hiring women and minorities is finding and identifying potential administrators. An institution that systematically stores and disseminates such information would be invaluable.

In addition, Margaret Weber, Jean Feldman, and Eve Poling have suggested that to precipitate a reversal of the current underrepresentation of women in educational administration in the eighties, responsibility must also be placed with women. These authors urge that more women

- obtain credentials in educational administration
- apply for positions in educational administration

- encourage other women to aspire to positions in educational leadership

These same recommendations would also apply to members of minority groups.

Recruiting policies are similarly important. A study, "The Elusive Black Educator," found that, though potential black administrators may not be highly visible, they can be located by any organization that seeks them resourcefully. This demands aggressive recruiting, including the establishment of informal contacts in schools of education and acceptance of the occasional need to train the right person to meet the formal requirements of a position. School systems must develop ways to determine which candidates will be successful, to find them, and to hire them.

One place where potential administrative talent should be plentiful is, of course, in schools of education. Unfortunately, this does not seem to be the case if the sought-after talent happens to be black or female. "The Elusive Black Educator" quotes Dr. Donald J. Leu, dean of the San Jose State college of education:

> We recognize, now, that there is an increasing number of job opportunities for the well-educated black person. But a real holdup is that colleges and universities aren't recruiting, accepting or producing *enough* of them.

Similarly, Catherine Lyon and Terry Saario point out that

> schools of education, specifically departments of educational administration, have not until quite recently made the commitment necessary to support the upward mobility of women students in public education.

Another useful and effective way of finding and developing administrative talent is through internship programs. At any level of administration, such programs will work in the same way. Laval Wilson describes one project in which he participated. It was funded by a private grant and designed for the specific purpose of training nonwhite men for the superintendency. The participants, chosen for commitment to urban education, mobility, and professional potential, served five months in each of two systems, working with successful and innovative superintendents. Wilson felt that the chance to see the superintendency firsthand was invaluable for the insights it gave him into the realities of power in a school system.

Such experience not only offers the interns useful job preparation, but also gives them a chance to measure their real desire for the job in light of the actual responsibilities and pressures involved. In addition, it gives evidence of practical ability rather than abstract potential and so should promote better hiring decisions. Unfortunately, some such programs are remarkably shortsighted; the program Wilson participated in was for minority men, which apparently means that all women, including minority women, were excluded. Such a program may be combatting racism, but it is also perpetuating sexism.

Ultimately, the solution to the problem of discrimination depends on the willingness of public education to commit itself to change. Once such a commitment has been made, a specific program, based on the circumstances in each school system, should not be difficult to devise.

CONCLUSION

The status of women and minorities in school administration seems clearly inconsistent with the ideals of a democratic, egalitarian society. But discrimination in this area is not merely morally repugnant; practically it is destructive, since it narrows the base from which school leadership can be drawn.

Blacks and women alike suffer from stereotypes, but those stereotypes are not identical. The fundamental assumption that limits the role of blacks in administration is that the races should be separated. There are jobs for black administrators, but few of these jobs include supervising white teachers or students.

The primary role assigned to women remains that of the mother. According to this role stereotype, women cannot have leadership responsibilities because they might conflict with the primary commitment of all women, bearing and raising children.

There are two ways in which this situation can change. The first requires a great deal of time; it demands the changing of attitudes throughout society. The second requires an institutional commitment, by public school systems, to implementing new hiring policies. Finally, though, the problem will cease only when sex or race is irrelevant in hiring, when qualified women and minorities are as routinely included in the decision-making process as white males are today.

CHAPTER 3
LEADERSHIP STYLES
Jo Ann Mazzarella

INTRODUCTION

In an era when educational leaders are worried about their survival, when they and their colleagues are the victims of personnel cutbacks, severe mental stress, and public criticism, a concern for leadership style may seem at best academic and at worst a waste of time. What is a leadership style and why does it matter?

Reduced to its simplest terms, a leadership style is the way a leader leads. In a chapter on the principal's leadership behavior, Thomas Sergiovanni and David Elliott speak of the "ways in which the principal expresses leadership, uses power and authority, arrives at decisions, and in general interacts with teachers and others." These activities — some of the most important things educational administrators do — have enormous implications for administrators' survival. If leaders choose inappropriate ways of leading, they will often fail to accomplish the task at hand, reach long-range organizational goals, or maintain positive relationships with subordinates. These kinds of failure can lead to ultimate loss of position or loss of peace of mind.

E. Mark Hanson notes that leadership style "might be thought of as a particular behavior emphasized by the leader to motivate his or her group to accomplish some end." For most of those who have studied leadership, motivation is an important component of leadership style. Effective leadership means that others are influenced to accomplish something.

Paul Hersey and Kenneth Blanchard have presented their view of why studying leadership style and motivation is so important:

> Knowledge about motivation and leader behavior will continue to be of great concern to practitioners of management for several reasons: It can help improve the effective utilization of human resources; it can help in preventing resistance to change, restriction of output, and labor disputes; and often it can lead to a more profitable organization.

Learning about leadership style can help managers be better supervisors, institute needed changes, and inspire subordinates to be happier and produce more.

HISTORY OF STYLE THEORY

Views of leadership have changed radically over the last forty or fifty years. The earliest leadership research tried to determine what makes a leader and what makes a good leader by examining the inherent traits of leaders. After the collection of leadership traits became too large to manage or make sense of, researchers began to focus on leadership behavior, on what leaders do in their capacities as leaders. The assumption was that leadership was something almost anyone could accomplish if he or she took the trouble to learn how it was done effectively.

The concept of leadership style was born, and the research began to focus on which leadership style was best, often comparing autocratic, democratic, and laissez-faire styles. Although democratic style frequently appeared to be the most effective, the theory began to emerge than no style of leadership was best in all situations. Situational theories of leadership style then appeared on the scene, introducing the idea that the most effective style would fit the particular situation at hand.

In later years the view that leadership is merely a behavior (like swimming or running) that anyone can learn has been modified. New studies of effective leaders suggest that effective leadership results from an interaction of style and inherent traits. In other words, leadership ability is partly learned and partly inborn.

PRACTICAL APPLICATIONS

Athough most authors on leadership style agree that it is an important component of leadership and something leaders ought to become aware of, there is very little more that they agree about. Experts disagree about the major elements of leadership style, whether style varies or ought to vary according to situation, whether a leader's style is flexible at all, and whether personality traits have any effect on style.

All this disagreement is very confusing and not very helpful to those who must work in leadership positions every day. Leaders want to know what leadership styles are effective and where, how they can become better leaders, what kind of leadership training is useful, and how to select coworkers and subordinates who have the ability to be good leaders.

Although at this state there are no definitive right answers to these style dilemmas, this chapter is written with these practical, everyday needs of leaders in mind. An attempt is made to present the elements of leadership style theory that have useful and helpful implications for administrators. Near the end of the chapter is a section including practical implications of each of the major leadership style theories; the theme of this section is how to select, to train, and to be a better leader.

WHAT IS IT?

It seems logical that leadership style does not include everything a leader does or thinks; the way the leader sharpens pencils is not a facet of leadership style nor are particular religious beliefs. Which activities and beliefs *should* be focused on when assessing one's own or someone else's style?

COMPONENTS OF STYLE

One superintendent may let staff make most of the decisions about how the district is run; another superintendent may feel that she alone has the expertise and ability to make important decisions. Somewhere between these two extremes lie the styles of most school leaders.

One way of looking at and classifying the dimensions of leadership style has been proposed by Robert Tannenbaum and Warren Schmidt, who see leadership style as a continuum stretching from "subordinate-centered" to "boss-centered." The most subordinate-centered leadership involves giving subordinates great freedom to make decisions within very flexible limits. With the most boss-centered leadership, the manager alone makes the decision and either merely announces it or attempts to "sell" the decision. While Tannenbaum and Schmidt admit that there are times when more boss-centered leadership is necessary, clearly they see more subordinate-centered behavior as the most effective. They advocate making a continuing effort to confront subordinates with the "challenge of freedom."

As well as differing about who makes decisions, leaders may also vary in the way they view employees. One principal may see staff members as lacking in motivation, needing to be constantly pushed, and holding their own interest above that of the school. Another principal may assume that staff are just the opposite: motivated to improve the school, self-starting, and giving prime importance to school needs.

This way of classifying leaders' views of employees is found in the writing of Douglas McGregor, who formulated the now famous concept of Theory X and Theory Y. McGregor believed each person holds one of two opposing theories of human behavior. One, Theory X, holds that people are basically lazy, need to be prodded to action, and are motivated only by material or other rewards and punishments. The other, Theory Y, holds that people enjoy accomplishment, are self-motivated (except when thwarted), and have a desire to make a real contribution to their organization.

McGregor classified leaders as following either Theory X or Theory Y, with Theory Y leaders cast as modern, enlightened, humanitarian, and compassionate leaders who succeed in motivating people.

According to McGregor, each view of human nature is a self-fulfilling prophecy. If one treats workers as being responsible and self-motivated, they will be. If one treats them as lazy or without motivation, they will be that too. A realization that this is so has been the basis of a movement toward more democratic determination of organizational objectives and participative management as part of an attempt to increase employee commitment to organizational goals.

McGregor's theories have made an important contribution toward making leadership more humanistic. Yet some critics have maintained that too much participative management can impede accomplishment of organizational goals.

61

One of these, Philip DeTurk (headmaster of Shepherd Knapp School in Massachusetts) expressed his fears that leaders who insist on always sharing power may be abdicating their responsibility to meet the institution's needs for authority, may be endangering their own health through personal overcommitment to time-consuming decision-making practices, and may be ignoring the urgency of month-to-month financial survival. DeTurk feels that McGregor himself came to a similar conclusion in a speech he gave when resigning as president of Antioch College.

> I thought that maybe I could operate so that everyone would like me, that "good human relations" would eliminate all discord and disagreement. I couldn't have been more wrong. It took a couple of years, but I finally began to realize that a leader cannot avoid the exercise of authority any more than he can avoid responsibility for what happens to his organization.

In spite of the undeniable value of McGregor's theories, it may be that too slavishly dedicating oneself to Theory Y-oriented leadership in the organization may cause decision-making to be slighted and survival of the individual leader or the organization to be threatened. The balance is a difficult one.

Decision-making is often an important component of leadership style. Mr. Smith and Mr. Jones are both principals who are faced with massive budget cuts. Mr. Smith spends the weekend alone in his office wrestling with the budget. At Monday afternoon's faculty meeting he announces what and whom must be cut. Mr. Jones, however, uses the Monday meeting to explain the problem, ask for suggestions as to what might be cut, and then calls for a vote on each suggestion.

These two leaders would be called the "autocrat" and the "consultative manager" by Thomas Bonoma and Dennis Slevin, who have identified four leadership styles based on where the authority for decisions is placed and where information about the decision comes from.

Another example of leadership style might be Mrs. Green (the "consultative autocrat") who asks for faculty suggestions and then makes the decision alone or Mr. Blue (the "shareholder") who elicits no information exchange from his faculty but leaves it up to them to make the decision. From these examples, it remains clear that how people habitually make decisions is one component of leadership style.

PEOPLE OR WORK?

Some people have more interest in what they are doing than in the people they are working with. Others give more importance to their relationship with coworkers than to the job. Whether one emphasizes the task or human relations is often thought to be central to leadership style.

For leaders, an important aspect of the task at hand often includes establishing ways of doing things, channels of communication, or organizational patterns. Andrew Halpin (along with Ralph Stogdill and others at The Ohio State University) called such activities "initiating structure." He found that effective leaders place a lot of importance on initiating structure. But he found too that they also are very much concerned about their relationships with people. Effective leaders evidenced a lot of behavior indicative of friendship, mutual trust, respect, and warmth. Halpin called this sort of behavior "consideration."

In a study of fifty Ohio superintendents, Halpin found that both school board members and staff saw superintendents' leadership effectiveness as made up of behavior characterized by high scores on initiating structure and consideration. Ineffective superintendents had low scores in each.

It is hard to balance work concerns and people concerns. In fact some experts claim it is impossible. Fred Fiedler, who called these dimensions "task-orientation" and "relationship-orientation," believed that leaders were able to focus on either one or the other but not both. He saw task-orientation and relationship-orientation as two ends of a continuum (like thin and fat or tall and short) and believed it logically impossible to be at both ends of the continuum.

Fiedler in the research on his "contingency theory" (to be described in detail later in this chapter) ascertained that leaders who described their "least preferred coworker" in positive terms were "human relations oriented," whereas those who described the least liked coworker in negative terms were "task-oriented." (The nature of the instrument

63

used to measure the attitude toward this coworker did not allow for leaders who had both orientations.) Fiedler believed that both styles would be effective.

Are task orientation and human relations orientation mutually exclusive? Some authors, such as Sergiovanni, side with Fiedler in answering yes. William Reddin is an example of other writers who, siding with Halpin, answer no. Reddin saw four possible combinations of orientation: human relations orientation alone, task orientation alone, both of these orientations together, and neither one. Reddin believed that any one of these four styles could be effective depending on the situation. When to use which style will be discussed in the next section.

This section has discussed a number of ways of looking at leadership style. Some stress decision-making styles, some stress ways of looking at subordinates, and some stress whether leaders are more interested in the people or the job. Although some of these theories are overlapping, they are not identical and some directly conflict with each other. They necessitate a choice. Administrators must choose and make use of the theories that best fit their experiences, situations, personalities, and, not least, intuitive perceptions of themselves and others.

THE IDEAL STYLE

Many leaders or would-be leaders puzzle over which leadership style is the most effective. Wanting to know the ideal way to approach leadership, they debate such issues as whether they should strive for subordinate-centered leadership or boss-centered leadership, whether they should base their leadership on Theory X or Theory Y, or whether they should concentrate on the task or on human relations.

Some researchers on leadership style maintain that these dilemmas are not only unsolvable, but also the wrong questions to ask. These researchers believe that there is no ideal approach to leadership that fits all situations; rather, the best view of leadership style is that it must vary to fit the particular situation at hand.

While some leaders swear by the importance of relationship-oriented leadership and others proclaim the importance of a task-oriented style, Fiedler, using his contingency theory, maintains that either one of these styles can be appropriate, depending on the amount of control the leader has over the situation (sometimes called how "favorable" the situation is). Fiedler sees three important components in situational control: status or position power of the leader, quality of relations between the leader and members, and structure of the task. Fiedler's extensive research reveals that when a leader is extremely influential or extremely uninfluential, the most effective style will be a task-oriented style. Relationship-oriented leaders are more effective in the situations that fall in between.

RISK TAKING

A contingency-type theory also made sense to Cecil Miskel, who, like Fiedler, studied how style factors and leader effectiveness were related to the situation. Miskel, too, found that how well leaders perform is related to different combinations of style and situational components. Miskel, however, believed that style variables might be other than task-related or relationship-related. He also examined other style factors, including risk-taking propensity in leaders. Miskel found that those principals who tended to be risk takers (or had low security needs) were more successful at innovative efforts — at least when they also had fewer years of experience and worked in a school that used innovative management techniques.

Is success at innovation the same as success as a leader? Not necessarily perhaps, but Miskel's findings take on added significance when one recalls that James Lipham defined leadership as "that behavior of an individual which initiates a new structure in interaction within a social system." This definition is not just an idle theory; good leaders are always making things better. Implicit in the word "leader" is the idea of movement from one place to another. Leaders are not leading when they are standing still.

Other researchers too have looked at risk-taking behavior. William Holloway and Ghulam Niazi related risk-taking propensities of school administrators to Fiedler's concept of leader control over the situation. Holloway and Niazi found

65

that the more control school principals had over their work situation, the greater their disposition to take risks. They concluded that leaders' willingness to take risks can be increased by improving the leader's status or group support.

WHAT IS THE SITUATION?

Many authorities agree with Fiedler's view that the leadership style needed depends on the situation. Many disagree, however, about what the important elements of the situation are. Fiedler saw three important elements in the situation: status, leader-member relations, and task structure. William Reddin sees five important components of the work situation: organizational philosophy, technology (or how the work is done), the superior, the coworkers, and the subordinates.

Reddin identified four possible styles that were combinations of task-oriented behavior and relationship-oriented behavior. "Integrated style" is style that emphasizes both relationship-oriented and task-oriented behavior. "Separated" style is deficient in both. "Related" style emphasizes relationship-oriented behavior but neglects task-oriented. "Dedicated" style emphasizes task but neglects relationship.

Reddin believed that each one of these four styles (even separated style) could be effective or ineffective depending on the situation, and he coined descriptive terms to describe the possible managerial types embodying the eight effective and ineffective styles. For example, the "autocrat" uses the dedicated (high task, low relationship) style inappropriately and is ineffective as a leader; the "benevolent autocrat" uses the dedicated style appropriately and is an effective leader. Figure 1 shows the effective and ineffective manifestations of each style.

Reddin explained that an appropriate time to use the dedicated style (or to be a benevolent autocrat) is when the manager knows more about the job than the subordinates do, when unscheduled events are likely to occur, when directions must be given, or where the subordinates' performance is easily measurable.

Robert Tannenbaum and Warren Schmidt describe "forces" a leader should consider in deciding how to manage. Although some theorists would lump all these forces into the

FIGURE 1. EFFECTIVE AND INEFFECTIVE MANIFESTATIONS OF THE FOUR POSSIBLE LEADERSHIP STYLES ACCORDING TO REDDIN

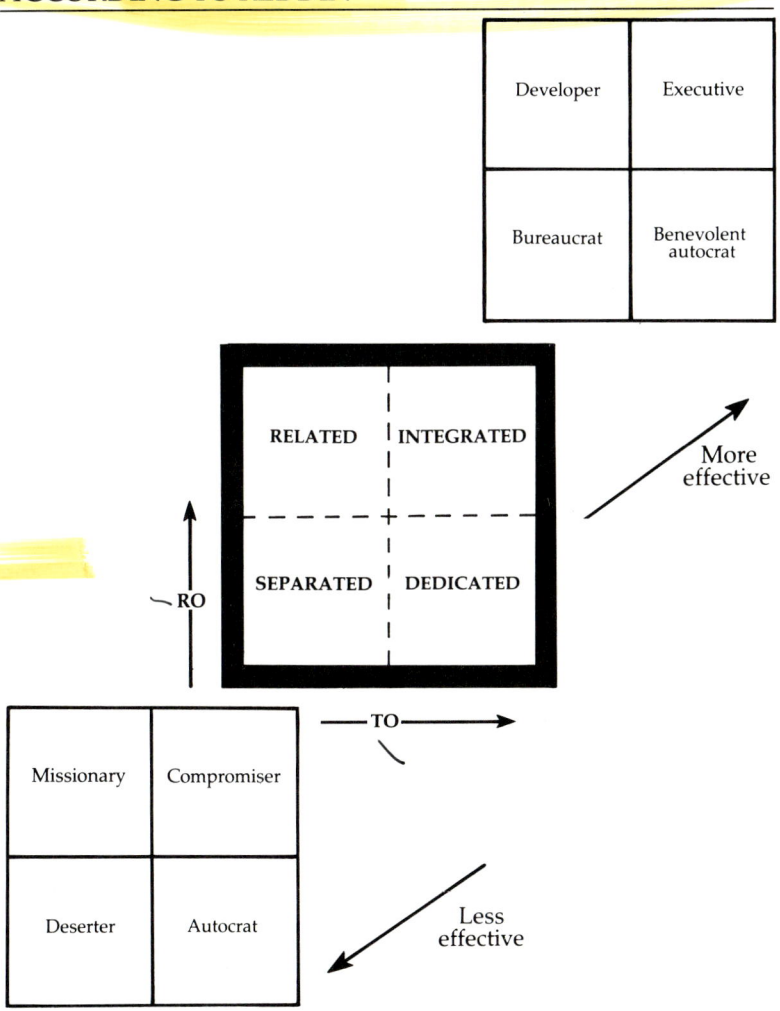

Developer	Executive
Bureaucrat	Benevolent autocrat

RELATED	INTEGRATED
SEPARATED	DEDICATED

RO ↑   TO →   More effective ↗   Less effective ↘

Missionary	Compromiser
Deserter	Autocrat

From *Managerial Effectiveness* by William Reddin. ©1970. Reprinted by permission of McGraw-Hill Book Company.

category "situational," Tannenbaum and Schmidt call them "forces in the manager," "forces in the subordinates," and "forces in the situation."

Forces within managers include their value systems

67

(How do they feel about the worth of participative decision-making?), their confidence in subordinates, their inclinations toward a particular style, and their feelings of security (Can they feel comfortable releasing control?).

Forces in the subordinates include such things as needs for independence, readiness to assume responsibility, and tolerance for ambiguity. The forces that Tannenbaum and Schmidt call "forces in the situation" include type of organization (Will participative decision-making be accepted and appropriate?), group effectiveness (Can employees work together?), the problem itself (Is it simple or complex, minor or important?), and time pressure.

In contrast to Reddin and Tannenbaum and Schmidt, who examined several components of the situation, Philip Gates, Kenneth Blanchard, and Paul Hersey looked at only one aspect of one of these components (subordinates) as being the most important and called this aspect "follower maturity." In the view of these authors, the leadership style a leader chooses ought to depend on the maturity of the followers. By maturity, they meant three things:

- a capacity to set high but attainable goals
- a willingness and ability to take responsibility
- education or experience

Because follower maturity can change over time, these authors believed that appropriate leader behavior should also change over time. When followers are low in maturity, they need leaders who are heavily task-oriented. As follower maturity increases, leaders can shift their emphasis from tasks to relationships. Then as followers come to have above average maturity, even their need for relationship behavior decreases.

But "maturity of followers (or any other single factor of which I am aware) is too simple a construct around which to build a contingency theory of leadership," maintains Thomas Sergiovanni in an article criticizing leader training programs focusing on only one situational variable. Sergiovanni cites a number of other contingencies that leadership style has been found to rest on, including Reddin's job characteristics, Fiedler's leader influence, and such concepts from other authors as role expectations of followers, peers, and superordinates; personality characteristics of leaders and followers;

time constraints in achieving objectives; political considerations; and interpersonal tension within the group.

In an earlier work, Sergiovanni and David Elliott cited the aspects of the situation they felt were most important for leaders to consider: the kinds of demands the job makes on leadership, the nature and distribution of power and authority, and the expectations held by significant others. Sergiovanni and Elliott noted that educational settings (particularly leadership situations in elementary schools) only occasionally call for separated and dedicated styles. According to these authors, therefore, styles that emphasize human relations will be the most effective in schools. They explain that with separated and dedicated styles "the human dimension is neglected." "The focus of leadership in general" ought to be related or integrated in schools that "wish to make a human difference."

SITUATION AND PERSONALITY

If leadership effectiveness depends on the situation, does it follow that who the leader is has no importance? Some authors think so. Stephen Hencley, in a survey of recent leadership theories, noted that to many authors "the situational approach maintains that leadership is determined not so much by the characters of individuals as by the requirements of social situations." Hencley feels that the situational approach focuses on "relationships and variables in social and environmental situations that appear to generate leader behavior." Individual capacity for leadership is not important.

But this view is certainly not held by all authors on leadership. Fiedler saw propensity for task-oriented or relationship-oriented behavior as a function of personality and noted that the leader's personality was one factor in determining success. He described his theory of leadership effectiveness as one that "takes account of the leader's personality as well as the situational factors in the leadership situation."

Andrew Halpin, too, whose theories were examined earlier, saw leadership as being determined in part by the situation and in part by leader characteristics. E. Mark Hanson, in a review of leadership style theories, defined situational theory in general as the view that situational factors and personality variables interact in determining leader effectiveness.

Leader personality does make a difference in leadership style; in fact, many authors believe that leadership style is determined by personality and is as difficult to change. This idea does not, however, negate the important contribution of situational theory and research that no leadership style is ideal for every leadership situation.

CAN YOU CHANGE YOUR STYLE?

If the situationists are right, if leadership style ought to vary to fit the situation, then it follows that leaders need to be able to change their styles at will. Is this possible? Is leadership style flexible enough to be changed to fit the situation? Or should leaders attempt to change the situation instead?

IDENTIFYING YOUR STYLE

The first step for a leader wanting to change his or her style is to become aware of what that style is. Yet identifying one's style is not simple. Fiedler, in a 1979 article, cited two studies that found that most leaders are not able to see their styles as others see them. In fact, one study found a zero correlation between leader and subordinate style ratings. Since it is assumed that others' perceptions are more objective than one's own, it seems likely that most leaders do not see themselves accurately.

All is not lost, however. Fiedler believes that leaders can be taught to recognize their styles. Together with Martin Chemers and Linda Mahar, Fiedler developed a teaching guide that helps leaders identify whether they are relationship-motivated or task-motivated. This guide asks leaders to look at their own behaviors and helps them to rate themselves on a number of specific style factors, rather than asking them to make guesses about their overall styles.

Much of Fiedler's own research used the Least-preferred Coworker scale as an instrument to measure style. Leaders are asked to describe the colleague whom they have most disliked. Those who describe this coworker in very negative terms have been found to be task-motivated, whereas those who describe him or her in positive or less critical terms have been found to be relationship-motivated.

Sergiovanni and Elliott also have formulated a questionnaire to help leaders identify their styles. Those who take this questionnaire are asked to describe how they would act if they were leaders of a work group. Respondents mark "always," "frequently," "occasionally," "seldom," or "never" to such statements as "I would allow members complete freedom in their work,""I would needle members for greater effort," and "I would schedule the work to be done."

Sergiovanni and Elliott suggest that leaders might find it helpful to have their coworkers or subordinates describe the leaders on the same questionnaire. They warn, "Don't be surprised if others see you differently than you see yourself."

Thomas Bonoma and Dennis Slevin display their leadership model on a grid to help leaders diagnose their styles. This grid, reproduced in figure 2, rests on their belief that leadership style is a mixture of where information for decisions comes from and where decision authority is placed. One recommendation is to keep a daily diary of decision-making activities and to place each decision on the grid by indicating where information input comes from and where decision authority is placed. Bonoma and Slevin quote a reader who reported that this method "confirmed that my actual leadership style was inconsistent with my preconceived image of leadership style."

STYLE FLEX

Even if style can be identified, it does not necessarily follow that it can be changed at will. Certainly Fiedler's contingency theory admits for very little style flexibility in leaders.

As mentioned earlier, Fiedler sees leaders as either task-motivated or relationship-motivated but not both. Fiedler saw this basic style motivation as part of one's personality and, as such, very difficult to change, especially through a short training program.

> At best it takes one, two, or three years of intensive psychotherapy to effect lasting changes in personality

structure. It is difficult to see how we can change in more than a few cases an equally important set of core values in a few hours of lectures and role-playing or even in ...one or two weeks.

Yet at the same time Fiedler maintains that neither style is appropriate for all situations. Are some leaders thus doomed to failure simply because they find themselves in a situation incompatible with their styles? The answer is no; Fiedler believed that those leaders in incompatible situations could change the situation.

Sergiovanni too, resting his case heavily on Fiedler's findings, has maintained that style, like personality, is very difficult to change. Although he admits that "some leaders are able to change styles with ease," he believes that "trainers

FIGURE 2. BONOMA-SLEVIN LEADERSHIP MODEL GRID

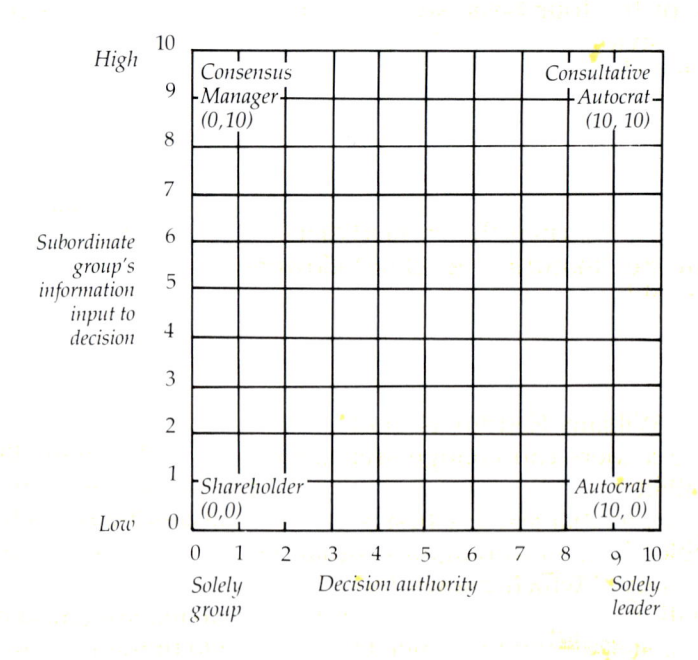

Subordinate group's information input to decision (Low to High, 0–10 vertical axis)

Decision authority (Solely group to Solely leader, 0–10 horizontal axis)

- Consensus Manager (0, 10)
- Consultative Autocrat (10, 10)
- Shareholder (0, 0)
- Autocrat (10, 0)

From *Executive Survival Manual, A Program for Managerial Effectiveness* by Thomas V. Bonoma and Dennis P. Slevin.
© 1978 by Wadsworth Publishing Company, Inc. Reprinted by permission of Wadsworth Publishing Company, Belmont, California 94002.

overestimate style flexibility and do not account sufficiently for those of us (perhaps the majority of us) with more limited style ranges."

"Successful leaders can adapt their leader behavior to meet the needs of the group," insist Paul Hersey and Kenneth Blanchard, who see four possible combinations of task-oriented and relationship-oriented behavior:

- task-oriented behavior
- relationship-oriented behavior
- task-oriented and relationship-oriented behavior combined
- neither task-oriented nor relationship-oriented

Like Reddin, Hersey and Blanchard believed that any of the four styles could be effective. But Hersey and Blanchard did not believe that every leader used or even could use all four styles. "Some leaders are able to modify their behavior to fit any of the four basic styles, while others can utilize two or three styles." In other words some leaders have the ability to be flexible in style and others are more rigid; the most flexible are the most likely to be effective in jobs that require a lot of adaptability.

Probably the theory of leadership style that allows for the greatest style flexibility was developed by Gates, Blanchard, and Hersey. Their theory held that leader behavior must vary to fit the "maturity" level of followers. As followers became more able to operate on their own, these researchers believed that leaders would be forced to change their styles. The successful leaders could change, whereas the unsuccessful ones could not.

William Reddin is another author who believes that some leaders can change style and other leaders have little flexibility. According to Reddin, the best leaders have three important abilities. The first is "situational sensitivity," which enables leaders to diagnose situations. The second is "style flexibility," which allows them to match their styles to the situation, and the third is "situational management skill," which helps them to change the situation to fit their styles.

Reddin also saw another side to style flexibility. He saw the negative effects of a "high-flex" manager in a situation that calls for a lower degree of flexibility. This situation Reddin

73

described as "style drift"; "drift managers" are those who are perceived as having no minds of their own, who fail to organize their situation, and who allow change to overwhelm them. Thus Reddin saw that the need for style flexibility, like the need for a particular style, varies to fit the situation.

There are so many diverse components of a principal's job that the situation may change from minute to minute. If we analyze the situation in Fiedler's terms, we find that at times the "task structure" is clearly spelled out (such as in organizing a bus schedule), at times it is extremely vague (as when improving school climate). At times "position power" is high (such as when hiring a new teacher) and at times very low (as in implementing a request from the central office). Only "leader-member relations" may stay fairly stable, and these vary from school to school.

In the face of this complex situation and the conflicting theories reviewed here, only one conclusion seems clear: school administrators are going to have to be able to be flexible about something — either their styles or their situations — or they are not going to be able to cope with their jobs. It is up to each individual administrator to decide, based on the theories presented so far, which aspect can most easily be changed.

SYNTHESIZING THE THEORIES

The preceding sections have presented important aspects of some (but certainly not all) well-known leadership theories. At this point it may seem appropriate to ask how these theories fit together. Can they all be coordinated to form a more all-encompassing theory?

It is quite tempting to think that we now have all the pieces of a giant puzzle that can be fitted together into a coherent whole. And at first glance it may appear that many of these theories are quite compatible. Certainly, all those that emphasize concern for task or human relations as elements of style have something in common, as do those that emphasize decision-making.

But after we have made these rather elementary connections, we are blocked from taking the logical next step of making generalities about all the theories. For instance, at first it seems to make sense that leadership styles that stress human relations are quite similar to those that stress participative decision-making, but the analogy does not hold up. A leader with a democratic or subordinate-centered style may (or even must) also have a concern for the task according to some of these theories (notably Halpin's).

Other seeming similarities turn out to be superficial. Although both Fiedler and Reddin see task and human relations as important components of style, they are diametrically opposed about whether leaders can change their styles — and this difference has big implications for the practice of leadership.

Unfortunately, it is not yet time for an overarching theory of leadership. The data are not all in on important questions like whether leaders can change styles or what the most important components of style should be.

The kind of synthesis that *is* possible with leadership style theories is one that compares and contrasts the theories in a way that shows graphically how they are alike and how they differ. This we have attempted to do in the form of table 1. In addition to listing the theories according to the components of style they emphasize, the table also gives each theory's answer to the questions of whether the components are mutually exclusive, whether the style ought to vary with the situation, and whether the style is flexible.

SO WHAT?

None of the theories of leadership style discussed so far has much value to leaders unless it can be used to improve leader performance. Whether styles can or should vary to fit the situation or how one determines the important characteristics of the situation are questions that do not really matter unless the answers can be used to select or train better leaders or to be a better leader.

Researchers and theoreticians do not always share this pragmatic view. Their work is not always aimed at practitioners, and even when it is, they are often more concerned about discovering "truths" than they are about being helpful. Thus, the theories discussed in this chapter do not always easily or

TABLE 1: COMPARISON OF LEADERSHIP STYLE THEORIES ACCORDING TO COMPONENTS, EXCLUSIVITY, VARIABILITY, AND FLEXIBILITY

	Authors	How many styles?	Components or Elements of Style
DECISION-MAKING	Tannenbaum and Schmidt	2	*Decision-Making* "Subordinate-centered vs. boss-centered" (Democratic vs. autocratic) (former most effective)
	Bonoma and Slevin	4	*Decision-Making* (where authority is placed and where information comes from) Four possible styles: autocrat, consultative manager, consultative autocrat, shareholder (all but the last are effective)
	McGregor	2	*View of employees* Theory X (need extrinsic motivators) vs. Theory Y (self-motivated) (Latter view most effective)
TASK AND HUMAN RELATIONS	Halpin	2	*Task and Human Relations* Concern for initiating structure or consideration
	Fiedler	2	*Task and Human Relations* Task-oriented vs. Human relationship oriented (either can be effective)
	Reddin	4	*Task and Human Relations* Four combinations of human relations orientation and task orientation. Four possible styles: integrated, separated, related, dedicated (each can be effective)
	Gates, Blanchard, and Hersey Hersey and Blanchard	4	*Task and Human Relations* (both can be effective)
	Sergiovanni and Elliott	4	*Task and Human Relations* (same as Reddin above) Integrated, separated, related, dedicated (each can be effective)
RISK TAKING	Miskel	-	Several, including risk-taking propensity of leaders
	Holloway and Niazi	-	

Are Components Mutually Esclusive?	Does the Style Needed Vary With the Situation?	Is the Leader's Style Flexible?
Yes (leader cannot use both at the same time)	Yes (components are forces in the manager, forces in the subordinates and forces in the situation)	Yes, leader chooses the style appropriate at the time
No (all possible combinations of the components are possible)	Yes	Yes
Yes	No	Not applicable
No (effective leaders have both concerns)	Not applicable	Not applicable
Yes	Yes (most important component is leader situational control, made up of position power, leader-member relations, task structure)	No
No	Yes (components are organizational philosophy, technology, superior, co-workers, subordinates)	Some leaders are flexible and some are not.
Yes (although leader can change from one to the other, does not use both simultaneously)	Yes (most important component is follower maturity)	Yes (must change with time)
No	Yes (components are the demands of the job, nature and distribution of power and authority, expectations held by significant others)	Usually no, and not without great difficulty
Not applicable	Yes (components are leader years of experience and innovative management techniques)	Not applicable
Not applicable	Yes (most important component is leader control)	Not applicable

neatly lend themselves to practice. Nevertheless, the following section is an attempt to pick out those practical implications that *can* be taken from the theories and studies discussed so far.

BECOMING A BETTER LEADER

How one uses leadership style theories depends on two things: what beliefs and assumptions about leadership one holds and what one's goals are. Below are listed some goals that leaders may have, each followed by a brief discussion of strategies for accomplishing the goal suggested by the pertinent theories. The leader will want to weigh each strategy according to his or her philosophy of leadership. The first and largest group of goals and strategies is based on the assumption that leaders can, indeed, change their leadership styles when it is necessary.

Goals That Assume Flexible Style

Raise Motivation of Workers, Help Them Accept Changes, and Improve Morale. If the leader holds these goals, then more "subordinate-centered" leadership, as defined by Tannenbaum and Schmidt, may be appropriate. Although Tannenbaum and Schmidt do not offer a recipe for how to become more subordinate-centered, they do offer guidelines for determining whether this style will be appropriate for particular subordinates. This style of leadership may indeed be in order if the subordinates have the following characteristics:

- high needs for independence
- readiness to assume responsibility
- high tolerance for ambiguity
- interest in the problem at hand
- understanding of and identification with the goals of the organization
- necessary knowledge and experience
- a history of sharing in decision-making

Besides depending on subordinates, the decision to change to more subordinate-centered leadership must also consider other factors: the manager's feelings and values, and situational forces. Is subordinate-centered leadership valued by the manager? Does the manager have confidence in subordinates? Will more participative decision-making be accepted in the particular organization and are the employees compatible enough to work together? All these questions must be answered before a switch to more subordinate-centered leadership is clearly called for. An acceptance of McGregor's theories and a desire to increase employee motivation will probably also prompt a similar type of move toward more participative management.

Remove Stress, Reduce Workload, and Assure the Survival of the Organization. If the leader is, however, in the position of some principals today who have for a long time been committed to participative management, who already ask employees to help with every decision — from which teacher to hire to which waste basket to buy — and who feel overwhelmed by the process, then DeTurk's suggestions may be more appropriate. For participative managers who feel under great stress, overworked, and worried about the very survival of the organization, a return to more leader autonomy may be in order. This does not mean a return to Theory X, but rather a realization that leaders must make some independent decisions.

Determine If the Leader's Style Fits a Particular Situation. Some leaders may feel that leadership style ought to vary to fit the work situation but may not know how to determine whether their style is appropriate for their own particular work situation. Their goal thus becomes one of assessing the compatibility of their style and situation. Like Tannenbaum and Schmidt, Reddin does not specify how to change style, but his theory is very helpful in determining if there is a fit between style and situation.

The leader can first determine which one of Reddin's categories (dedicated, related, separated, or integrated) describes his or her style. The next step is to look at the important components of the situation as outlined by Reddin (superior, subordinates, technology, organizational philosophy, and co-workers) and determine whether the style used is appropriate to fit these.

For instance, if the manager knows more about the job than do the subordinates, if unscheduled events are likely to occur, if directions must be given, or if performance is easily measurable, then an effective dedicated style (benevolent autocrat) will contribute to the manager's success. But if the leader in this situation is not "dedicated," he or she may have to make some changes in either the style or the situation.

Adapt Style to Maturity of Followers. Some leaders are going to find that their experience, beliefs, and abilities cause them to lean toward the theories of Gates, Blanchard, and Hersey, who hold that style should change with follower maturity. These leaders will closely assess their follower's capacity to set goals, willingness to take responsibility, education, and experience and choose their styles accordingly (task-oriented when maturity is low, relationship-oriented when it is moderate, and as little leadership behavior as possible if maturity is high). They will remember too the warning that follower maturity may regress (especially when new tasks are presented) and that style must change to fit.

Improve Decision-Making. Some leaders have trouble making leadership decisions or even deciding how these decisions *ought* to be made. These leaders may find it helpful to borrow Bonoma and Slevin's idea of looking at both information input and decision-making authority and determining for each decision who ought to supply information relevant to the decision and who ought to actually make the decision. Based on this assessment, the leader may decide to increase or decrease staff involvement in decision-making.

Those interested may also find it helpful to use Bonoma and Slevin's leadership checklist to help them think through how well their styles fit with organization's needs. This checklist asks things like, "Am I developing my subordinates by letting them participate in decisions affecting them?" and "Does the organization management information system work for me or do I work for it?"

We must add to all these suggestions Sergiovanni's warning that situations are extremely complex and that any system that looks at only one or two components of the situation is much too limited. Leaders who focus on only one situational component may run into trouble with the others. Worth repeating too is Sergiovanni's warning that for many, style may not be easy to change. Those who expect to change it overnight are in for a frustrating time.

The preceding suggestions have all been based on the supposition that leaders have some control over and can change their styles. The next group of suggestions is based on the opposite assumption: leaders' styles usually cannot be changed.

Goals That Assume Inflexible Style

Change the Situation to Fit One's Style. If one accepts Fred Fiedler's assumptions about the necessity of changing the situation when style and situation are incompatible, his theories are extremely useful in improving one's leadership abilities. In the book written with Martin Chemers and Linda Mahar, Fiedler has supplied specific techniques for making needed changes.

After explaining how to categorize both style and situation and providing instruments for use in the process, these authors advise leaders on how to change the situation to fit their style. Fiedler, as we recall, believes that relationship-oriented leaders work best in situations of moderate control, and task-oriented leaders work best in situations of very great or very little control. According to the authors, the most important step a leader can take to increase control is to improve leader-member relations. This might be done through socializing more with members of the group or requesting particular people to work in the group. The second most effective way to increase control is to change the task structure. This might be done by structuring the task more tightly or asking superiors for more structured tasks or detailed instructions. Obtaining more training often serves to make the task more structured. The final method of increasing control would be to change one's status or "position power." This might involve developing more expertise in the job or using more fully one's decision-making power.

Fiedler, Chemers, and Mahar also explain how to *decrease* control of the situation through such tactics as socializing less with workers, loosening task structure, and asking for more participative decision-making. They also note that those who accept Fiedler's theories about the difficulty of changing style and yet who nevertheless feel their styles must change may want to embark on a program (probably lengthy) of therapy.

Increase Innovativeness. The implications of Miskel's theoretical and empirical work are that leaders who want to become more innovative in their leadership will have to increase their risk-taking behavior or make their organization's management techniques more innovative. How can risk taking be strengthened? According to the findings of Holloway and Niazi, one way is to increase control of the situation using Fiedler's techniques, especially by improving leader status or group support.

Improve Human Relations. If school leaders accept Sergiovanni and Elliott's theory that a style stressing human relations is most effective in schools, then they will want to assess their styles (using the Sergiovanni and Elliott questionnaire) in attempting to determine whether their styles do indeed have this kind of emphasis. Most people believe they have human relations skills, but without an instrument they are unable objectively to assess how they compare to others on this dimension. Those who discover that they have the required related or integrated styles will be reassured. Those who are very weak in human relations will face a difficult decision. They may have to reassess whether a school leadership position is the best place for them to be.

TRAINING PROGRAMS

Any theory of leadership style that makes it possible to become a better leader also has implications for leadership training programs. If a theory can be used to improve leadership behavior, it can also be the basis for a training program. Anyone who wants to institute a training program for leaders can begin by going back over this chapter, extracting the theories that would be helpful along with the new behavior these theories imply, and using those as the basis for training leaders. Aside from these obvious applications a few more specific applications need to be made.

Hersey and Blanchard, who prefer to view leadership as "an observed behavior" not dependent on inborn abilities or potentials, believe individuals can be trained to adapt their leadership styles to fit varying situations. They argue that "most people can increase their effectiveness in leadership roles through education, training, and development." Nevertheless, these authors are not naive. They do not believe that leadership training is easy and they warn that most training programs do not take into consideration that it is difficult to change styles quickly.

Fiedler likewise is critical of leadership training programs, but for other reasons. Fiedler notes that most training programs are never evaluated objectively, so that it is impossible to tell whether they were really effective or not. Most programs that *have* been evaluated "throw considerable doubt on the efficacy of these training programs for increasing organizational and group performance." Fiedler's theories offer an explanation of why this finding may be so. Assuming that most leadership training programs teach leaders to be more relationship-oriented or more task-oriented, Fiedler notes that even if it were effective, each kind of training would be useful only to some leaders and not to others, depending on their situations. A leader trained to be more task-oriented will become better suited for situations where the leader has much or little control but will become less suited for situations involving intermediate amounts of control. Those trained to be more relationship-oriented would be better suited for situations intermediate in control but poorly suited for high- and low-control situations.

Fiedler offers an alternative. "If leadership training is to be successful, the present theory would argue that it should focus on providing the individual with methods for diagnosing the favorableness of the leadership situation and for adapting the leadership situations to the individual's style of leadership."

The leadership training guide written by Fiedler, Chemers, and Mahar attempts to do exactly that. This guide, mentioned in the previous section, is designed as a self-instructional program to help leaders become more effective. Part 1 is concerned with identifying leadership style, part 2 provides tools for accurately diagnosing and classifying leadership situations, and part 3 discusses how to match leadership style with the situation and, if necessary, change the situation. The guide contains numerous exercises, each usually consisting of a short case study or incident presenting a problem in leadership and asking the participant to choose the best of several solutions. Average time for completion of the entire guide is five hours. In a 1979 article, Fiedler noted that objective evaluation techniques have proved this program to be extremely effective.

Another training program that also shows evidence of being effective has been described by Leverne Barrett and Edgar Yoder. Unlike the programs criticized by Fiedler, this program was carefully evaluated with pre- and post-test data collection and (something unusual in most evaluation efforts) a control group.

The program was based on the theories of researchers like Halpin who make two assumptions not held by Fiedler: that effective leadership requires both task-oriented and human relations-oriented behavior and that leadership style can be changed by a leadership training program.

Barrett and Yoder emphasize that an important component of the program was its first step: principals were given feedback about how their teachers saw them as leaders through the teachers' responses on the Supervisory Behavior Development Questionnaire, the Likert Profile, and the Job Objectives Questionnaire. Barrett and Yoder maintain that this information helped leaders realize the need to change and made them more receptive to training. The program sought to teach human relations skills through such workshop activities as communicating, instituting administrative structures that promote communication, and establishing a working climate in which teachers and students have feelings of self-worth. Task-oriented activities included showing the principals how to help teachers learn and achieve the goals of the school.

According to a posttraining survey of teachers, the administrators improved their leadership behavior in both task-oriented and human relations-oriented areas, especially in adequacy of communication and work facilitation.

These successful examples should not obscure the fact that some training programs on leadership style have serious problems. Those who choose a program should remember the warnings of Sergiovanni, who objected not only to the simplistic nature of many programs (especially those that looked at only one situational variable) but to the very goals of the programs.

The leadership models themselves are too simple, the claims of most leadership trainers are unrealistic and the assumptions basic to the models and to training programs are conceptually flawed on the one hand and emphasize instrumental and mechanistic aspects of leadership at the acute expense of the substantive on the other.

Administrators looking for a good program should be wary when promises of success are too sweeping, when instantaneous changes are promised, and when the true goals of leadership appear to be forgotten.

LEADER SELECTION

Just as they have implications for leadership training programs, the leadership style theories discussed here all have implications for leader selection. Any theory that includes ideas about the most effective style can be adapted to choosing the most effective leader.

Some of the theories and findings have specific application to leader selection in schools. For example, Miskel's research with principals implies that propensity for risk taking may be one good indicator of the performance potential of principals. This finding seems especially noteworthy in light of the fact that quite often those who are considered the most promising candidates are conformists who follow all the rules and never take risks.

CONCLUSION

This brief survey of theories and research on leadership styles reveals that the subject is not a simple one. The theories are complex and varied and encompass such things as personalities, attitudes, decision-making techniques, risk taking, and orientation toward work and people. They include such areas as leaders' control of the situation, subordinates' maturity, and technology. Some rest firmly on the belief that leadership style can be changed, whereas others assume that it cannot. Some theorists maintain that an effective leader has a style that emphasizes a concern for both the "task" and for "human relations," whereas others believe that these concerns are incompatible and are not found within the same person. Some theories stress an ideal leadership style, but others hold that the best style varies to fit the situation.

How can such diverse and conflicting theories be helpful to leaders? After the initial smoke and confusion have cleared and administrators are actually able to make sense of and differentiate among these theories, their usefulness begins to become apparent.

Because leadership by definition includes action, any theory of leadership is helpful only if it can be used to guide action. Each of these theories has implications for better leadership. Each can be used as a basis for training leaders, for selecting leaders, and most importantly for becoming a better leader.

Although the theories disagree significantly, basing one's actions on any one of them is more effective than following no theory at all. This is because action based on a coherent theory is more consistent than action that is purely blind. It tends to be more economical of effort and less wasteful of physical and psychic energy because it is based on a clearer logic and vision than is blind action.

So then the question becomes how to to use these leadership style theories as a basis for one's leadership behavior. Although there is no magic recipe, some criteria and ways of evaluating the theories are better than others. The first step is to understand the major leadership style theories. The second step is to weight the evidence, look at the research findings, and examine the logic and internal consistency of each theory.

And what is the final step? It might seem that the final step is simply to choose a theory to follow. But of course it is not that easy. Leaders do not choose the theories they follow like dishes from a smorgasbord. Rather, choosing a theory is like buying a new pair of shoes — it has to fit the person who is going to use it.

So rather than intellectually determining the "best" theory, the final step is to look closely at yourself and your situation. Do you believe you can change your style or does that sound extremely difficult or impossible? Are you already aware that your style changes from situation to situation?

What are the most important components of your situation? What is the most important aspect of your style, and what do you believe it ought to be? In short, which theory makes the most sense to you and fits best with your needs?

It may be that, in the face of so much conflicting evidence, the only way out of the leadership maze is to rely on intuition. In the end, it is simply the informed intuition of the leader that is the intended outcome of this analysis of leadership concepts and theories.

PART 2
THE STRUCTURE

PART 2: THE STRUCTURE
INTRODUCTION

How are decisions made in a school or school district, and who makes them? What groups meet together to discuss problems and organize strategies for change? How are the actions of different persons in the school or district organized and coordinated? What are the underlying norms that dictate appropriate behavior for individuals in the organization?

Each of these questions is one of organizational structure, and each is important because structure can largely determine the success of both an organization and its leaders. Even the most skilled and charismatic leader may fail if the "organizational deck" is stacked against him or her. On the other hand, an appropriate organizational structure can be a powerful tool for helping a leader guide the organization toward its objectives.

Several aspects of organizational structure are dealt with in this part of the book, ranging from decentralization of power to community involvement to the influence of schools on student achievement. In chapters 4, 5, and 6, the central issue is decision-making: who has the power to make what decisions, and who is accountable for the decisions made. In chapter 7, the focus is broadened to view the overall patterns of behavior and interaction in a school and their product, school climate.

Chapter 4 addresses the relationship between a school district's central office and the individual schools in the district. In traditional forms of district management, the central office makes the great majority of substantive educational decisions and passes orders "down" to the individual schools. Chapter 4 proposes a different form of district organization in which the school replaces the district as the primary unit of educational decision-making.

In school-based management, the personnel and clients of each individual school collectively make most decisions regarding personnel, budget, and curriculum at that school. The central office recedes from the traditional role of "dictating" the individual schools' actions to a role of facilitating those actions. The central office also acts as a coordinator, evaluator, and "watchdog" over individual schools' actions.

The principal becomes a central figure in school-based management systems. He or she finally inherits enough authority to balance the overburden of responsibility that the principalship now bears. In short, the organizational structure is shifted in school-based management systems to enable the principal to become a true leader of the school. This new balance of powers has proven quite successful in the numerous districts where it has been implemented, as chapter 4 shows.

Chapter 5 outlines another reform of school district governance: team management. The term *team management* has been used to describe participative decision-making arrangements at many levels of educational governance. In chapter 5, however, it refers to a system of district governance in which central office and middle-echelon administrators — especially principals — share the authority for making decisions regarding district governance.

Although decision-making power is shared in team management systems, the superintendent retains both the final authority for decisions and ultimate responsibility for the team's decisions. Thus, the success of team management depends heavily on the superintendent's willingness to "take the risk" of sharing power with others.

In districts utilizing team management, all central and middle-echelon administrators usually meet together periodically as a team. In small districts, useful work may be done at team meetings. In larger districts, however, the total team sessions are primarily informational and ritualistic in nature, or they serve as forums for reaching final agreement on team decisions. The real work in these larger districts is done by various subgroups of the team that meet at additional times, much as legislative committees do. Numerous districts have successfully implemented team management, three of which are reviewed in chapter 5.

A natural extension of team management at the district level is participative decision-making (PDM) at the school site, discussed in chapter 6. PDM has been shown to have numerous advantages over traditional, hierarchical systems of command, including better decisions, better implementation of decisions, higher employee satisfaction, and better relationships between management and staff. In chapter 6, the research confirming these advantages is discussed. This chapter also outlines several guidelines for implementing PDM at the school site and describes the experiences of some schools with PDM systems.

The final chapter of part 2 takes a broader look at structure. In this chapter, the patterns of behavior, communication, and social interaction in a school are discussed as contributors to the overall "climate" of the school.

School climate can be conceptualized as the "feel" one gets from being within a school's social system. This feeling is the "global summation" of an individual's perceptions of how school personnel and students behave and interact. These behaviors, in turn, are largely determined by the underlying norms in the school, which dictate the kinds of behavior that are considered appropriate.

Chapter 7 explains how the self-perpetuating "norm-behavior" cycle works and how administrators can intervene in the cycle with behavior modification or organization development techniques to improve school climate. Several instruments for characterizing school climate are explained, and the experiences of several administrators in climate improvement are discussed.

An understanding of the structure of school governance and school climate as provided in this part of the book can help school leaders conceptualize their relationship to the larger school organization and work effectively within it.

CHAPTER 4
SCHOOL-BASED MANAGEMENT
John Lindelow

School-based management is a system of educational administration in which the school is the primary unit of educational decision-making. It differs from most current forms of school district organization in which the central office dominates the decision-making process.

In districts utilizing school-based management, each school is a relatively autonomous unit. Most decisions regarding expenditures, curricula, and personnel are made by school-site personnel in consultation with parents, students, and other community members. The school board continues to formulate and define the district's general policies and educational objectives. The role of the central office, however, is altered from that of "dictator" of individual schools' actions to that of "facilitator" of those actions.

This chapter will present the case for school-based management as put forth by its proponents, with particular attention given to the key role of the principal in such a management system. Because school-based management is in large part a reaction to what many educators perceive as an overcentralization of power within school districts, these pages necessarily contain criticisms of the centralized systems of school governance that most districts now employ.

The site management concept has great promise and has proved successful in numerous districts where it has been implemented. In the following pages, the school-based management concept will be examined in some detail. The rationale underlying decentralized management will be examined, and numerous school systems that have successfully implemented school-based management will be described. The key role of the principal in school-based management will be discussed, along with the complementary role of the central office. The school site's control over curriculum, personnel, and budget matters will be examined, followed by a review of the roles of the staff and community in the decision-making process.

THE RATIONALE

In many districts the administration of education has been centralized to the point of diminishing returns, say critics. A new balance of decentralization and centralization—autonomy and control—needs to be struck. School-based management is designed to redress the current overemphasis on centralization and control by reassigning a good deal of decision-making authority to the school site.

In this chapter, the history of American education will be briefly examined to determine how school districts became so centralized in the first place. The deficiencies of this over-centralization will be outlined, followed by the merits of decentralization to the building level.

AUTONOMY AND CONTROL THROUGH HISTORY

To gain perspective on the current interest in school-based management, it is useful to examine the past history of the centralization-decentralization debate, not only in education but in society in general.

For as long as there has been government, there has been a constant tug-of-war between the concepts of autonomy and control. Indeed, Amitai Etzioni attributes the failures of both past empires and contemporary organizations to an inability "to locate a productive balance between autonomy and control" (quoted by Luvern Cunningham). It is really no surprise, then, that today's educators have not yet found the perfect blend of freedom and form.

One view of the long-term oscillations of centralization and decentralization is provided by Alvin Toffler in his new book *The Third Wave*. Toffler believes society is on the brink of a new "post-industrial" age that will be characterized by decentralization and the encouragement of individual variation. In Toffler's view, the ancient agrarian civilization was washed over about three hundred years ago by a "second wave" of industrialization. According to Andrew P. Zale's review of Toffler's book, "the overriding principles of standardization and centralization along with a 'covert curriculum' of punctuality, rote learning, and obedience (set up and encouraged by industry and governments) helped train the young for work in the new [industrial] society." The second wave moved children from the fields to regimented schools "designed to meet the needs of the industrial age."

The coming third wave, characterized by "a highly developed informational grid, home computers, and other electronic devices" will challenge today's notions of centralized and standardized education. The large bureaucratic educational institutions will break up as the centers of knowledge disperse into the informational grid. Society will become more democratic, and the family home will be restored as a teaching and social institution.

Whether or not Toffler's analysis of the long-range waxings and wanings of centralization is correct, there appear to be shorter-range oscillations of the concept's popularity as well. American education, for example, has seen a change from a decentralized to a centralized organization, and now appears to be becoming more decentralized again.

In the early years of the United States and up until about 1900, local control and representation in the governance of education were in vogue. According to Michael W. Kirst, "a decentralized, ward-based committee system for administering the public schools provided effective linkages to community opinion." There were more board members per district than there are today, and each represented the population of an unambiguous geographical area. Some large cities had hundreds of neighborhood boards.

Unfortunately, this kind of decentralized system lent itself to political corruption, particularly in the large urban centers. According to Kirst, "many politicians at the time regarded the schools as a useful support for the spoils system and awarded teaching jobs and contracts in return for political favors." Educational policies were often adopted not for the public good, but for the self-serving interests of politicians. In short, state Harvey J. Tucker and L. Harmon Zeigler, "school politics, like the machine politics of the urban area of which it was a part, provided responsiveness *and* corruption."

Public school reformers argued that the cure for these problems was to depoliticize education by transferring the power then held by politicians (and citizens, as Dee Schofield notes) to a professional group of educators. The reformers advocated that educational management be modeled after "the large-scale industrial bureaucracy that rapidly emerged in the turn-of-the-century economy," explains Kirst. The watchwords of reform were "centralization, expertise, professionalism, nonpolitical control, and efficiency."

Between 1920 and 1970, as the reformers' efforts came to fruition, the management of education became more and more centralized and insulated from community politics. School boards became smaller while districts were enlarged. Superintendents and other professional educators gained increasingly greater control over education, while the representative governance of lay boards slowly melted away.

How has the principal's role changed in response to these radical changes in educational governance? "Up until about 1920," states Paul L. Houts, "the principal possessed near total autonomy," including total authority for "teacher selection, placement, promotion, and salaries." As the reform movement progressed, however, the new central school boards transformed superintendents from clerks into major policy-makers. While the power of the central office swelled, the autonomy of the building principal slowly eroded, so that today the principals and not the superintendents are often considered to be the "clerks." Today, school boards and superintendents continue to relinquish principals' powers in collective negotiations with teachers' unions, often with little or no consultation with principals.

Sometime in the last decade or two, the swing of the pendulum apparently reached its limit, and it now appears that education may be moving back toward a more decentralized system of governance. Community involvement, decentralization, diversity, shared governance, and school-based management are the key words of this new reform movement. For the principal, this new movement may well mean a return to a true leadership role.

THE DEFICIENCIES OF CENTRALIZATION

Most present-day advocates of decentralization and school-based management begin their arguments, logically enough, with an exposé of the evils of centralization. John Gasson, for example, has this view of the status quo:

> The central office hierarchy regards the school principal as an agent of the superintendent. The principal may ostensibly run the school, but in reality he acts as a vehicle to transmit and implement edicts from the office. As a result, the principal and his teachers have become cogs fixed into a large, impersonal machine that depends on the machinist (superintendent) to keep every cog uniformly lubricated.

Centralized educational management, states Lawrence C. Pierce, operates on the premise "that education is a science and that with enough information, educational professionals can agree on the best school program for all children." Although these programs are designed with good intentions, critics maintain that their imposition from on high fosters expectations of uniformity and an intolerance for difference. Programs are designed for either the "mythical average" or for the majority, with the result that the special needs of individuals and minority groups are frequently overlooked.

A rigid, hierarchical structure extending from central office to classroom, critics continue, does little to foster innovation and creativity, which require a flexible and supportive atmosphere. "Inflexible bureaucratic structures," states Houts, "can often serve as the best innoculation against individuality and originality."

The above criticisms are reactions, it seems, to the overapplication of the "large-scale industrial bureaucracy" model to the field of education. Now, the tide of public opinion has turned; community involvement and decentralization of power are again in demand.

THE EFFICIENCY OF DECENTRALIZATION

Proponents of centralizing and consolidating school districts often claim that such actions can reduce the cost of education, and thus increase its "efficiency." Pierce and other proponents of school-based management, however, have criticized this definition of efficiency because it takes only dollars into account.

Pierce believes educational efficiency should be defined "in terms of matching available resources with the educational needs of children in schools." Thus, centralized administration, geared to provide uniform services, is efficient only if the needs of its clientele are uniform. "If they are different," states Pierce, "then centralized provision may be inefficient." Decentralized administration, on the other hand, is much more capable of matching educational services with the changing needs of students and parents. Its flexible nature allows it to be efficient in the sense that Pierce defines.

The push for equal opportunity has tended to accentuate the inefficiency of centralized administration. As long as districts are providing equal expenditures per student, equal class size, and the same course offerings, they feel as if they have fulfilled the requirements for equal opportunity.

But to more and more citizens, argues Pierce, equal educational opportunity has come to mean more than just superficial dollar equality or program uniformity. It has come to imply instead a condition in which all students—regardless of social or economic background—can realize their full potential. School-based management, says Pierce, answers this call by encouraging "school program diversity so as to promote equality of educational outcomes rather than inputs."

Pierce also advocates the coupling of school-based management, which gives parents and students a larger "voice" in education, with districtwide open enrollment plans, which would provide greater "choice." As autonomous schools gained more freedom from centrally mandated philosophies, they would tend to diverge in their approaches to education. If open enrollment plans were instituted, the consumers of education would then have the long-awaited ideals of diversity and choice within the public system.

EXAMPLES OF IMPLEMENTATION TO DATE

School-based management has been implemented primarily in Florida and California, in part because legislation in these states encourages or requires the decentralization of some aspects of school management. We will outline the development of school-based management in Florida and California, looking closely at two districts in each state. Then we will describe the systems in Lansing (Michigan), Edmonton (Alberta), and Cherry Creek School District (Colorado). But the concept has also sprung up in other districts around the United States and Canada without the provocation of state legislation.

FLORIDA

In the early 1970s, Florida's legislature passed a series of acts designed to transfer decision-making authority to the school site. This legislation was part of a broader legislative reform of state education and school finance that took place starting in the late 1960s. The legislative acts set "guidelines for educational accountability, comprehensive planning, annual progress reports, school advisory committees, and a comprehensive information, accounting, and reporting system," states a National Urban Coalition (NUC) document *(Four Case Studies of School Site Lump Sum Budgeting)*. The legislature did *not*, however, "mandate specifically that decisionmaking be decentralized to the school level," as Pierce notes, though it did significantly prune the state education codes to facilitate local control.

Since 1971 several Florida school districts have implemented elements of school-based management, often with the help of grants from the state's Department of Education. Since 1978, the state has funded districts wishing to implement or experiment with school-based management. In both the 1978-1979 and 1979-1980 school years, five of the state's sixty-seven county school districts were given grants. In 1979-1980 those grants totaled about $250,000. Several more districts will be given grants again in 1980-81, according to Larry Brown of the Florida Department of Education.

The implementation of school-based management in Florida has been uneven, despite the legislative mandates and the state funding. The Monroe County School District—reviewed below along with the Alachua County system—remains one of the few shining examples of school-based management in the United States, while most of the rest of the state's school districts still move slowly toward decentralized decision-making.

Even though the implementation of school-based management has had only scattered success in Florida, the state is probably the furthest along of any in implementing the system. "School site management is most often talked about in those states that have either large, diverse school districts or a highly centralized state school system," said Pierce in an interview. In Florida, the sixty-seven school districts are county based. Thus, within one county there can be a wide range of communities that have very different educational needs. The weaknesses of centralization come to the fore in systems, such as Florida's, where the diversity within one district can be great.

School-based management began in Florida—as it has elsewhere—not as a grassroots movement, but as a reform movement promoted by legislative policy-makers, said Pierce. Where it has been successful or partially successful—as in Monroe and Alachua counties—it has been so because of a superintendent who strongly believed in the concept. It seems, as is often the case, that it takes a great deal of energy and persuasion to break down people's conceptions of what can or should be.

Monroe County

Between 1971 and 1976, the Monroe County School District (1980-81 enrollment about 8,000) moved from a centralized to a school-based management system. The change was stimulated both by the state's reform legislation and by the unique geography of the county. Monroe County—composed of a long chain of islands (the Florida Keys)—stretches over one hundred miles from the Florida mainland out into the Gulf of Mexico. The islands are connected by bridges and causeways, and the school centers are clustered in three geographic areas about fifty miles apart.

Armando Henriquez has been the superintendent of Monroe County School District since January 1969. He has been a major factor in the successful implementation of school-based management in that district.

Soon after coming to Monroe, Henriquez—whose training was in centralized management—tried to improve education in the district by traditional means: inservice teacher training, adding curriculum coordinators, and so forth. The central office staff grew, but after three years no significant improvement could be seen.

Henriquez started to ask consultants about the district's problems and began to look at the research literature on school management. Together with the central office staff and the principals, he began to look for ways to reorganize the district. When the group ran across the concept of school-based management, said Henriquez in a telephone interview, "there was kind of an enlightenment that took place among all of us, and we thought this might be the direction to go." The principals, Henriquez noted, did not have to have decentralized decision-making imposed on them by the district, because they were involved in the decision from the very start.

Starting in the 1972-73 school year, the district shifted its training emphasis from central office personnel to building personnel and elevated principals from middle management to top management, with commensurate increases in both salary and responsibility. Prior to the change, the principals were "just carrying out edicts and directives from the central office," said Henriquez, "and there was no chance for the principals to really become managers or exercise any ingenuity or creativity."

School-based management concepts, including shared decision-making with teachers, were phased in slowly over a five-year period, so that teachers, principals, and central office administrators could adjust to the new power structure. During the first year, principals spent more than eighty days outside of their buildings undergoing extensive training in team management and decision-making skills. The training was supported by a grant from the National Institute of Education, grants from the Florida Department of Education, and some of the district's own funds. Four of the state's universities collaborated in the development activities, and an organizational development consultant was hired to help in the training and evaluation. The district benefited because its move toward school-based management coincided with the state's interest in implementing the concept.

During the changeover, the number of central office staff fell from twenty-eight to sixteen, partially because of inflation and partially because the schools were deciding what services they needed. The fifteen principals actively participated in deciding which district-level positions would be eliminated or combined with other positions. Despite this central office reduction, the amount of paperwork and communication between the schools and the district office increased. Community involvement also demanded more time and effort. In short, the new system generated a lot more work.

In the Monroe County system, funds are allocated to schools according to both number of students and special school needs. Each school decides how it will spend its funds and what its educational goals will be.

The schools are run by school "teams" that usually consist of the principal, assistant principal, guidance counselor, department heads, and other inhouse personnel. According to Henriquez, 99.9 percent of the decisions reached by the team are based on consensus. If the principal decides to make the decision himself or herself, the other team members must be informed beforehand that they are only offering advice. The same decision-making process is used by district management teams headed by the superintendent.

Besides a school team, each school has an advisory committee composed of parents, teachers, students (at the secondary level), and nonparent citizens. The authority of the fifteen-to-twenty-five member committees depends on the relationship between the professional staff and the community, according to Henriquez. In some schools, the committees are heavily involved in decision-making with the school team, while in other schools the committee's influence is quite restricted. Although state law requires that these committees be involved in establishing goals and plans, their real influence is determined by the principal and school team.

The teachers' union did not fully understand school-based management in its early days, but the contract with the union now contains a clause stating that "they agree with and recognize school-based management as the form of management within our district," said Henriquez. The district negotiates salaries, hours and conditions, fringe benefits, grievance procedures, and other related matters with the union. But "the district itself does not hire teachers or other school staff," said Henriquez. "That is strictly the principal's prerogative."

The union, stated Henriquez, is reacting very favorably to the system. Teachers have the highest starting salary in the state, have a favorable student-teacher ratio, and can buy their own materials and supplies. Henriquez believes that over 99 percent of the teachers would say they prefer his district to any other, mainly because they have a sense of "ownership" in the decisions made at the school. "That's what school-based management is really all about," said Henriquez, "It's giving people an opportunity to have an input." The trade-off for that input, however, is that it takes a lot of extra time and effort to make the participatory process work.

Henriquez feels that one of his important duties is selecting the right principals. When a principal is needed, central office administrators screen and interview applicants and present three qualified applicants to Henriquez, who makes the final decision. Henriquez says he wants principals to have an allegiance to him and the school board, rather than to the parents, because if the principal is not functioning properly, he wants to have the authority to remove that principal without creating an uproar in the community. When the community is involved in selecting the principal, there might be more compatibility between the principal and the community, but, says Henriquez, "we just haven't felt comfortable enough to go that way yet."

Henriquez believes the role of the school board has changed very little. The board still has the legal responsibility for assuring quality education in the district, and it is still responsible for setting the broad policy objectives within which the district will operate. Its main functions remain "ratifying recommendations or actions that have been delegated to other people" and serving as a decision-making body of last resort. Apparently, the community is quite pleased with the system: in the last election, two board members and Henriquez (an elected superintendent) ran unopposed.

Alachua County

The Alachua County School District (1975-76 enrollment, about 22,000) in north central Florida started moving toward school-based management in 1972, when James Longstreth became superintendent in the district. According to a National Urban Coalition (NUC) document, Longstreth "strongly believed that principals and schools should become the keys to management of the district."

During the 1973-74 school year, the superintendent and principals developed and refined a management model for school-based budgeting. According to the NUC document, Longstreth emphasized these points: that as long as principals "were receiving management salaries, their management-budget authority should match their program responsibilities"; and that as managers, principals should become a part of a district management team. By 1974-75, the district was operating under school-based management.

In the summer of 1974, school staffs in cooperation with their citizen advisory councils prepared a budget for the coming year. The district then "made adjustments or corrections for inflation, pupil-teacher ratio or accreditation minimums," according to the NUC document, and finally the state reviewed the budget and made its allocations in October or November.

The central office staff made the "total operating budget decisions," and the comptroller's office monitored and audited the spending of the individual schools. A key function of the comptroller's office was to offer technical assistance to managers for making budget projections.

In accordance with a state mandate accompanying the Florida Educational Finance Act of 1973, each school established a citizens advisory committee. At least half of the eleven to twenty-five members had to be parents, while the remaining members were teachers, nonparent citizens, students (in middle and high schools), and members of the PTA or other school support groups. The principal was also a member of the committee, but did not have a vote.

The NUC report states that the administrators of the district "offered strong evidence that a great deal of time and effort had been put into expanding opportunities for parents to gain information" about the schools. This effort apparently paid off, for parents reported that information was readily available to them. Parents also indicated that they wanted the school to be open to them, but wanted the professionals to keep running the school.

The superintendent and school board no longer made decisions about how to utilize funds at individual schools. The superintendent viewed his most important functions as selecting site managers, making as much money for the district as possible, "developing standards of service for school programs," and "district planning and continuing evaluation."

The school board members, states the NUC report, were "struggling to redefine their positions." They were supportive of the changes in district management, and were trying to "stay out of administrative issues and housekeeping." The board was also attempting to refocus its energies on "serving as a public forum for concerns about education, taking a strong hand in shaping policy and working with the superintendent in the selection of school site and district leaders."

The central office staff shifted from control functions to functions of "assistance and advisorship to school managers and staff." For example, the assistant superintendent for personnel maintained a pool of qualified personnel for the schools, instead of allocating personnel to the schools. The number of central office staff was halved during the reorganization, but many of these staff members were sent out to the school sites.

One of the problems of implementing school-based management, said Longstreth in a telephone interview, is that "you really strip some authority from the central staff, and they're not too happy about that." In Alachua County, if central administrators were dissatisfied with their new support roles, Longstreth offered them the opportunity to take one of the new top-level management positions as principal.

Principals, states the NUC report, "had truly become school site managers and participants in the district's management team in Alachua." They reported that they were more cost conscious, did more planning, and had more flexibility to work toward their schools' goals.

Principals who survived the changeover were those who enjoyed their new responsibility and authority, said Longstreth. But about 20 to 30 percent of the principals did not want to take on, or couldn't handle, the new decision-making role. Such principals, said Longstreth, are best moved to non-decision-making roles.

In Alachua County, school-based management appeared to encourage experimentation and diversity of program offerings. All schools designed instructional programs that were within the guidelines set by the district. But within those guidelines, the schools could vary their programs, without prior approval from the central office.

A policy of open enrollment couldn't be implemented with the school-based management system, said Longstreth, because the district was interested in maintaining desegregation. Open enrollment, Longstreth believes, would have led to increased segregation.

Since Longstreth left Alachua County in 1977, the district has drifted back to a more centralized structure.

CALIFORNIA

A 1977 publication of the California Department of Education (see Decker) lists sixty-one California school districts that have "implemented, to some degree, one or more concepts of a decentralized management plan." In thirteen of these districts, the principals "have moderate to substantial latitude in decision-making."

As in Florida, the move toward decentralization in California was stimulated in part by state legislation. The Early Childhood Education Act directed state funds to individual schools that used the money to improve education in the first three grades. The act also had "well defined requisites for parent involvement in the planning, implementation and evaluation of related school programs," states a National Urban Coalition document.

California's most recent school finance reform legislation (AB 65), which incorporated the Early Childhood Education Act, requires that each school in the California School Improvement Program have a school site council. The councils are to be composed of the principal, teachers, other school personnel, parents, and students (at the secondary level). The California State Department of Education, in a document designed to help districts and schools establish councils, outlines these council responsibilities: "developing a school improvement plan, continuously reviewing the implementation of the plan, assessing the effectiveness of the school program, reviewing and updating the school improvement plan, and establishing the annual school improvement budget."

Encouragement for California's move toward school-based management was also provided by a loose-knit consortium of twenty-five superintendents, according to James Guthrie, who was interviewed by telephone. In the late 1960s and early 1970s, the superintendents—most of whom were from Southern California—started to meet informally to work on the idea of school-by-school budgeting with the hope that it could improve the delivery of educational services and increase accountability.

As in Florida, the implementation of school-based management has been slow in California. According to Guthrie, school site management is "not going at all" in California, or at the very best is "not expanding." Some districts that started the system, such as Newport-Mesa, have gone back to centralized systems. In a few scattered districts, though, school-based management has been a success. Two of these successful districts—Fairfield-Suisun Unified, and Irvine Unified—will be reviewed below.

Fairfield-Suisun Unified

The Fairfield-Suisun Unified School District (1980-81 enrollment about 13,000) began its move toward a decentralized management system in March 1973, after a "careful assessment of its needs," according to Barbara Wells and Larry Carr, principals in the district. The district's objectives included finding the best management system for the district, developing school-based budgeting, providing for community and staff input to the budgetary process, and "improving the community's knowledge of the school district by establishing a district informational system."

Prior to the change to decentralized budgeting, say Wells and Carr, principals had two budgetary functions: they maintained records for a small amount of restricted money given them by the district, and they "learned and used persuasive techniques in obtaining additional 'special money' that a district administrator controlled to use for a local school project."

The district revamped its management system so that site administrators had more control over their budgets. This new control, state Wells and Carr, gave the principals "the substance to change priorities that affect the quality of education at the school site."

The schools are funded on an enrollment basis, but the schools design their own budgets, according to Ernest Moretti, assistant superintendent for instruction. "We encourage the involvement of staff and parents in the decision-making process," said Moretti in a telephone interview, but "the degree of involvement in the schools is really up to the principal." The central office doesn't advocate any one method of involvement, so there are all varieties and extents of involvement. When teachers are more involved in decision-making, though, they become much more aware of what different programs cost, Moretti noted.

Moretti has found some changes in his role as assistant superintendent of instruction. Instead of telling a principal what to do, he has to *convince* the principal to change. He also finds that he has to examine particular problems at school sites in more depth, so he can offer the principal sound advice and convince the principal when a change is needed. "If we're going to hold the principal responsible for the instructional program," said Moretti, "he or she has to have that expertise from the central office available."

In the personnel area, the central office maintains a pool of qualified applicants. Principals make the final personnel selection, with the restriction that intradistrict transfers must be placed first. The principal is required to put together a panel of teachers and community members to help in the selection process. However, the principal has the final hiring authority.

The district has established the departments of maintenance, data processing, printing, food services, transportation, and personnel as independent budgeting units. Schools buy the services out of their budgets. Large maintenance expenditures and other emergency expenses, however, come out of the district's undistributed reserve. Schools can carry over any budget surpluses they have, said Moretti. Since schools have control over their budget, building personnel have learned to be very ingenious in using and saving funds, particularly on utilities.

Moretti reports that as a result of the decentralization, there's a lot more communication between the central office and the school sites. "There isn't one central place that has all the answers," said Moretti, so the principals and central staff have to talk a lot more.

Principals have responded favorably to the new system and like their new autonomy. Even though the central staff sometimes thinks it might be easier the old way, said Moretti, "I don't believe there's an administrator out there who would like to go back to the centralized system."

Irvine Unified

The Irvine Unified School District (1980-81 enrollment about 15,000) was created by election in 1972. It consisted at that time of six elementary schools and one high school, with a total enrollment of about 6,000. Today, there are twenty-five schools in the district, and the district's enrollment is continuing to grow at a rate of 10 percent per year.

"From the district's inception," states an NUC document, "the superintendent and school board had agreed that the school site was to be the basic unit of management." According to Superintendent Stan Corey, the district wanted a management model that would take them through the period of turbulent growth that lay ahead. After eight years, said Corey in a telephone interview, school-based management is working "very well."

The school site is given a good deal of autonomy at Irvine, a finding confirmed by the NUC study group, which found "patterns of management and budgeting that were substantially different from centralized school systems." The principal is responsible for goal setting, needs assessment, reporting educational results to the community, budgeting, program planning, and staff selection, development, and evaluation. But the principal must fully involve the staff in all important decisions or he or she gets in trouble with the central office. "That's the trade-off," said Corey. "He can have lots of autonomy as long as he shows me it's participative. If he can't handle that, then we have to get a new principal."

At Irvine, resources are allocated to the school sites according to a staffing formula that is, in turn, based on the average daily attendance at the school. This method is used to get the resources to the schools in an equitable manner. Once the money is at the school site, said Corey, "the principal can move money around, as long as he can show that the decisions were made participatively and the bottom line is black."

The staff must also be involved in personnel selection. The central office maintains a pool of qualified applicants, and the principal, with staff input, makes the final choice. The school's staff can hire paraprofessionals instead of professionals if they so desire, or they can eliminate a position and buy books, as long as they stay within state laws.

School sites also have substantial latitude over curriculum matters, resulting in a variety of educational approaches. "One of our maxims is that diversity is good," said Corey, so "we try to offer people significant choices between the kinds of schools they send their kids to." To further enhance educational choice, the district maintains a policy of open enrollment.

Each school in the district participating in the California School Improvement Program has a site council, while all other schools have a school advisory forum. The principal, said Corey, is heavily accountable to these community-involvement bodies, but the principal retains final decision-making authority. The extent of community involvement varies with the principal and with the community the school is in.

To date, said Corey, the teacher association's response has been very good. "So far, we've avoided the separation into 'we' and 'they.' They can't separate themselves from management because they were co-mingled in decision-making tasks."

According to Corey, participative management has paid off in commitment from the district's staff: "We have a lot of people out there who not only view themselves as workers in the vineyard but as decision-makers as well. To the degree that their decision-making is real, then, their commitment is real."

LANSING, MICHIGAN

In the Lansing, Michigan, schools, the essential elements of school-based management have been in effect since 1971, and the system is operating smoothly now. The individual schools have considerable autonomy, according to Superintendent Matthew Prophet.

Each school has a twelve-to-thirty-five member citizen involvement committee, consisting of parents, teachers, students (at the secondary level), and building administrators, including the principal. Decisions are arrived at through a "modified" consensus model. Prophet explained in a telephone interview: "The principal is encouraged and, in fact, is obligated to involve citizens and staff in all of the critical decisions made at the building, but the principal retains 51 percent of the stock. In other words, the ultimate decision is made by the principal." However, when a principal is found to be habitually or continually exercising his or her 51 percent, the district intervenes and counsels the principal.

To help this consensus model work, the district has developed a manual on consensus-based decision-making, which gives several examples of how a group might apply the consensus model in attempting to reach decisions. The consensus method is successful 90 percent of the time, Prophet stated, but in about 10 percent of the decisions, there is nonacceptance by community or staff members, who feel that the principal is being too dictatorial.

Even with these problems, Prophet contends, the advantages of a school-based system far outweigh the advantages of a centralized system, which has proved itself time and again to be unresponsive to individual needs. Parents, teachers, and students have all expressed their satisfaction with the decentralized system.

The results of a 1973 study of the district by Throop "showed a centralization of some administrative functions but generally most decisions are forced to the lowest possible level through the philosophy of building autonomy." The overriding philosophy of the autonomy movement in Lansing, continues Throop, is that "decisions affecting the activities, organization, and curriculum of a school community (the staff and parents of that school) may not be made at the central office." As Prophet put it, the function of the central office is to "facilitate, not dictate."

The diversity of program offerings has increased greatly since school-based management was implemented. Given the diversity of the community, said Prophet, "no single program is needed by all buildings, so each building has to adapt its program to what it perceives its needs to be." The central office staff believe they cannot determine what each building needs relative to other buildings, and they do not tell the schools how to teach math or how to teach reading. "We make available to the schools, however, the opportunity to select from some forty to forty-five different curriculum management systems," said Prophet.

"But while the buildings have that kind of latitude," Prophet continued, "that doesn't mean they have the latitude to determine what the final products are." The central office, in other words, maintains educational standards that the schools must meet, and the central staff measures annually to determine the effectiveness of each school's program. If a school is not living up to district expectations, the central office intervenes.

The central office maintains a pool of qualified applicants for district jobs, but the principals make the decisions about whom they want to work in their schools. Each building must hire staff according to a staffing formula. Through mutual agreement with the school's staff, however, the principal can, for example, exchange a professional for two or three paraprofessionals.

Busing is still centralized in Lansing, as is payroll. The schools determine their own budgets, but purchases are made through the central office, except for certain items under $100.

Over the years, the principal population has shifted, as those principals who have been incompatible with Lansing's system have left. The principals, said Prophet, "must have the ability and the inclination to be humanistic and humanitarian in their whole management approach. It takes a very strong and sincere person to exercise this management model. A weaker person can always fall back on the authoritarian model."

EDMONTON, ALBERTA

The Edmonton Public School District (1980-81 enrollment 65,000) decided to implement school-based budgeting in all of its 160 schools in December 1979, after a three-year pilot project in seven volunteer schools in the district. The implementation of school-based budgeting was one part of a major district reorganization.

In the Edmonton system, the school site is responsible for budgeting for certificated and support staff, supplies, equipment, and services. The parts of the budget that remain centralized include building maintenance and renovation, substitute teachers to cover long-term illness, and utilities.

Allocations to the school sites are determined by a method that "is one of the most elaborate of any system with school-based budgeting," states Caldwell. Allocations vary according to such factors as special education needs of students, type of program, size of school (schools with fewer than 100 students receive more funding), rate of student transience, and enrollment in such programs as home economics, industrial arts, and extended French programs.

Despite initial fears to the contrary, the principal's role has become "more that of instructional planner than bookkeeper or business manager," states Caldwell. The successful change to instructional planner, Caldwell notes, is dependent on the provision of support services from the central office.

It is too soon, states Caldwell, to assess the impact of decentralized budgeting in Edmonton. However, "experience in the three-year pilot and in other jurisdictions suggests that it will be favorably received at all levels following stabilization of the change." The district is taking pains to retrain its staff in school-based budgeting, an action that seems imperative to the success of any major management change.

CHERRY CREEK SCHOOL DISTRICT, COLORADO

The Cherry Creek School District (1980-81 enrollment about 21,000) in suburban-metropolitan Denver has developed and refined its school-based management system over a long period. "It is to the point that when the district opens a new school, the principal gets a shell and must design and develop everything in it," said Principal Doug Gowler in a telephone interview. He estimated that he had "95 percent or more autonomy" over personnel and curriculum in the Sagebrush Elementary School that he heads.

The central office staff remains very small, even though the district has expanded from eleven to thirty-one schools in the past eight years. Thus, the individual schools perform many of the traditional central office functions. With a smaller central office staff, the principals can be paid well for their extra duties.

"Our superintendent sees principals as curriculum directors, directors of special education, directors of finance, and so on, as well as principals," states Gowler in a *National Elementary Principal* article. "He hires us to do all those things, and he gives us the freedom to do them. In other words, he lets us rise or fall on our own strengths and abilities."

When Sagebrush Elementary needs to hire a new teacher, Gowler sits down with the teacher team with which the new teacher will work, and together they work out a job description that is then advertised. The district's personnel department does the initial screening, Gowler interviews the applicants he thinks may be good for the job, then he sends the best of these — those who could "teach under a tree" — to the teacher team and the team makes the final choice.

When a teacher slot opens up, the school can hire paraprofessionals or a professional. The teachers' union would not argue with this, said Gowler, and "would challenge any union to challenge them." Both the teachers and Gowler believe that their primary responsibility is "to design appropriately to meet the needs of the kids, and if that means that we buy *only* paraprofessionals, we can do that."

Gowler and the school's staff design and continually refine most of their own instructional materials, and they design according to the students' needs. They do not use any major publisher's curricula in the building.

Other principals in the district also have the opportunity to run their schools the way they see fit. Gowler admits he is disappointed with some of them because they have simply adopted a published curriculum system, even though they have the opportunity to design their own system "and show what education is really all about."

Parents have been very much involved in Sagebrush Elementary ever since it was built, even before it was built. Community support, said Gowler, is "fantastically strong." Gowler works with parents through the parent-teacher organization, and parents work closely with Gowler in developing school policy.

What makes the difference in Cherry Creek are commitment and trust, said Gowler. The staff is extremely committed to their school and spend extra time to make it work. Superintendent Richard Koeppe trusts the staffs of Sagebrush Elementary and the other schools in the district to do their job. The result is a newfound sense of freedom for the principal, which Gowler described as "absolutely fantastic."

THE TRANSFER OF AUTHORITY

In a school-based management system, the principal becomes the central actor. The great responsibility that the principal now shoulders is—finally—matched by an equivalent measure of authority. With both the responsibility and the authority, the principal is free to become the leader of his or her school.

The relationship that will be most changed by the implementation of school-based management is that between the central office and the school site. Because the site administrator will inherit power and authority from the central office, the roles of the central office administrators will change nearly as much as the role of the principal. Thus, before the principal's new role is described in detail, the complementary role of the central office will be outlined. And prior to that, the school board's role in a school-based management system will be briefly reviewed.

THE SCHOOL BOARD

In a change to school-based management, the role of the school board would not change significantly. The board's primary duties would be providing general direction for the district by establishing goals and policy statements, keeping informed about the district's progress toward goals, and acting as a decision-maker of last resort.

According to Paul Cunningham, a school board member in Cambridge, Maryland, the school board would not relinquish any of its power in a change to a decentralized budgeting system. The board's role would remain that of developing broad policies for the operation of the school district. As Cunningham notes, "when the board makes the decision to decentralize the decision-making process, it is exercising policy development of the highest order." Once the decision has been made, continues Cunningham,

> it is the responsibility of the superintendent to submit a plan for board approval. The board is not relinquishing any of its authority to fix the budget. In the event that a budget must be reduced, the superintendent is given the directive and the amount by which it is to be cut. The staff (including building principals), on the other hand, should determine where the cuts are to be made.

Advocates of school-based management point out that redistributing the power in the district can work to the advantage of the school board because, as Barbara Parker states, "the total school system becomes more accountable and those at the top can get more results." Parker quotes Oron South, an organizational development consultant to Monroe County during its change to school-based management, as saying that decentralized management gives board members "a greater sense of power—not so much to order people around, but finally to get something done."

Support from the school board is vital to the success of school-based management. As James Longstreth points out, districts that have tried to initiate school site management "without school board endorsement or with their grudging acceptance of the program have not generally received continuing support" from the board.

If the new management system is to stick, the board members—after giving their approval for the system—should be involved in a continuing education and training program, to ensure their uninterrupted support. Without such a program, Longstreth continues, the board, when faced with a crisis, may revert to its accustomed behavior and take "centralized district-wide action. Although such action may not be appropriate for all schools within the district, it will be taken to demonstrate to the community that the board is 'on top' of the educational needs of the system."

THE CENTRAL OFFICE: FACILITATOR

In a school-based management system, central administrators shed some of their authority and become managers of the school system instead of its bosses. They become support and evaluative staff for the schools instead of directors. In short, they "facilitate, not dictate," as Matthew Prophet put it.

The principal and other school site personnel design the budget, hire instructors and other school personnel, and work out the curriculum. The central office focuses on "developing student and staff performance standards, offering technical assistance to schools," determining how much funding each school should get, and "carrying out systemwide planning, monitoring and evaluation," states a National Urban Coalition document.

The role of the chief business official in the district has traditionally been a combination of three functions—maintaining tight fiscal control over school budgets, providing technical assistance to the schools, and acting as the comptroller, or monitor, of district expenditures. In a school-based management system, tight fiscal control becomes the responsibility of the principal, but the business officer continues the other two functions.

William Dickey, business administrator for the Alachua County (Florida) School District in 1977, reports that decentralized budgeting "greatly reduces the responsibility of the school business official and substantially modifies his traditional role." Under a school-based management system, says Dickey,

> The school business official becomes a coordinator and controller of the budget and soon realizes, to his surprise, that he has an ally in the school principal. Whereas previously the school business official was one of the few employees in the school district who worried about enrollment fluctuation, utility costs, and the budget in general, he now has each principal worrying about those things for him.

The school site determines what items it would like to purchase and then forwards a requisition order to the purchasing officer at the central office. The purchasing officer orders the items, pays the vendor, and charges the school's budget accordingly. The central office can keep an eye on the schools' purchases in this way and make sure that the schools don't overshoot their submitted budget.

The personnel officer is still responsible for recruiting employees, collecting information about applicants, maintaining personnel records, and providing technical assistance to the school site. But the principal and other building level personnel are responsible for selecting staff for their school.

The chief instructional officer of the district should maintain the traditional functions of that office—providing technical assistance and general direction to the schools, and monitoring the school's effectiveness—but should not dictate the details of the curriculum. The district should continue to require that students become competent in basic skills, and should monitor the schools with both standardized tests and visitation. But the individual schools should be free to meet the district's educational goals in whatever way they see fit.

The superintendent continues to be the chief administrator of the district and the one person responsible to the board for administrative decisions. Experience in district after district has shown that strong support for school-based management from the superintendent is absolutely necessary for its proper implementation. Superintendents will support the concept once they realize that it can help them meet the responsibilities of their office in a more effective and efficient manner; when the entire system becomes more accountable and responsive to client needs, say proponents of school-based management, the job at the top gets easier and easier.

THE PRINCIPAL: SCHOOL LEADER

> The renewal or remaking of society is imaged in the remaking, the restructuring of education, which, in turn, is epitomized by the remaking of the principalship.

These words of John Bremer reflect the growing consensus among educators that the leadership role of the principal must be exhumed and revived if education—and society—are ever to find new vitality. The importance of the principal to quality schooling is attested to by legions of educators and researchers. "One of the few uncontested findings in educational research," states the chief executive officer of the NASSP (See "An Interview with Scott Thomson"), "is that the principal makes the difference between a mediocre and a good school."

Both Bremer and Thomson believe that an effective principalship demands considerable autonomy and authority for the building administrator. Common sense and modern management theory agree, continues Thomson, that true educational leadership can only be achieved when the principal is "freed from the blanket of directives and reports and meetings which now suffocate performance." Within the limits of general objectives established by the central office and board, the principal and school staff "should enjoy considerable latitude in decision making about program, personnel, and budget."

For a school system to be truly accountable, says James W. Guthrie, "it is imperative that there be a chief executive, the principal." Only when the responsibility for educational outcomes and the authority for making educational decisions reside in the same unit can true accountability be established. Presently, most important decisions are made in the central office and passed down the line to principals and then to teachers. But the responsibility for educational outcomes is a hot potato, juggled from principal to teacher to central office and never seeming to come to rest. School-based management seeks to fix responsibilities where they belong and thus close "the gap between the authority for initiating and operating school programs and the responsibility for their success or failure," as Albert H. Shuster states.

From all accounts, it appears that school-based management would mean work for the principal. The building site administrator, states the National Urban Coalition document, "would have to attend a much larger set of managerial tasks tied to the delivery of educational services," including "program planning, development and evaluation, personnel selection and assignment, staff development and evaluation, and budget management." In addition, the principal would be further burdened by the extra time and effort required by shared decision-making processes at the school site.

This added burden may discourage some already overworked principals from trying the system. But it should be remembered that along with the extra burden, the principal is gaining authority and autonomy to guide his or her own school. The rewards of leadership and authority may well be sufficient compensation for the added administrative burden.

Although most principals will respond positively to the opportunity to become autonomous school leaders, some will not. A common figure given by school-based management consultants is that 20 to 30 percent of principals will not find the system satisfactory. Many in this fraction would rather continue to be middle managers for the district, and they may view the new management system as a threat.

The dramatic change in the principal's role necessitates extensive retraining of principals. Without retraining, the new management system will probably not survive its first real challenge. Instead of working with the new system when a crisis arises, people will tend to fall back on the workings of the familiar centralized system.

To further help principals adjust, Longstreth recommends that districts develop guidebooks for principals. In districts where guidebooks have been used, "some uniformity of management" has been created in the district, states Longstreth, while some of the "isolation problems" that sometimes accompany autonomous schools have been avoided.

THREE CRITICAL CONTROL AREAS

Which kinds of decisions should be decentralized to the school site, and which should remain centralized? Results of a survey of California educators, states Pierce, support "the conclusion that decisions related to the delivery of school programs (personnel, curriculum and budgeting) can be effectively decentralized while those decisions which provide supportive service (transportation, maintenance, warehousing, data processing, etc.) should remain centralized." These perceptions were shared by the administrators in school-based management districts interviewed for this chapter.

The three main areas in which principals and their staffs would gain authority in a school-based management system are curriculum, personnel, and budget. Each of these critical areas is reviewed separately below.

CURRICULUM

In a school-based management system, the school site has near total autonomy over curriculum matters. Within broad outlines defined by the board, the individual schools are free to teach in any manner they see fit. As long as a school is attaining the educational goals set by the board, the district does not intervene. The district provides technical assistance to the school sites in instructional matters and monitors the schools' effectiveness. The principal works with staff and parents to determine educational needs and designs the school's curruculum around these needs. In some site management schools, the staff has diversified its curricula by selecting a variety of published materials, as opposed to using the district's suggested curricula. In Lansing, the district maintains a large number of curricula systems from which the schools can choose. In other districts, the schools can use whatever curricula they choose, but they must be screened by the central office first. In most school-based management districts, though, the board and central office establish an outline of educational objectives and leave the schools free to meet those objectives in any way they see fit.

In general, a district's implementation of school-based management has led to an increase in the diversity of educational approaches in that district. Teachers and principals gain more freedom to design their own instructional programs, and parents gain more influence on the design of those programs. Some schools may opt for a back-to-basics focus, others for open classrooms. Still others may adopt both approaches and have "schools within schools."

PERSONNEL

If principals are to tailor their schools' educational programs to the needs and desires of the community, they must have control of their major resource—teachers. In most existing districts with school-based management, principals make the final choice of who will work in their schools.

The most common practice at present is for the central office to maintain a pool of qualified applicants. When a position opens up, the principal—often with involvement from staff and community—selects from the pool. The district negotiates such matters as salaries, working conditions, fringe benefits, and grievance procedures with the union, but the actual decision to hire is made by the principal.

In many school-based management districts, the principal has some flexibility to hire paraprofessionals instead of certificated teachers. In some districts, the decision must be reached mutually between the principal and school staff. In other districts, the decision can be made by the principal alone, as long as the school stays within state staffing laws.

So far, resistance from teachers unions to school-based management has been minimal. One fear expressed by teachers is that principals might start acting as dictators if given more authority, so some unions want protection against this kind of mismanagement. Essentially, however, the concerns of teachers unions do not significantly conflict with the concerns of school-based management.

BUDGET

Budget control is at the heart of school-based management, as is attested to by some of the alternative names for the concept, such as "school based budgeting" and "school site lump sum budgeting." Control of the curricula and of personnel are largely dependent on the control of the budget. Thus, as Longstreth notes, "the extent to which a school district may be determined to practice school-based management is the extent to which the principal is allowed total budgetary discretion."

Many traditional districts allow principals control over expenditures for supplies and equipment only. Many school-based management districts, on the other hand, give the school a "lump sum," which the school site can spend in any way it sees fit. Individual schools, it should be pointed out, are not given the money outright. Instead, they purchase the services and products they need through or from the central office. The schools generate the decision to spend, and the central office carries out the schools' orders. The central office, however, also functions as a monitor of school spending and can intervene when a school is exceeding its budget or has other budget problems.

What kinds of restraints should be put on the school site's authority to make budget decisions? Longstreth, a former superintendent in a school-based management district, believes that *no* restrictions should be placed on the schools, except, of course, that they not exceed their budget. In practice, certain constraints will remain on the schools. The district's general educational objectives must be met, and student-teacher ratios must be kept within limits set by state law or collective bargaining agreements.

In the first step of the budgeting process, the central office allocates lump sums to the individual schools. In many districts, this is carried out with the aid of various pupil weighting schemes, some of which are quite elaborate.

The second major step of the budgeting process is for the school site to actually budget its lump sum. This is the most critical process in school-based management, for it is from this process that most of the advantages of decentralized management stem, in particular the flexibility of the school to meet students' needs, and the feelings of "ownership" that people derive from making decisions at the school site. The budget should be prepared with input from the school's staff and—according to most proponents of school-based management—from parents and students (at the secondary level) as well.

Budgeting at the school site, say proponents, increases the efficiency of resource allocation. Teachers and other school staff become more aware of the costs of programs, the school's financial status, and its spending limitations. Old programs "fade away to permit the establishment of alternative new ones," says Charles W. Fowler. Budgeting becomes "markedly more realistic," continues Fowler, because the charade "of requesting more money than expected in hopes of receiving a reduced amount still sufficient for program goals" is ended.

SHARED DECISION-MAKING

Increased community and staff participation in school decision-making has been an important component of school-based management wherever it has been implemented. In general, teachers, parents, and oftentimes students (at the secondary level) participate in decision-making as members of school advisory councils, which are usually distinct from the traditional PTAs or PTOs. Advisory councils vary widely in form, but generally they are composed of the principal, classroom teachers, other school personnel, parents, nonparent citizens, and students (at the secondary level). In some districts, the principal meets separately with a staff council as well as with an advisory council. Although their input usually comes by way of the same council, the involvement of staff and community members will be considered separately here.

STAFF INVOLVEMENT

It is possible, as noted earlier, to shift power from the central office to the school site without decentralizing it further. As Edward W. Beaubier and Arthur N. Thayer note, however, "it makes very little difference to a teacher if decision making has been decentralized to the school unit if he has not gained freedom to make a decision in an area that was verboten before a decentralization decision."

Some districts and collective negotiation agreements require that principals involve teachers in decision-making. Other site management districts only encourage the principal to involve others. Thus, the extent of teacher involvement varies widely from district to district and from school to school. In general, though, all site management schools have involved teachers to some extent.

Sharing decision-making authority at the school site, states Longstreth, "enables faculty to be personally involved in decisions crucial to them, which directly relate to their day-to-day activities within the school." As a result, faculty members develop a sense of "individual partnership or ownership" with the school.

Thus, it behooves the principal to involve teachers in policy decisions and give them more authority to design, develop, and evaluate their own curricula. To match this new authority, teachers should also be held responsible for their students' performance, states Pierce.

"As the climate created by decentralization demanded that teachers be significant decision makers, they would gradually become more educationally responsible," states John Gasson. "They would teach according to their own beliefs, using the instructional materials that they had individually chosen for their particular setting." Eventually, they would become the "major recognized determiners of the curriculum."

COMMUNITY INVOLVEMENT

School-based management often allies itself with the community involvement movement. Both are decentralization movements, but school-based management is more of an "administrative" decentralization that preserves the notion of professional control of education. The community involvement movement, on the other hand, is more "political" in nature and seeks to transfer real power to the community level. This discussion will confine itself to community involvement within a school-based management system.

The advantages of involving parents and other community members in school decision-making are many and well acknowledged. Public involvement enhances public support of the schools. The school becomes more responsive to community and student needs. Parents have more of a sense of "ownership" of their school. Parents can participate in decisions that affect their children.

The question that remains is how to achieve community input while retaining an accountable education system. Longstreth notes that "after advisory councils are formed and begin operation it is often discovered that the members serve no real function except as window dressing for the community providing only the appearance of lay involvement." On the other hand, "there is no general mechanism by which advisory councils can be held accountable for their decisions" if they are given real authority.

The only avenue left open—while still retaining the general structure of the educational governance system—is for school administrators to voluntarily accept and adopt the advice offered by community advisory councils. If the recommendations of the councils are repeatedly ignored or rejected, states Longstreth, "the council will quickly lose its membership and its effectiveness, or there will be a concerted effort to seek decision-making or veto power for it." Thus, it becomes vital for principals and other staff members "to ensure a visible acceptance of implementation of the recommendations offered by the council."

One way to encourage the principal to involve the council in decisions would be to allow the council to participate in the selection of the principal. James W. Guthrie recommends that parent councils have principal selection as their only real authority and be advisory in all other matters. Principals would be given a three- or four-year contract, "a period of time sufficient to implement programs and be evaluated," states Guthrie. Thereafter, the continuation of the principal's contract would be a joint decision between the council and the superintendent, with each having veto power.

Advisory councils, states Pierce, should be "intimately involved in designing and evaluating the school program." The council, Pierce continues, should "decide what students need to learn, assess the capabilities of both the school's teachers and programs to teach those competencies, recommend changes for improving the effectiveness of school programs, and design a system for evaluating school programs."

Whatever the duties of the parent advisory council, those duties should be clearly defined. Without guidelines, states Longstreth, two major problems arise: "The councils frequently become involved in mundane school operations or in activities such as fund raising (generally not considered an appropriate council role)," or they go to the other extreme and start influencing "matters normally considered beyond the scope of effective participation."

Council members could be selected by a variety of means. Longstreth advises that not all members be appointed by the principal, or the council may be viewed as a "hand-picked, rubber stamp" group. Some members should be elected to assure representation of interested community members, but others should be appointed to ensure "representation by persons from segments of the community which might not be included in the election process," such as minorities and the disadvantaged.

CONCLUSION

In the preceding pages, the essential elements of school-based management have been described, with special emphasis on the principal's role in a decentralized management system. In brief, the role of the principal in a shift to school-based management would change from that of middle manager for the district to leader of the school. The school site would replace the district as the basic unit of educational governance, and the principal would become the central actor in school management, with authority over curricula, staffing, and budget matters. The central office, which now dictates so many of the actions that individual schools take, would become the facilitator of decisions made at the school site. Parents, teachers, and students would work with the principal to develop educational goals and implement decisions they helped make.

Numerous examples of working school-based management systems already exist, and much can be learned by studying these districts. Successful implementation requires, first of all, extensive retraining of central office and school site personnel. The biggest stumbling block in implementing school-based mangement is breaking down the conventions that people hold about what should or can be. With extensive retraining and education, so that all school and central office personnel understand the new system, the change can be made smoothly and the school system can stabilize in its new management mode.

Successful implementation also requires strong support from the school board and superintendent. In fact, as Brian J. Caldwell notes, the initiative to implement decentralized budgeting "has invariably been taken by superintendents who have contended that better decisions will be made if resources are allocated with a high degree of school involvement."

Before it starts, the district must have a clear idea on the extent to which power will be decentralized. The authority that is to be given to the school site and to staff and community members should be decided in advance, to avoid confusion and conflict.

Finally, successful implementation requires a good deal of trust and commitment. The superintendent must trust school site personnel to do their jobs, and all concerned must be committed to making the system work. By all accounts, the system takes more work at the school site, but many educators believe that the rewards of autonomy and feelings of ownership are well worth the extra time and effort spent.

CHAPTER 5
TEAM MANAGEMENT
John Lindelow

Few concepts in the recent history of public education have been as widely promoted and endorsed as team management. Nearly every major educational organization and most school districts now support the notion of sharing district decision-making through team management, or team administration, as it is often called.

Team management has been used to describe various shared or consultative decision-making arrangements among school-site personnel, among central office personnel, or among a mixture of central office and building administrators. In this chapter, the focus will be on the latter form of team management. We will follow Harold J. McNally's definition of the "management team" as "a group formally constituted by the board of education and superintendent, comprising both central office and middle echelon administrative-supervisory personnel, with expressly stated responsibility and authority for participation in school system decision making."

The practice of using a collaborative group or "team" of administrators to manage a school district is not a new idea. There have always been some innovative districts that have quietly used what is now called team management. The concept has also been promoted for decades by educators and social reformers intent on opening school district decision-making to building administrators.

Recently, however, the team management concept has sky-rocketed to prominence. Why this sudden interest in the team concept? Many observers trace the cause back to the advent of collective bargaining with teachers in the 1960s.

The rise of teachers unions and collective bargaining in the 1960s significantly altered the "power structure" of public education. Using union tactics, teachers associations acquired powers that had formerly been held exclusively by boards and administrators. Teachers thus quite suddenly became major forces in shaping district policy.

"Early in the negotiations game," says Ray Cross, "it

became apparent that teachers and superintendents, by the very nature of their respective roles, were on opposite sides of the table." In response, superintendents "reached out to enlist all of the allies that they could get — particularly principals."

According to Robert C. Duncan, the management team concept has often appeared

> in "position papers" published by state organizations of administrators, usually in response or reaction to passage of a collective bargaining bill which enables teachers to bargain collectively. Such papers usually take a position indicating that one or more levels of principalships are and should be considered to be managerial in nature, and thus elementary, junior high and senior high school principals are said to properly belong to the school system's "administrative team."

It is unfortunate, Duncan continues, that the concept was revitalized as a reaction to collective negotiations instead of as a result of purposeful and rational deliberation by school boards and administrators. "However, for the sake of better leadership of the school enterprise, the institution of a team approach to administration may well result in such improvement as to owe a debt of gratitude to the catalyst — whatever it is."

Another stimulus for the recent rush to team management has been the threat of principal unionization. Principals have been increasingly "squeezed" from both above and below by the collective bargaining process with teachers. School boards have traded away building administrators' prerogatives to teachers — often without consulting with principals — while holding the principals responsible for carrying out the terms of teacher contracts.

Building administrators justifiably feel that they have been bypassed in the negotiations process, that their former authority has been significantly encroached upon, and that their professional stature has been diminished. In response, principals in many districts have unionized or threatened to unionize, both to protect what authority they have left and to redefine their relationship to the school board.

Rather than risk another forced rearrangement of the power structure through principal unionization, many boards and superintendents have agreed to share some of their power with middle-echelon administrators through team management. In many cases, however, the power has not really been redistributed; boards and superintendents in many districts have simply used team management to co-opt or pacify principal unionization movements.

The rapid adoption of team management for purely political purposes such as these has given the concept a bad image among principals. For example, a nationwide survey of principals conducted by *the American School Board Journal* (see "The Brewing...") in 1975 found that principals "seem plainly on the verge of bolting the school district's 'management team' by which they feel unaccepted and from which they see themselves becoming increasingly alienated." In many instances, principals believe their district's team to be a sham. And "an overwhelming 86 percent of responding principals are in favor of state laws that will guarantee their right to bargain directly with school boards and will force boards to negotiate in good faith with principals," states the *Journal*.

Even where superintendents and boards have attempted to implement team management with honest intentions of sharing power, the system has often not worked. Because team management has become somewhat of a fad, many school districts have rushed to implement it without a full understanding of the concept and without the commitment, trust, and training required for the team's success. The failure of the team — even when implemented with good intentions — serves only to exacerbate principals' feelings of distrust and alienation.

In some districts, however, team management has been a success. Three of these successful team management systems will be reviewed later in this chapter. First, however, the team management concept will be more fully explained.

ORGANIZATIONAL CONSIDERATIONS

"Team management" has recently become one of the most overworked terms in the educational literature. Universities, community colleges, school districts, and individual schools are all employing the term or some variation of it to describe a myriad of different shared decision-making arrangements.

Even among public school districts that use the term, the meaning of team management can vary "radically from district to district and state to state," as a publication of the American Association of School Administrators (AASA) notes. "Some approaches work very well," while "others are merely labels attached to existing hierarchical structures."

It is no surprise, then, that there is confusion about what team management really is. Of course, there is no one "right" model for team management that can be applied to all districts. Each district must find the team structure that is most appropriate for its desires and needs. There are, however, several features that most successful management teams share. These features and other organizational considerations are discussed below.

POWER AND TRUST

As mentioned earlier, teacher unionization caused a significant rearrangement of the power structure of most school districts starting in the 1960s. Other redistributions of power — though not as radical — have taken place in districts that have implemented either school-based management (discussed in the previous chapter) or team management.

In team management systems, the "formal" power structure changes very little. The school board remains the primary policy-making and governing body of the district. The superintendent remains the one person responsible to the board for the district's proper functioning and retains authority for making the final decisions. Principals continue to perform their primary function of managing the local schools.

The changes that do take place in the power structure of team management districts are informal in nature and depend on the willingness of the superintendent and central office administrators to share their powers. Although principal participation may be mandated by district policy, the real extent of principal influence is up to the superintendent, who retains both final power and final responsibility for the team's decisions. Thus — unlike the "brute force" type of power redistributions caused by teacher unionization — changes to team management depend on "enlightened" boards and (especially) superintendents to make them work.

Most proponents of team management, then, are not promoting a legal transfer of power to building administrators. Rather, they are calling on superintendents to open communications channels from the "bottom" to the "top" of the administrative hierarchy. They are, first and foremost, promoting the adoption of a structure that would enhance building administrator input into the district's decision-making process.

The success of team management, though, depends on more than a superintendent willing to share power. It also depends in large part on such factors as trust and commitment. Team members must trust the superintendent to respect and implement the team's decisions. Team members must also feel free to disagree with the superintendent without the fear of falling into disfavor. The superintendent, in turn, must have trust and confidence in the team to make intelligent decisions for the district. Each team member must trust that the others are working primarily for the good of the district.

Like school-based management, team management requires an increased amount of time and effort to make it work. It is always more difficult to make group decisions than it is for a lone administrator to make a command decision. But it is from this investment of extra time and effort that the benefits of team management spring. Thus, successful team management depends on the commitment of all team members to the system and on their willingness to spend the extra time and effort needed for shared decision-making.

In districts where strong adversary relationships already exist between factions of the administration, team management will likely travel a rocky road and may end up doing more harm than good. This does not necessarily mean, however, that team management and principal bargaining units cannot peacefully coexist, as Attleboro's (Massachusetts) management system demonstrates (reviewed in next section).

THE BOARD-ADMINISTRATOR AGREEMENT

McNally's definition of the management team emphasizes that it be "a formally constituted group" with "formally recognized responsibility and authority for making important decisions on school system policy interpretation and operational matters." Lester W. Anderson emphasizes that a crucial factor in implementing a management team is "the adoption of a formal structure which assures a system of open communication with all administrators."

Several other authors stress that the team should be clearly defined in writing. For example, Paul B. Salmon, veteran director of the AASA, recommends that a "management manifesto" be drawn up that would formalize the team concept and would make it possible to be quite specific about:
- the perimeters of its authority
- the nature of its composition
- working relationships among its members and components
- the limits of its rights and responsibilities
- how it will be held accountable for its actions
- the types of matters that may comprise its agenda.

A clearly written team definition, Salmon continues, would "more nearly guarantee that its implications be thoughtfully considered, its structure carefully designed, and its potentialities fully anticipated."

A 1971 monograph of the National Association of Secondary School Principals contains an example of a written board-administrator agreement, along with explanations of many of its sections. The material in this "typical agreement" was extracted from a number of board-administrator agreements from throughout the country.

Most of the agreement outlines the conditions of employment for school administrators. Included are sections on working conditions, leave, termination of employment, fringe benefits, salary provision, evaluation of administrators, transfer and promotion policies, grievance procedures, job descriptions, participation in professional meetings, and the like. Another section guarantees "that administrators shall have the right to form a local organization for the purpose of representing them in describing and defining their professional relationships in the district."

The management team is defined broadly in the agreement as all management and supervisory personnel. One section provides that regular meetings be held "between administrative team personnel and the board of education."

Another section states that "the board agrees to involve administrative team representatives in an advisory capacity to the board in all negotiating or collective bargaining sessions with employees who are subject to their supervision or under their administration."

The finer details of the team's composition, structure, and decision-making processes are not described in the NASSP agreement. This is in accord with an AASA document, which recommends that the agreement "should not spell out operational details" but "should address the basic philosophical issues, leaving no doubt of the board's commitment and the staff's obligations."

A written board-administrator agreement sounds good in theory and may be the best procedure to follow in some districts. Yet in numerous successful team management systems — including the three reviewed in the next section — most of the board-administrator agreement is neither formalized nor written. Instead, these districts depend primarily on trust, good faith, and informal understandings between board and administrators and among team members to make their team systems work. Whether or not a formal agreement exists, however, all team members should clearly understand the team's objectives, organization, and operating procedures.

MEMBERSHIP AND ORGANIZATION

The management team, according to most proponents of the concept, should include all central office and middle-level administrative personnel, including principals, assistant principals, and supervisors at the building level.

In small districts, the entire team can regularly meet and work together. Recommendations vary, but fifteen to twenty members is generally considered the outer limit for efficient team operation.

In larger districts, says Richard Schmuck, the term *management team* "usually refers to a *class* of administrative personnel including assistant principals, principals, and district-office administrators and not to a functioning *team*." In these districts, the total team must be divided into interlocking subgroups capable of getting useful work done, which may or may not meet together as a "total" team.

Each of the management teams described later is divided into working subgroups, but each also meets together regularly as a total team. These twenty- to eighty-member sessions are primarily informational and ritualistic in nature, or they serve as forums for reaching final agreement on team decisions. The real problem-solving is done in the subgroups or working committees that meet at additional times. The total management teams in these districts, then, resemble legislative bodies (though they rarely take votes) more than they do true working "teams."

Management teams can be organized in a large variety of ways, depending on the needs and desires of the district. No one model or set of models can adequately describe the possibilities for team organization, and thus districts must formulate their own team models according to their own local circumstances.

The best source for ideas on team organization is descriptions of successful team management systems. Another source is descriptions of general team models, which have been attempted by a few writers.

Kenneth A. Erickson and Walter H. Gmelch, for example, outline three team models that depend on representation to keep the central "leadership team" at the authors' preferred membership level of five to ten. In the "conventional" model, representatives from central office areas meet with representatives of various principal groups, or with all principals if the district is small. In large districts, the principal representatives are also members of other "interlocking" management teams from their geographical areas.

In the "crossbred" model, the leadership team consists of "one representative from each of the major functional categories in the organization," such as classified support, principals, special education, finance, and staff development.

And in the "cocoon" model, the leadership team forms an ad hoc team for each specific problem that arises, each with an "executive secretary" who reports back to the leadership team. Once the ad hoc team's report has been accepted by the leadership team, it is disbanded. The utilization of ad hoc teams of various sorts is common to many successful team systems, as will be seen below.

DECISION-MAKING

The primary purpose of the management team is to bring middle-echelon administrators into the district's decision-making and policy-development processes. Numerous advantages — many documented by research — are thought to accompany the kind of shared decision-making present in team management systems.

For example, participation in decision-making increases job satisfaction for most (but not necessarily all) employees and gives them a sense of "ownership" in the organization. Also, decisions made by a group are likely to be better than decisions made by one person. Collaborative decision-making also increases the coordination of tasks and enhances the general quality of communications in an organization. These advantages and others will be discussed more fully in the next chapter.

Although middle-echelon administrators are involved in district decision-making in team management systems, they should not necessarily be involved in *every* decision made by the district. Some problems of a technical or legal nature should be delegated to the person or persons with the greatest expertise. Other routine decisions should not be brought before the team unless they could significantly alter the district's operations.

The power to make some decisions might also be reserved by the superintendent or be delegated to a particular administrator. In the Attleboro (Massachusetts) team, for example, Superintendent Coelho reserves the power to make decisions in the special subjects areas. Coelho was careful, however, to inform the team that this would be one of his ground rules.

Even if the team is involved in decision-making, the decisions it reaches may not necessarily be binding. The superintendent in team management districts almost always retains final "veto" power over team decisions.

Superintendents, though, should be careful in exercising their ultimate power over the decision-making process. If they restrict decision-making too severely or exercise their veto power unwisely, the fragile trust that makes the team work will be destroyed. The team may be considered a fraud by its members, who might then withdraw their support and seek other ways to gain influence in the decision-making process.

Superintendents should also be careful to clarify the team's role in each decision before the team begins work on a problem. If the superintendent intends to let the team decision be binding, he or she should clearly communicate that fact to the team. If the team's input is to be considered advice only, that, too, should be clearly communicated. In short, the superintendent should decide on a "leadership style" (as discussed in chapter 3) for each problem area the team tackles and then let the team members know what their role will be.

Although votes may sometimes be taken, decisions reached by management teams are most often based on consensus. This does not necessarily mean that every team member agrees totally with the decision reached. Instead, the "informal" consensus often reached by teams implies that all members agree to abide by the terms of the decision reached. Even though some members may have reservations about a decision reached, they agree, in effect, not to work against the decision's implementation.

EXAMPLES OF SUCCESSFUL TEAMS

Although the ideas of organizational theorists are useful for providing general ideas about the structures and functions of management teams, the most useful and practical ideas often come from working team management districts. In the following pages, three districts with successful management teams are described. Each team is unique in its organization and operation, yet all have certain features in common, including a superintendent dedicated to the concept, the division of the team into working subgroups, the lack of a written board-administrator agreement, the separation of principal welfare issues from other district decision-making issues, a decision-making process based primarily on consensus, an organizational structure open to input from all members, and an atmosphere of professionalism and trust that permeates the team.

YAKIMA, WASHINGTON

In the mid-1970s, principals in the Yakima Public School District (1980-81 enrollment, about 11,000 with twenty-one schools) were being excluded from negotiations with teachers and "felt a need to restructure their role," according to Mark Bontrager, a former principal in the district and now administrative assistant to the superintendent. When Warren Starr became superintendent in Yakima in 1975, the restructuring the principals desired began to take place. Starr — a proponent of team management — began moving the district toward a new management system that now provides substantial opportunity for principals and other administrators to influence the district's decision-making and policy-development processes.

The team management system at Yakima is organized somewhat like a legislative body, with numerous working groups within the larger team. The total team — with about eighty members — meets once each month. Membership includes the superintendent, central office personnel, all principals and assistant principals, and various supervisors and directors. The meetings are run not by the superintendent but by an elected meeting manager.

"Most of what happens in the meetings of the total team is information dispersal," Bontrager told the writer. "The real action takes place in small groups within the team that receive assignments to carry out specific functions or activities."

Once one of the small groups decides on a course of action, it presents its suggestions to the entire team for approval. Votes are rare, Bontrager reports; most agreements are based on an informal consensus. The superintendent, however, reserves the right to make the final decision.

All the team's members are involved formally or informally with one or more of the team's subgroups, according to Dale Sayler, a principal in the district. "You kind of pick up assignments depending on what comes up and where you are," said Sayler, who has been active in many of the subgroups.

In addition to these small "workhorse" groups, there are two other subgroups of the total team that meet separately. The "superintendent's cabinet" meets once a week and consists of the superintendent, central office managers, one principal representative each from the elementary, junior high, and senior high levels, and one person each from the curriculum and federal program areas. Another subgroup — consisting of the cabinet and all building principals — meets together once a month.

"Occasionally," Sayler told the writer, "some principals get the feeling that a decision has been made by the superintendent's cabinet" before the issue has been reviewed by the entire team. Team members, though, are generally quite satisfied with the system, Sayler added.

To facilitate policy development, the Yakima management team uses a "position paper" process. A position paper, according to Starr, is a written agreement between the chief administrator and the management team on some policy issue.

In a 1978 article in the *NASSP Bulletin,* Starr gives an example of one such position paper on "administrative hiring." An opening statement describes the problem and the philosophy behind the proposed solution. The next section details the proposed hiring process. A final section outlines how the process will be evaluated.

Any team member can develop and propose position papers. Thus, a team member's opportunities for contributing to district policy development are potentially unlimited: "I could put out a lot of position papers if I took the time to sit down and write them," said Sayler. "We work under a system where if you've got something interesting and it's worthwhile and you can back it up, it's more than likely going to happen."

Position papers also formally define a few of the relationships between the board and team members. For example, one position paper outlines the process of working out agreements on salaries, working conditions, and related issues.

By and large, however, agreements between the board and the team are informal. "We deal with the board on an informal basis," said Bontrager, "and use position papers to give us guidelines for our total operation."

The team takes pains to avoid adversary relationships among its members, said Bontrager. Dialogues about welfare issues take place between subgroups of the team and central office managers. The superintendent separates himself from this process and acts, in a sense, as a negotiator

Principals also have input into the negotiations process

with teachers. Principal representatives sit at the negotiating table. "The teachers," said Sayler, "ask us for more input than we give."

In some areas, circumstances have limited the team's latitude in making decisions. For example, declining enrollment has forced the district to fill vacancies with district personnel instead of with new employees. Excluding these special areas, however, Sayler and Bontrager both believe that principals have a significant role in the decision-making process in Yakima. "The group feels very positive about the process," said Sayler. "None would have reservations about it."

By and large, then, the management team system at Yakima appears to be working quite well. "If I were to interpret how a management team ought to operate," Bontrager concluded, "we would be as close to it as anything I've run into so far."

RIO LINDA, CALIFORNIA

The Rio Linda Elementary School District (1980-81 enrollment, about 7,000 with seventeen schools) started its move toward team management in 1975, when Nick Floratos began his superintendency there. According to a 1978 article in *Thrust for Educational Leadership* by Floratos and other district personnel, one of the new superintendent's first actions was to appoint a committee of principals and central office personnel "to develop an organizational structure and process that would allow our district administration to function as a management team."

Presently, the district has a forty-member team that meets twice monthly. Membership includes all central office and building-site administrators.

The internal organization of Rio Linda's team is similar to that of Yakima's team, in which various smaller groups do much of the real work and then present their suggestions to the larger team. The meetings of the total team, state Floratos and his colleagues, provide a setting for the "presentation of concerns, questions and problems"; "decision making by consensus"; inservice training; and "dissemination of information and sharing of ideas."

Subgroups include three "area councils," whose membership includes the principals, vice principals, coordinators, and psychologists from the same geographical area; a "cabinet" that includes the "Superintendent, Deputy Superintendent, Directors, Area Council Representatives (as needed)," and "Classified Management (as needed)"; and various other "Sub Groups" in such areas as funded programs, curriculum personnel, and classified management. In these small groups, problems are identified and discussed and solutions are developed. The meetings of these groups also serve as a setting for both inservice training and "the support of individuals."

When a problem arises that cannot be dealt with easily by the total team, a "study committee" is formed. Each of these committees includes one representative from each area council, a representative from the cabinet, and other nonmanagement personnel as needed. "The study committee's role is to make an in-depth investigation, explore alternatives and make a final recommendation to the total management team."

The recommendations can either be accepted by the total team or sent back to the committee for more work. Once the solution is accepted, however, the committee is disbanded.

According to principal Jay Baumgartner, who was interviewed by telephone, the team never takes a vote on an issue. But decisions are not based strictly on consensus either. The team simply "works toward a solution," said Baumgartner, until general agreement is reached.

Conflicts — when they do occur — are caused by a breakdown in the team's well-defined problem-solving process. "The only time we've had problems was when, for some reason, that process was bypassed," said Baumgartner. "If the process is working as it should, the study committee's report is not really news to anyone."

Salary and related issues are worked out in a fairly informal way, said Baumgartner: "The superintendent asks for input once a year from the area councils regarding building administrators' needs and concerns. Then he comes back to the councils and says, 'Here's what I can live with and what I plan on giving to the board. Do you have any problems with this?'"

Previous to the implementation of the management team, Baumgartner and other administrators were meeting informally "because we didn't feel that we were being involved in decision-making. But that group has disbanded since we've gone to the team," and the district now has no administrators union.

One of the management team's most important functions, write Floratos and his colleagues, "is that of establishing the district's posture as it relates to collective bargaining." The district's negotiating group includes a psychologist, two principals, the director of personnel, and the assistant supervisor of maintenance and operations.

Proposals from the teachers association are first reviewed by the board and the district's legal counsel and are then sent to the area councils for review. The management team then discusses concerns brought up by the area councils. Finally, the negotiations group formulates counter proposals that are reviewed by the board and then presented to the teachers. Following each negotiation session, each management team member receives a publication that "abstracts all proposals and counter proposals and summarizes negotiation progress."

Once the contract is ratified, the negotiations group "provides each member of the staff with a written interpretation of each article to help further clarify the meaning of the terms of the contract." The negotiations group also provides inservice training on contract management and grievance processing. "The end result of this process," state Floratos and his colleagues, "is a contract which has been developed and reviewed by all the management team."

This kind of intricate communication may seem time and energy consuming, and it is. But "frequent, complete and meaningful" communication of this sort is "a key element in the central administration of a school district." It provides both staff unity and clarity of purpose, not only when dealing with teacher negotiations, but in all other areas as well.

Another key to the success of team management at Rio Linda is support from the school board. "The importance of a supportive board cannot be over-estimated as an imperative in the building of a management team," stress the authors. The board must be actively interested in the district's staff and consistently support the decisions made by the team.

The team management system at Rio Linda demands

extra time and effort from each team member, said Baumgartner. Principals who are comfortable just following orders will be dissatisfied in such a system. But, Baumgartner concluded, "I could not name one principal in this district who is truly dissatisfied with the system."

ATTLEBORO, MASSACHUSETTS

The team management system in the Attleboro Public School District (1980-81 enrollment, about 6,600 with thirteen schools) has been functioning smoothly for over ten years and recently withstood a severe test of its strength. In November 1980, a property tax limitation measure was passed in Massachusetts that reduced the district's operating budget for 1981-82 from a projected fifteen million to less than thirteen million dollars. The management team carried the district through the difficult period of staff and program cutbacks, which included reductions in the administrative ranks and the closing of two elementary schools.

Starting in October 1980, the team began to plan for the impending budget cut. Within two weeks after "Proposition 2½" passed in November, the team had formulated three possible budgets for the 1981-82 school year—one for "drastic" budget cuts, one for "moderate" cuts, and one for a "status quo" budget.

The effects of the different cuts were projected, including the likelihood of school closings and the loss of administrative personnel. "Some administrators knew they were bound to go," Superintendent Robert Coelho told the writer, "but the group's cohesiveness remained strong. And difficult as it is now, they're still with it."

Coelho has been building the management team in Attleboro since 1969, when he became superintendent there. He had previously worked in the district for fourteen years as a teacher, principal, and assistant superintendent, which gave him "the opportunity to observe the system's growth mechanisms" and formulate some plans for changing the district's organization, according to a publication he wrote in 1975.

With two other members of the central administration, Coelho "analyzed the organization's planning, organizing, staffing, directing, controlling and evaluating processes against the system's human abilities to communicate, make decisions and solve problems." Coelho and other members of the "central office team" read widely about organizational development, "organic models of organization," and related topics, and they enrolled in courses in human relations and organizational analysis and decision-making.

Then the team sought "the expertise and use of outside consultants," which Coelho believes was "probably the most strategically advantageous decision by the central team during its early stage of development." A series of training seminars on group dynamics, team development, and related topics were held for building administrators and the central office team.

Coelho emphasizes the importance of this kind of "team training" for the successful implementation of a management team. Training strategies employed "must aim at changing the entire system, not merely one part of it," he writes. Unless "the culture of the system" is changed "to allow for new ideas and technologies to be introduced and examined, the people and their problems will still exist: the same communication blockages will persist and the same clinging to staid, security-bound values will tend to keep the system" from becoming the adaptive organization it needs to be.

Presently, the Attleboro district has six basic subgroups within its total team. The central office team consists of the superintendent and other central office personnel. The K-5 team, the middle school team, the high school team, the 6-12 team, and the K-12 team consist of the principals, assistant principals, and other building administrators from each group of schools. Every week the central office team meets with one of the other groups, while the other four groups meet by themselves or with each other, as needed. The "total" team — consisting of the K-12 and central office team combined — has about twenty-two members.

Each team conducts its meetings in the same manner: A "convener" or chairman leads the meeting, a "process observer" attends to the way members are interacting, and a "recorder" writes out the meeting's minutes on an easel visible to all members. These positions — including the convener of the central office team — are rotated to encourage member participation and to emphasize the democratic nature of the meetings.

Decisions are made by consensus, though the superintendent retains the final authority for decisions because, Coelho told the writer, "he has to answer to the board as the chief executive." Coelho also reserves the right to make decisions in the special subject areas, such as guidance, physical education, art, music, and athletics. "I chose to take the system-wide supervisor's view of these special subjects," Coelho explained, "and I told the principals that would be the ground rule."

The Attleboro district has no formal board-administrator agreement regarding the management team. "We never got into the policy statement as a method of operation," said Coelho. "It's been based on the good-faith effort of all of us working together to develop the system. Now that we've got to dismantle part of the system because of the budget cuts, the same kind of ground rules prevail. There's a professional awareness or agreement that we've got to work these problems out together."

The management team in Attleboro coexists peacefully with a principals bargaining unit, which has existed since the 1960s. The threat of a powerful principals union was not a factor in the implementation of a management team system, Coelho reports.

The relationship between the building administrators and the central ofice is still very positive, Coelho told the writer, primarily because of the nature and attitudes of the principals group: "They're quite professional people and they deal separately with working condition issues and district decision-making issues." Coelho never bargains directly with the principals group. This is left to other central office administrators. No salary or working condition issues have come up in regular team meetings, even though agenda items can be contributed by any team member.

Coelho attributed the strength of the management team in the face of this year's budget cuts to the extensive training in communications skills the administrators received in the 1970s: "The general structure of the system — the skills we taught each other and that we learned from our trainers in the mid-seventies — have paid off in this budget crisis," Coelho concluded.

CONCLUSION

For decades, reform-minded educators have promoted shared school district management as an alternative to the traditional hierarchical arrangement of district governance. In a few scattered districts, shared management has been a reality for many years, usually due to the leadership of a superintendent who is convinced of the merits of shared decision-making.

Since the advent of collective bargaining with teachers, however, shared or "team" management has received much greater emphasis. Many districts have rushed to implement team management to "unify" management against the teachers associations, to co-opt or prevent principal unionization, or to provide a greater role in district management for dissatisfied principals. In the many districts where team management has been implemented for mainly political reasons — and not out of a real desire for shared decision-making — team management has not often been successful.

As illustrated in the preceding section, however, team management has been successful in some districts. Whether more districts are successfully utilizing shared district decision-making now than before the advent of collective bargaining remains open to question. The recent deluge of rhetoric promoting shared decision-making and team management, though, has undoubtedly pushed more districts toward the real implementation of management teams.

In team management systems, the superintendent continues to be the one person responsible to the board for the team's decisions and also retains final authority in decision-making. Thus, successful team management is highly dependent on a superintendent who is honestly interested in sharing decision-making power with middle-echelon administrators.

Of course, it is not just the superintendent who must desire shared district governance. The success of the team depends on "the extent to which all parties involved really want a working relationship based on a philosophy of involvement in policy formulation of all individuals affected by the policy," as Lester W. Anderson notes.

The design of the team management system is another important factor in its success. As Anderson states, the extent to which the concept is implemented is dependent on "the skill with which the superintendent and his staff design a structure which assures a process of open communications among all administrators in the decision-making process." Successful implementation may thus require substantial training of team members in the communication skills required for shared decision-making, a topic addressed more fully in chapter 8.

The most important factor in the success of team management, however, is the existence of an atmosphere of trust among team members, especially between the superintendent and building administrators. When this trust is present and when all parties truly desire a management system based on shared decision-making, team management has a good chance of success.

CHAPTER 6
PARTICIPATIVE DECISION-MAKING

John Lindelow
David Coursen
Jo Ann Mazzarella

The present structure of educational governance is modeled after the industrial bureaucracy that emerged in the economy at the turn of the century. The educational reformers of this period believed that centralization of power and dependence on professional expertise were the solutions to the problems facing the schools. As a result of the reformers' efforts, a centralized and authoritative power structure — which Harold McNally has likened to a "royal hierarchy" — became firmly established in the public schools.

In hierarchical organizations, decisions are characteristically made near the top of a pyramidal power structure and are passed down a chain of command to lower levels. Information flows primarily from the "top" to the "bottom" of the structure. Subordinates are assumed to be incapable, unqualified, or uninterested in contributing to the organization's decision-making process.

Although such a structure may be valuable for some purposes — such as a military command — it is inappropriate, say critics, for the governance of schools. An authoritative structure is "undemocratic" and ignores the worth of individuals. Furthermore, hierarchical structures do not have well-defined channels for the flow of information from the bottom to the top of the pyramid. Thus, an inevitable gap exists between problems and decisions made to resolve them.

In recent decades, a new reform movement has been building momentum both in public education and in other sectors of society, notably business. This reform movement can be seen as a broad attempt to make organizations more "democratic" and less authoritarian in their operation. A cornerstone of this reform movement is participative decision-making (PDM).

PDM is an ambiguous term at best and can refer to a variety of decision-making arrangements. In chapter 3, the notion of a continuum of leadership styles was introduced, with the authoritative and "boss-centered" model on one end of the continuum and the democratic and "subordinate-centered" model on the other. In this chapter, PDM will refer, in general, to those leadership behaviors toward the democratic end of the spectrum.

The school leader can exercise PDM in a number of ways. He or she can consult with subordinates before making a decision or can allow the group to make the decisions via consensus or majority vote. If the group makes the decision, the leader can act as an "equal" with no special authority, or the leader can retain the final "veto" power for decisions. As will be discussed later, however, the effective leader will use a variety of decision-making styles, including, at times, an autocratic style.

PDM is an essential feature of both team management and school-based management, as discussed in the two previous chapters. PDM is the central element of the management team — its *raison d'être*. In school-based management, decentralization of decision-making authority to the school site is the central theme, but PDM at the school site is also essential to the system's proper function.

In both team management and PDM at the school site, the formal and legal power structure of school governance is not significantly altered. The person in the traditional and legal position of power — whether it be the superintendent or the principal — retains both the authority and the responsibility for decisions made through the participative process.

Thus, the power of position in PDM systems is *voluntarily* shared with those in traditionally subordinate positions. Essentially, authority to make decisions is shared, but there is usually no concomitant dispersal of responsibility for the decisions made. Thus, PDM is often referred to as a "high-risk" undertaking for the administrator involved.

There are three good reasons, though, for believing that this risk is worth taking. First, PDM has been shown to have numerous advantages over traditional, authority-based systems of command, including better decisions, higher employee satisfaction, and better relationships between management and staff. These advantages and some of the research confirming them will be discussed in the next section.

Second, the "democratic" reform movement referred to

earlier has not subsided and is not likely to in the near future. Teachers, parents, and other community members are clamoring for a piece of the decision-making pie. The rights of citizens and teachers to participate in school governance are being written into state laws and collective bargaining agreements.

The writing is on the wall: If school administrators do not voluntarily share their power, they risk forced rearrangement of the power structure of education through political means. If, however, educational administrators do voluntarily share their power with subordinates and the clients of the school system, they can have the best of both worlds: professional control of the schools and access to the huge potential for improved education that participative management provides.

The third reason the "risk" of PDM is worth taking is that it can prevent the development of adversarial relationships between administrators and teachers. A recent study of Montana educators, reported by James Keef, found that much of the discontent and "restlessness" of teachers stems not from low pay but from "a lack of teacher involvement in the decision-making process at the building-site level."

The major goals of teachers, Keef states, are to "have some control over their jobs and profession, and to be professionally consulted on matters that affect children in their classrooms." When teachers are denied input at the building-site level, they try to obtain a voice in decision-making through collective bargaining. And if this fails — which it often does because administrators are afraid they will lose control of the schools — teachers focus on money and fringe benefits, because, states Keef, money can act as a temporary substitute for the fulfillment of higher needs.

Administrators should not fear sharing power, however. According to recent research reviewed by James Lipham, "teachers do not wish to usurp the role of administrators to make final decisions. In fact, participative decision making in schools still is seen [by teachers] as rightfully occurring within an authoritative organizational context."

Of course, just "sharing power" sounds easy enough, yet there are many pitfalls to avoid when implementing PDM. Some of these pitfalls and guidelines for avoiding them will be discussed later in this chapter. Then several schools' experiences with PDM will be described.

Decision-making at the school site can, of course, be shared with parents, other community members, and students, as well as with teachers. This chapter, however, will focus on decision-making that is shared between a school's principal and its faculty. Most of the principles of PDM discussed below, however, are equally applicable to PDM with other groups.

ADVANTAGES OF PARTICIPATION

One of the fundamental arguments for PDM is that it is the method of school governance most consistent with democratic principles. The belief that those affected by public institutions should have some voice in how they are run is deeply rooted in America's laws and traditions. Making the governance of schools more participative is an expression of belief in the democratic system and is a useful means of teaching both students and educators the principles of the democratic process.

Participative decision-making can also improve schools in more specific ways, say proponents, by promoting both better decisions and their more effective implementation. Broader participation increases the number of different viewpoints and interests that are expressed and considered while a decision is being made, and this, in turn, may encourage better decisions. PDM also helps improve communication within a school by providing formal channels for the exchange of information and ideas, particularly for the "upward" movement of information from the bottom to the top of the administrative hierarchy. Finally, PDM can lead to better decisions because it allows a school to make fuller use of its human resources, particularly the expertise and problem-solving skills of its teachers.

PDM leads to better implementation of decisions, in part because the distance between where a decision is made and where it is put into practice is reduced. If persons implementing policy have participated in the development of that policy, they are more likely to understand it better. In addition, they are likely to have a greater sense of "ownership" in the decision and thus will feel more committed to its successful implementation.

Many writers also suggest that PDM can improve both employee satisfaction and school climate. For example, the fact that teachers are consulted about decisions shows them that the school values their opinions; they, in turn, develop greater feelings of professional pride and job satisfaction. An adversarial relationship between administrators and teachers is less likely. With better communications and more satisfied personnel, the school's overall "climate" (discussed in the next chapter) can be significantly improved.

QUALITY OF DECISIONS

Many of the above advantages of PDM have been confirmed either directly or indirectly by research. Donald Piper, for example, compared the quality of decisions made by individuals acting alone with those they made in groups. He first gave each individual subject a test that required making a series of decisions. While members of a control group simply retook the test individually, the remaining subjects were divided into three types of groups for retesting. One type (consensus) had no leaders; group members discussed the problems until they reached solutions that were accepted — though not necessarily agreed upon — by everyone in the group. In the second type of group (participative-best), the individual who had scored highest on the test was chosen group leader and given the responsibility for making decisions after eliciting advice from the rest of the group. The third type (participative-worst) worked the same way, except that individuals with the lowest scores were designated as leaders.

The results of the testing strongly favored group decisions. While the individuals who retook the test actually scored slightly worse on a second try, each type of group did much better than the average of its members' initial scores. The consensus group decisions were better than the individual averages, and several groups actually outperformed even their best individuals. In each participative-best group, the leaders made better decisions with help than they had made acting alone. The decisions of the participative-worst leaders improved dramatically, though only one such group was able to surpass its best individual.

Although the exercise used for this test was not related to education, its results are significant because they form such a consistent pattern. All the leaders — good test-takers and bad — gained from the participation of others, and in no case did listening to the advice of others cause a leader to make decisions that were less correct. Thus, as Piper suggests, the results indicate that "if arriving at the most correct decision is the primary goal, the involvement of several people . . . will provide better results than the 'one-man-deciding alone' model."

ORGANIZATIONAL EFFECTIVENESS

In a recent article, Jane and Rensis Likert review some of the research that shows schools run more smoothly with participative leadership. These authors classify systems of management as follows: system 1 is an "exploitive, authoritarian model"; system 2 is a "benevolent, authoritarian model"; system 3 is a "consultative model"; and system 4 is a "participative, goal directed model."

The Likerts summarize several studies illustrating the applicability of the system 4 model to educational administration. A 1972 study by Haynes of twenty Michigan school districts showed that districts that had never had a teachers' strike were significantly closer to system 4 management than were a matched set of school districts that had recently had a teachers' strike. "The teachers in the school system where work stoppages occurred were more frustrated than were teachers in the systems where work stoppages did not occur," say the Likerts. "This frustration was measured by the differences between the expectations of being involved in decisions affecting them and their actual experience."

Bernhardt's 1972 study of sixty-seven New York State schools also examined the relationship between management style and teacher militancy. Results indicated that "the closer to System 4 the teachers perceived the school's administration to be, the less they displayed militant orientation."

Gibson's 1974 study found that in schools perceived by teachers and principals as being close to the system 4 model, "boys attain higher achievement test scores in relation to their intelligence test scores than do boys in schools with administrative systems more toward System 1."

Miller's 1970 study of six California districts showed that in school systems or individual schools closer to system 4, the motivation of students and teachers was higher, their frustration with the decision-making process was lower, the confidence and trust among persons in the school were greater, and the school had better communications "in all directions." Other studies reported by the Likerts corroborate the findings discussed above.

TEACHER SATISFACTION

Several researchers have tried to determine how teachers feel about involvement in decision-making. Joseph Alutto and James Belasco, for example, did pioneering work on the relationship between level of participation and teacher satisfaction. Comparing teachers' actual and desired levels of participation in decision-making, they identified three different conditions: deprivation (too little involvement), saturation (too much involvement — recent research indicates this is a relatively rare phenomenon), and equilibrium (neither too much nor too little involvement). Test results indicated that teachers in a state of equilibrium were the most satisfied group. Teachers who experienced either deprivation or saturation were less satisfied. Thus it may be more important to offer a teacher the right amount of participation than it is simply to increase participation.

Important as it is, Alutto and Belasco's work is limited by its exclusive focus on the amount — rather than the type — of participation offered to teachers. Other research has considered whether teachers are more interested in participating in certain types of decisions than in other types. Allan Mohrman, Jr., Robert Cooke, and Susan Mohrman, for example, divided decisions into technical (relating to teaching or the instructional process) and managerial (relating to support functions) domains. The authors found that teachers desired and experienced higher levels of participation in the technical than the managerial domain.

Noel Speed attempted to measure the effects on satisfaction of the amount (extent and frequency) as well as the domain of the decision-making power teachers were offered. His study covered only schools with individualized instructional programs, which, he concedes, may not be typical of all schools. However, several of his findings were consistent with those of other researchers: either equilibrium or slight deprivation in either domain or amount of participation was correlated with higher levels of satisfaction than was severe deprivation; and teachers' ideal and actual levels of participation were higher in technical than in managerial domains. Nevertheless, teachers apparently derived considerable satisfaction from their limited participation in managerial decision-making. Speed also found that teachers' satisfaction was affected more by how *extensively* they participated in decision-making than by how *frequently* they did so.

Further evidence that teachers desire a greater decision-making role in certain areas than in others is provided by the work of Robert Knoop and Robert O'Reilly. They asked 192 teachers how they felt decisions should be made about textbook selection, curriculum planning, and curriculum evaluation. While most teachers felt they should have sole responsibility for selecting textbooks, in the other areas teachers did not want sole responsibility nor did they want to give principals total responsibility. Instead, most favored some sort of shared decision-making, either through majority rule or a system of "consultation" in which the principal makes the decision with a lot of input from teachers. Another researcher's findings emphasize how important it is that teachers be offered the right forms of participation. Carl Lowell studied the relative effectiveness of three different types of decision-making groups — consensus, majority vote, and centralist (leader dominated). He specifically focused on the effect these different decision-making processes would have on the members' attitudes toward the process itself, their willingness to alter their own initial private opinions, and their satisfaction with the group solution.

The consensus groups, with all the members sharing the power equally, showed the highest level of satisfaction with the group solution. The members also had highly favorable attitudes toward the process the group followed in reaching its decision and were quite willing to change their opinions in the course of reaching consensus. The leaders of consensus groups tended to take the role of synthesizers by helping communication to flow openly and by working to involve all group members in the decision-making process.

Members of centralist groups, in which decisions were made by a leader after consulting with the group, also tended to be satisfied with the groups' decisions, positive toward the decision-making and group interaction processes, and willing to change their opinions about the value of their initial solutions. Lowell had not expected these groups to work so well. Apparently, the primary reason for their success was that the group leaders, although they had final responsibility for decisions, chose to share their power with the group. They worked collaboratively by collecting a variety of ideas and opinions and "synthesizing them into a solution that requires at the most an informal approval from the group."

In practice, therefore, centralist groups worked very much like consensus groups. Their members felt free to participate, perceived that the group was moving toward a solution, and were pleased that the leader incorporated their ideas into the group decision. It appears, in fact, that the centralist group leaders actually assumed a role similar to what teachers in Knoop and O'Reilly's study considered ideal and that, in practice, this ideal role proved to be highly functional.

The majority-vote groups in Lowell's study, however, were far less successful. Members were generally less satisfied with the solutions the group reached, less willing to change their initial opinions, and less favorable toward the decision-making process than members of other groups. Group leaders often acted as arbitrators between group members endorsing different solutions. The atmosphere in these groups became competitive, with little of the give-and-take that characterized consensus groups. Lowell suggests that poor communication may have caused these groups to function ineffectively, since concentration "on the alternative solutions to the case hinders the development of a common understanding of the facts and clarification of the problem(s)."

Taken together, the above studies constitute a remarkably strong endorsement for participative decision-making. They show that PDM can enhance the quality of decisions, increase employees' job satisfaction, prevent adversarial relationships, and, in general, improve the school's climate.

The primary disadvantage of the participative approach is that it requires more time and effort on everyone's part to make it work. Although it often slows down the efficiency of the decision-making process, the advantages accrued through PDM appear to easily outweigh the disadvantages.

GUIDELINES FOR IMPLEMENTATION

Many building administrators are convinced of the desirability of PDM at the school site, yet they are not sure how to proceed. How should the organizational structures for involvement be designed? Who should be included in the decision-making process? What kinds of decisions should be shared with others? How should agreements be reached?

Of course, there are no pat answers to these questions. Each school is unique and has different needs, resources, and restrictions that will influence the final form of its PDM system. There are, however, several basic guidelines that should be considered before setting up any shared decision-making system.

VARYING DECISION-MAKING STYLE

Although PDM has many advantages over autocratic decision-making, it does not necessarily follow that all decisions should be made collectively. In some instances — such as when a crisis arises, when decisions are routine, or when special expertise is called for — an autocratic style might be best.

Consider the task facing the school's leader: he or she must maximize several variables — the efficiency of decision-making, the quality of decisions, the use of professional expertise, and the satisfaction of those affected by the decisions made — each of which may be at odds with the others. Simply increasing participation in decision-making without considering the other variables could ultimately be counterproductive. As management consultant Maneck Wadia states,

Participative management is but one tool in the management bag. An executive proclaiming to be a "participative manager" is tantamount to a carpenter proclaiming to be a "hammerer." Obviously, a carpenter has and needs a variety of tools in achieving objectives. Similarly, a manager needs a variety of techniques to achieve goals.

Instead of sharing all decisions, the astute school leader will make some decisions autocratically, will make some with input from the staff, and will allow the staff to make some decisions themselves. In short, the effective building administrator will utilize a "situational" style of leadership and will vary his or her decision-making style with the needs of the situation.

One useful exercise for making administrators more aware of their decision-making styles was explained by Robert DeVries in a telephone interview. The exercise is used by DeVries and colleague Mark Robert to train administrators in Los Angeles's staff development program for administrators. Decisions that administrators are faced with are classified as follows:

- consensus (when acceptance and trust of staff are needed)
- command (when constrained by time and need for special expertise)
- consultation (when more input is needed)
- convenience (when no one cares about the decision)

The goal of the activity is to show administrators that blindly insisting on only one kind of decision-making for every decision can be inefficient or destructive of trust.

Just as important as varying one's decision-making style is making it clear to staff members what their part in the decision-making process will be. "There is considerable evidence," states James Lipham in a recent research review, "that in effective schools, the principal defines clearly the boundaries of others' involvement, avoiding giving the impression that they have the power to make decisions when, in fact, they do not." When staff members understand the structure of the decision-making process and the bounds of their power, they can begin to work within that structure toward group goals, without continual doubt or haggling over power.

WHO SHOULD BE INVOLVED

The "classic rule of thumb" in this matter, as Robert Muccigrosso states, is "to involve all those in the decision-making who will be directly and significantly affected by the outcome of the decision." Although this general rule seems sensible enough, it is complicated by several considerations.

First, different individuals desire different levels of involvement. Some faculty members might desire a great deal of participation, while others might prefer to be told what to do. Thus, the first step in implementing a PDM program would be to determine just who does have the desire to be more involved in decision-making. An ideal program would be selective and voluntary, offering participation to those who want it, without forcing it on those who do not.

Involvement in the decision-making process should also be dictated by the situation. Research indicates that "total group decision making continues to be overutilized in schools," says James Lipham. "In the early stages of any change process, when awareness and support are critical, wide participation should be the rule. In later stages (i.e. implementation), participation should be limited because people weary of group meetings devoted to redeciding issues."

Another complication of involving all those affected by a decision in its making is that some individuals in the school may have special expertise in certain areas that gives them a special status in the decision-making process. This is the classic dilemma between "professionalism" and "populism" in a democratic system, a dilemma that never has reached — and probably never will reach — final resolution.

Of course, the input of others should always be sought and heard. The principal, however, will have to decide in each case whether following the advice of the "expert" (who may be the principal himself) or consenting to the desires of the larger group will do most to advance the school toward its goals. In any case, the principal should make clear to staff members what their role in the decision-making process will be before the process begins.

161

Another problem with the "classic rule of thumb" for involvement is that the decision-making group can quite quickly become too large and cumbersome for efficient operation. Thus, some form of representation may be called for.

So how should staff members be chosen for participation on a decision-making or advisory committee? James Longstreth has addressed this issue in a monograph on school-based management. If the faculty elects members to the committee, it will likely be more representative but "it can also result in the selection of the more popular faculty members ignoring those with the necessary expertise." If the principal appoints members, the necessary expertise will be available, yet the committee may not be representative. Despite the weaknesses of each method, Longstreth concludes, one or the other should be used, or perhaps a combination of the two.

EXTENT OF INVOLVEMENT

As discussed in the last section, research has shown that teachers who feel they have too little involvement and teachers who feel they have too much involvement are less satisfied than teachers who perceive their participation as appropriate.

According to Lipham, "excessive involvement causes frustration ('Why doesn't the principal just decide and leave us alone?'), whereas underinvolvement creates hard feelings ('Why wasn't I consulted?')." The sensitive principal, Lipham concludes, must give attention to both the frequency and the level of involvement and should strive for "a condition of equilibrium" between too little and too much involvement.

AREAS OF INVOLVEMENT

In general, participation should be offered in those areas of decision-making that are of most concern to teachers. As noted earlier, research has shown that teachers are more interested in those areas that are more immediate to their work — such as textbook selection, curriculum planning and evaluation, and classroom management — than they are in more general management areas. As Knoop and O'Reilly's work indicates, most teachers desire sole responsibility for selecting textbooks, but in other areas they desire only a strong consultative role, with the principal making the final decision.

Of course, different teachers have different areas of primary interest. PDM systems could be designed, however, so teachers could influence the policies that affect them most, without getting involved in other areas. In such systems, teachers who did wish to participate in a certain area would also be likely to be those with the greatest interest and expertise in that area, and therefore, presumably, they would have the greatest potential for contributing to better decision-making.

FORMS OF INVOLVEMENT

Since teachers seem to respond to participation when it takes forms they consider desirable, it is particularly important to identify the most effective forms of PDM. Unfortunately, the form of participation that teachers desire most — consensus — is not always practicable, primarily because it can take a great deal of time and may not work at all in large groups. This may indicate that what Lowell calls a centralist approach, with a single decision-maker extensively using the advice of others, could often be the most desirable form of PDM. The principal, however, should vary the forms of involvement according to his or her judgment of what will be best for the total operation of the school.

MOVING TO PDM

Several writers stress the importance of implementing a PDM system gradually. Jane and Rensis Likert, for example, advise organizations not to "attempt one big jump" from an authoritative to a participative system. In moving toward PDM, they state,

> a leader should make no greater shift at any one time than subordinates or members can adjust to comfortably and respond to positively. If a leader makes a

sizable shift, the members do not have the interaction skills to respond appropriately and usually are made insecure or frightened by the shift, responding to it negatively.

To develop a program that truly fits the needs of a specific school community, PDM should be introduced gradually, allowed to evolve, and evaluated regularly, with feedback from participants. As one result of such an evaluation, the participants may see that the program could be more effective if their own skills and expertise were improved. A natural next step might be the design of training sessions providing whatever content is needed.

Exercises to help schools and school groups assess their decision-making structures and learn more about how participative decision-making works have been collected by Richard Schmuck and his colleagues. For example, the "Card Discovery Problem" requires participants to find a unique card — something impossible without information-sharing by all members. The "Lost on the Moon" exercise (the same exercise used by Donald Piper in the decision-making experiment described previously) teaches participants to reach decisions by consensus by rank ordering equipment most useful for a two-hundred-mile trip across the moon. These exercises are helpful because they allow groups to learn participative decision-making by using it to solve hypothetical problems unlikely to arouse anxiety or strong feeling.

Some of the skills necessary to make PDM work are discussed in detail in the chapters on communicating and leading meetings.

Ultimately, the key to a successful PDM program is the development of trust and mutual respect among the participants. If these exist, they will foster the open exchange of ideas and feelings that is essential to effective policy-making. After all, no rules or theories can really identify what the most appropriate forms of PDM will be in a given situation. But when the formidable human resources of a school community are employed, a school will have little trouble developing a specific approach tailored to the needs, skills, and aspirations of those who are to participate in the decision-making process.

APPROACHES TO INVOLVEMENT

There are no "magic formulas" for implementing PDM at the school site. Each school is unique and must design a decision-making structure that will fit its own characteristics and needs.

The guidelines presented in the previous section can help administrators conceptualize the general outlines of their school's PDM system. Another valuable resource in the design process, presented here, is a description of the experiences of other schools with PDM systems.

Vincent Crockenberg and Woodrow Clark, Jr., in a 1979 article, describe what they believe to be the most important of the recent teacher participation experiments, namely the San Jose (California) Teacher Involvement Project (TIP). TIP — which was "modestly financed" by the National Institute of Education from 1974 to 1977 — sought "to train classroom teachers to participate with their building principals in identifying and resolving local school problems and to sustain that involvement by implementing formal decision-making procedures at each school site."

With the help of the TIP staff, teachers at each of the twelve participating San Jose schools identified both the decision-making areas they wished to be involved in and the levels at which they wanted to be involved. These preferences were then incorporated into a "constitution" that each school's faculty drew up, often in collaboration with the principal.

The constitutions described in detail "the basic structure of government" at the school, including "the composition and operation of the faculty council, the faculty's decision-making prerogatives, and the procedures for recourse in the event of differences between the councils and the school administration."

"As it turned out, the decision-making areas of particular concern to teachers were distinctly instructional rather than administrative," state Crockenberg and Clark. Most faculties indicated that they preferred to operate in an advisory or consultative capacity, though some faculties desired to have the power to reject and authorize decisions.

TIP had strong support from San Jose's superintendent, as well as support from the state and local teachers associations. In some schools, principals objected because they felt TIP undermined their authority as business managers. Some of these principals finally came out in favor of TIP, while those who remained opposed "were effectively neutralized by the superintendent's clear support of the project."

After three years, twelve of the district's schools had developed councils and constitutions that provided "legitimate and effective faculty participation in a wide variety of decision-making areas." Not surprisingly, however, TIP was most successful in those schools where the principal voluntarily shared power with the teachers.

Crockenberg and Clark identify five factors that led to TIP's success: strong support from both the superintendent and teachers; the involvement of teachers in the planning of TIP; appropriate training for school personnel; the establishment of formal mechanisms that "clearly specified who had legitimate authority to make what decisions in the new governance structure"; and the gradual implementation of the project, which proceeded "with due regard to the difficulties teachers and building principals would confront in reconstructing the long-established and well-entrenched governance structure of the public schools."

Although each school had achieved a significant degree of teacher participation at the end of the three-year grant period, two years later TIP was thriving in only six of the twelve original schools. Crockenberg and Clark blame TIP's languishing on adversarial relationships brought about by collective bargaining and budget cuts caused by Proposition 13.

Another approach to PDM is found in the Mansfield, Connecticut, public schools (enrollment: 1,200 students in three elementary schools and one middle school). In Mansfield, "teachers conceive and write curricula, help to screen and nominate professional staff, help prepare the budget, schedule their schools and bring recommendations to the Board of Education," according to David Weingast.

Teachers participate directly in the process of district-wide curriculum development by serving on curriculum councils, which are organized by subject. The councils identify curriculum work that needs to be done, develop the curriculum themselves or with the help of outside consultants, and then present their proposal to the board of education. Prior to their public session, Superintendent Bruce Caldwell meets with the council to help shape their proposal. Caldwell does not, however, force his thinking on the group, says Weingast.

Teachers also participate at the building level. When a new teacher is needed, for example, "the principal constitutes an in-house committee of teachers who, with him, develop specific job criteria, screen applications, interview candidates, observe them on the job, and make recommendations to the superintendent. Virtually without exception their proposals stick."

Principals retain a leadership role in the Mansfield system, though many teachers speak of the principals as "facilitators." The principals are happy with the district's new spirit, says Weingast, and they speak highly of the teachers' professional health in the PDM system. However, "an old fashioned principal, used to running everything, would be out of place here."

One of the district's principals, Margaret Anthony, had this to say about the Mansfield system in a recent article:

> Leadership in Mansfield may come from students, parents, teachers, administrators, school board members, and even the superintendent. Leadership is not structured in the traditional hierarchy of command, the pyramid of power with its pinnacle in the main office and its broad base resting in the powerless, voiceless teaching staff. Leadership is not permanently fixed, rigidly controlled, or jealously guarded. The entire staff is encouraged to contribute their best and indeed they do.

Mansfield's teachers work hard at making the PDM system work, concludes Weingast, "but there is no sign that they would trade their present responsibilities and gratifications for an easier life under a more traditional arrangement."

CONCLUSION

Recent research has confirmed what proponents of participative approaches have long claimed — that PDM can lead to better decisions, better implementation, greater job satisfaction, and improved school communications.

But simply increasing participation in decision-making is not enough to ensure a smoothly functioning school. As James Lipham stresses, "effective principals recognize the need for situational leadership" and will utilize a variety of decision-making styles according to the dictates of the situation.

When a participative approach is called for, the effective school leader will consider all the variables involved — who should be involved, their optimum level of involvement, what will be decided, and how it will be decided — and then will clearly communicate to the group the design of the decision-making process. When used in this way, PDM can be one of the most effective techniques a leader can use to motivate others to "strive willingly for group goals."

CHAPTER 7
SCHOOL CLIMATE
John Lindelow and Jo Ann Mazzarella

> There is a subtle spirit that exists in a school, both in the minds of the teachers and students and in every act, which may never be exactly described or analysed, but which even the most inexperienced observer recognizes when he enters a school or a classroom.
>
> L. J. Chamberlin

Ask any student, teacher, or administrator; indeed, ask anyone who has spent even a short amount of time in different schools: each has its own distinct "feel" or "personality" that can be recognized soon after entering its doors.

Some schools are perceived as "good" schools — desirable and perhaps even exciting places to work and learn. Others are perceived as just the opposite — places where one would probably not spend much time were it not for legal or financial compulsions to do so. Still other schools are considered "ordinary" by most observers — not particularly exciting, but not particularly threatening, either.

For decades, this "subtle spirit" of a school was generally referred to as "school morale" by researchers and practitioners. In the past twenty years or so, however, the concept has more often been called school or organizational "climate."

In a broad sense, organizational climate is the product of every aspect of an organization — the nature of the work that goes on there, the people, the architecture and surroundings, the history of the organization, the administrative policies in effect, and, especially, the patterns of interaction and communication among the members of the organization. Thus, Eugene Howard defines climate as "the aggregate of social and cultural conditions which influence individual behavior in the school — all the forces to which the individual responds, which are present in the school environment."

Most of the research and discussion on school climate, however, focuses on the "social" aspect of climate, which appears to be the major contributor to overall climate. In this chapter, then, discussion will center on that part of school climate which results from the ways organizational members

169

behave and interact with each other.

Definitions of the social aspect of school climate abound. Fritz Steele and Stephen Jenks, for example, define organizational climate as "what it feels like to spend time in a social system — the weather in that region of social space." Wilbur Brookover, Charles Beady, Patricia Flood, John Schweitzer, and Joe Wisenbaker conceive of climate as "the composite of norms, expectations, and beliefs which characterize the school social system as perceived by members of the social system." Andrew Halpin and Don Croft have another useful conceptualization of school climate; they call it the organizational "personality" of a school. " 'Climate' is to the organization," they state, what " 'personality' is to the individual."

For a given individual, climate is the "feel" he or she gets from being in an organization. This feeling is the product of the individual's "global" perception of the patterns of behavior and interaction in the organization. And these behaviors, in turn, are largely determined by the underlying structure of norms, expectations, and beliefs in the organization. Thus, norms determine behavior, which determines climate.

Because of the complexity of the underlying stratums of behaviors and norms, portraits of climate created by researchers are necessarily multidimensional in nature; that is, they usually have numerous variables. Climate is thus quite similar to human personality, as Halpin and Croft note. Just as personality has many "facets" to it, so does the climate of a school have many components.

And just as there are numerous ways to characterize personality, there are numerous ways to characterize climate. The science of "organizational climate," however, is in its infancy compared to the science of personality. Thus, the methods of characterizing climate — as will be seen below — are as yet rather undeveloped. Methods of climate "therapy" lag even further behind and are nearly on a par with "folk" medicine. Nevertheless, useful suggestions for improving climate exist and will be reviewed.

Of couse, it isn't just the school that has its characteristic climate. Both classrooms and school districts also have their "personalities." The climates of the classrooms in a school contribute to that school's overall climate, just as the climates of the various schools in a district contribute to the district's overall climate.

In this chapter discussion will center on climate at the school building level, for two reasons. First, most research to date has focused on this level. Second, the school has a more defined and independent climate than the district or classroom. Individual schools are rather loosely tied into the larger district structure, so individual schools can vary widely in their climates. Thus district climate is a somewhat disparate entity.

Classrooms within a school, however, are more closely associated and thus are more apt to share a common climate. "Although there is some variance in school climate between classrooms within the school," state Brookover and his colleagues, "the within school differences are not so great as to rule out the existence of a characteristic climate for the school."

MEASURING SCHOOL CLIMATE

Although there is vague agreement among researchers on what constitutes healthy school climate, there is little consensus on how climate should be measured. Several systems for characterizing organizational climate have been devised. Most of these systems focus on measuring patterns of interaction and communication among the school's staff members, particularly between teachers and administrators.

One of the earlier school climate assessment instruments was developed in 1962 by Andrew Halpin and Don Croft. Their "Organizational Climate Description Questionnaire" (OCDQ) focused on "the social interactions that occur between the teachers and the principal." Halpin and Croft recognized "the importance of other components" of school climate, but chose to start with the social component with the hope of dealing "with the others at a future time." Their OCDQ, meanwhile, has become the most commonly used instrument for measuring school climate.

Halpin and Croft examined elementary schools in the development of their OCDQ. They collected data from seventy-one schools in six different regions of the country, with climate descriptions from 1,151 respondents.

The items composing this questionnaire were selected for their ability to indicate consistencies in faculty members' perceptions within their schools and to allow for comparisons among different schools. From teachers' descriptions of their school experiences and from previous research, Halpin and Croft constructed a set of simple statements, such as "Teachers seek special favors from the principal" and "The principal schedules the work for the teachers." Respondents indicated to what extent these statements applied to their schools.

After certain refinements, the sixty-four-item OCDQ was divided into eight subtests; four of these tapped the characteristics of the faculty as a group, and the other four pertained to characteristics of the principal as leader. The group behavior subtests were intended to measure *disengagement* (teachers' tendency toward anomie), *hindrance* (Do the teachers feel the principal facilitates or hinders their work?), *esprit* (teachers' morale), and *intimacy* (social needs satisfaction).

The leader behavior subtests were intended to measure *aloofness* (Is the principal impersonal and formal, or emotionally involved with his staff?), *production emphasis* (Is the principal highly directive and not sensitive to staff feedback?), *thrust* (Does the principal motivate teachers by setting a good example and personally moving the organization?), and *consideration* (Does the principal treat teachers "humanly"?).

Of these eight characteristics, Halpin and Croft discovered that esprit and thrust possessed special significance. The combined OCDQ scores for these two characteristics is "the best single index of authenticity," as Halpin states. Esprit indicates the authenticity of group behavior, while thrust indicates the same for the principal's behavior. Halpin conceived of authentic behavior as reality-centered, open, and essentially honest. And his data indicate that authenticity is strongly associated with those organizational climates he and Croft class as "open."

Halpin and Croft discovered that the organizational profiles of their seventy-one elementary schools could be arrayed along a continuum from "open climate" at one end through "closed climate" at the other.

In the open climate, members experience high esprit, but have no need for a high degree of intimacy. The leader scores high on thrust, but does not have to emphasize production, since the teachers' productivity is already high. The behavior of both leader and group is "authentic." At the other end of the spectrum, the closed climate is "the least genuine" one. What the leader says and does are two separate things. Teachers are disengaged, esprit is low, and group achievement is minimal.

Halpin and Croft are careful to point out that their continuum, while it is useful for purposes of classification and convenience, has certain shortcomings. As Halpin notes, "the ranking scheme is, at best, only an approximation, and the use of a continuum — which, perforce, assumes a linearity of relationship — oversimplifies the facts." He acknowledges that, even though the six climate types were predicated on the research, "in a genuine sense we did not discover these Organizational Climates; we *invented* them."

Drea Zigarmi and Ron Sinclair have developed another instrument for characterizing school climate, which they call the Staff Development School Climate Questionnaire (SDSCQ). The SDSCQ, they explain, measures five "dimensions" of climate. Respondents are asked to indicate their level of agreement with fifty-eight statements on a six-point Likert-type scale.

The five dimensions of climate measured by the SDSCQ are *communication* — the extent to which "information is shared among groups such as the school board, the central office, the building principal," and the teachers; *innovativeness* — the extent to which "educational innovations have been supported in the past by the school board, the central office, the building principal," and the teachers; *advocacy* — the "rapport and professionalism that exists among professional staff members"; *decision-making* — the extent to which respondents can contribute to decisions; and *attitude toward staff development* — the feelings respondents have "toward inservice education in general and specific inservice activities sponsored by the school system."

Brookover and his colleagues have developed three questionnaires (for teachers, principals, and students) designed to measure their idea of school climate as the "complex of feelings, attitudes, beliefs, values, expectations, and norms of the school." The fourteen "climate variables" measured by

their questionnaire are as follows:
STUDENT
1. Student sense of academic futility
2. Future evaluations and expectations
3. Perceived present evaluations and expectations
4. Perception of teacher push and teacher norms
5. Student academic norms

TEACHER
1. Ability, evaluations, expectations, and quality of students' education for college
2. Present evaluations and expectations for students' high school completion
3. Teacher-students' commitment to improve
4. Perception of principal's expectations
5. Teacher's academic futility

PRINCIPAL
1. Parent concern and expectations for quality of education
2. Efforts to improve
3. Evaluations of present school quality
4. Present evaluations and expectations of students

The findings of these researchers will be discussed more fully in the next section.

George Litwin and Robert Stringer have developed a thirty-one-statement organizational climate questionnaire. As with the other instruments, the respondents indicate their level of agreement with the statements. Each item is intended to reflect one of the following "dimensions of climate":

1. *Structure* — the feeling the workers have about the constraints in their work situation; how many rules, regulations, and procedures there are
2. *Responsibility* — the feeling of "being your own boss"; not having to double-check all of your decisions
3. *Risk* — the sense of riskiness and challenge in the job and in the work situation
4. *Reward* — the feeling of being rewarded for a job well done; the emphasis on reward versus criticism and punishment
5. *Warmth and support* — the feeling of general good

fellowship and helpfulness that prevails in the organization
6. *Conflict* — the feeling that management is not afraid of different opinions or conflict; the emphasis placed on settling differences here and now

Of all these instruments for measuring climate, it is difficult to say which is the "best." Some instruments are better tested and have more internal consistency than others. But a better criterion for judging these methods is, perhaps, how useful they are as tools for helping educators accurately profile their school's climate as the first step in a climate improvement program.

THE IMPORTANCE OF SCHOOL CLIMATE

Does it really matter whether a school has a "healthy" climate? Is it worth taking the trouble to try to improve climate? What would be the rewards of such an undertaking?

Certainly the satisfaction and morale of students and staff are higher in schools with healthy climates than in schools with unhealthy climates; indeed, school climate measures are often a direct reflection of satisfaction with the school. But is there any hard evidence that climate influences the final outcomes of education — how much and how well children learn? A good deal of recent research — briefly reviewed in this section — indicates that it does.

The question of whether climate influences student outcomes is important, because, as Michael Rutter and his colleagues have noted, there has recently been "a widespread acceptance among academics that schools made little difference" in student outcomes. This view stemmed largely from James Coleman's *Equality of Educational Opportunity* (1966) and Christopher Jencks' *Inequality: A Reassessment of the Effect of Family and Schooling in America* (1972).

According to Brookover and his colleagues, the conclusion of Jencks and others "that schools do not and (or) cannot make a difference in the achievement outcomes has been based on inadequate evidence." These studies have used such variables as family origins, teachers' qualifications, and school expenditures to examine the impact of schools on achievement. But these studies "devoted little or no attention to the nature of the social interaction which occurs within the school social system."

Several new studies are challenging the notion that schools don't make a difference by showing that school climate and school achievement are closely correlated. Brookover and colleagues, for example, sought to test the hypothesis that "the cultural or social-psychological normative climate and the student status-role definitions which characterized the school social system explain much of the variance in achievement and other behavioral outcomes of the schools."

These researchers studied 91 elementary schools chosen at random from the 2,200 elementary schools in Michigan with fourth- and fifth-grade students. Altogether, 11,466 students, 453 teachers, and 91 principals participated in the study.

From school records and from questionnaires administered to the students, teachers, and principals, the researchers obtained data on socioeconomic status and racial composition of the students, teacher salaries, teacher qualifications, student-teacher ratio, average daily attendance, student population, and average length of teacher tenure in the school. The questionnaires also characterized some aspects of each school's social structure, such as the extent to which parents are known and involved in the school social system, the amount of time devoted to instruction, the teachers' satisfaction in school relationships, and two student "status-role definitions."

Finally, the questionnaires measured characteristics of each school's climate, which the researchers identify as the "normative social-psychological environment" of the school. Climate variables included students', teachers', and principals' perceptions of their abilities to function successfully in the system, their perceptions of others' expectations and evaluations of them, and the norms of the school social system.

All of the above data were regarded by the researchers as the "input" into the school system. The "outcome variables" were the achievement scores of the fourth-grade students on state-administered math and reading tests, measures of the students' self-concepts of academic ability, and measures of students' sense of "self-reliance."

The input variables, taken together, accounted for about

three-fourths of the variance in achievement between schools. The authors then attempted to determine which input variables accounted for most of the variance in achievement. Unfortunately, this attempt was frustrated by the fact that "measures of climate are highly correlated with the measures of socioeconomic and racial compositions of the student bodies."

Through various statistical analyses, however, the authors are able to show convincingly that their climate variables had a stronger influence on achievement than did the economic and racial factors. "Although it is not sufficient proof," they conclude, "these analyses suggest that school climate rather than family background as reflected in student body composition has the more direct impact on achievement."

Other recent studies have focused on the effect of the school on student achievement. James Coleman's new report *Public and Private Schools*, for example, contains "important data about the relationships of various educational practices to student achievement," according to Diane Ravitch. She explains the impact of the new Coleman report as follows:

> For 15 years, since the appearance of the original Coleman report in 1966, educators have been reminded repeatedly that "schools don't make a difference" and that family background heavily determines educational achievement. The new Coleman report dramatically reverses this pessimistic conclusion and finds instead that schools *do* make a difference, regardless of the family background of students.

Time and again, Ravitch continues, the new report "demonstrates that achievement follows from specific school policies, not from the particular family background of the students," findings that represent "a dramatic departure from the social determinism of the past 15 years."

Another study, this one conducted in Britain, came to similar conclusions. In *Fifteen Thousand Hours,* Michael Rutter, Barbara Maughan, Peter Mortimore, Janet Outson, and Alan Smith concluded that

> differences between schools in outcome *were* systematically related to their characteristics as social institutions. Factors as varied as the degree of academic emphasis, teacher actions in lessons, the availability of incentives and rewards, good conditions for pupils,

and the extent to which children were able to take responsibility were all significantly associated with outcome differences between schools. All of these factors were open to modification by the staff, rather than fixed by external constraints.

Rutter and cowriters suggest that school climate has a lot to do with these differences. They found that the combined effect on school outcomes of the school process variables they measured was much stronger than the effect of any individual process variable.

> This suggests that the *cumulative* effect of these various social factors was considerably greater than the effect of any of the individual factors on their own. The implication is that the individual actions or measures may combine to create a particular *ethos,* or set of values, attitudes and behaviours which will become characteristic of the school as a whole.

Thus, what happens in a school *does* appear to influence the "outcomes" of the school — student achievement, behavior, and attitudes. Improving school climate is, then, a worthwhile undertaking.

IMPROVING SCHOOL CLIMATE

Many principals would like to improve the climates of their schools but do not know how to proceed. They may understand quite well how to elicit changes in particular programs or policies. Yet how can they change something as pervasive and powerful as school climate?

As a first step, principals should gain an understanding of the cyclical and self-perpetuating nature of organizational climate. Then they should consider the process of changing climate and their place in that process. Finally, they might listen to the practical suggestions of researchers and practitioners to gain ideas to apply in their own schools. Each of these steps toward improving school climate will be discussed in turn.

THE STABILITY OF CLIMATE

Every organization develops norms of behavior that dictate how members of the organization are expected to behave. Each individual learns, through interacting with others in the organization, just what is considered appropriate behavior and what is not. When a person behaves in accordance with the norms, the norms are confirmed and reinforced.

In this kind of cyclical fashion, norms reinforce and perpetuate themselves. And the behavior that the norms dictate is what creates, in the minds of individuals, the organization's climate. Thus, climates, too, are self-perpetuating.

A useful analogy, again, is that of human personality. Each person has a self-image that dictates how that person will tend to behave. Behavior consistent with the self-image reinforces the self-image, which then dictates future behavior.

Habits and patterns of behavior become firmly entrenched in this way and are difficult — though not impossible — to change. Habits of behavior or of thought can be changed, for example, by forcing oneself to behave or think differently for a time, until new patterns become established. The key is to break the self-reinforcing cycle of self-concept and behavior.

Changing organization norms — and the climates they create — is exactly analogous. The change agent must somehow intervene in the self-perpetuating cycle of norms and behavior and establish a new "self-concept" for the school.

The new norms — once established — will to a large extent reinforce and perpetuate themselves. A useful conceptualization of this stability of a good school environment is provided by Edward Wynne, who studied some 140 schools in the Chicago area. The "good" schools Wynne found were like well-tended gardens:

> In an efficient garden, weeding is easier once the food plants are well rooted. A mature and vigorous crop chokes out the weeds. So too in highly coherent — or good — schools, the vitality of the total environment stifled occasional surges of inefficiency: Students kept peers from breaking rules; teachers went out of their way to help colleagues solve professional problems; things seemed to work out without obvious conflict and stress.

Do events create the leader, or does the leader create the events? Is it possible for the principal to modify climate, or will the climate of the school seep into the principal and modify his or her behavior?

The leader of the school is — like everyone else — subject to the norms of the school and the expectations of the school's personnel. Some authors contend that the power of the organizational norms is stronger than the power of the principal to change them. Thus, any attempt to improve the climate created by the norms can only end in frustration and defeat.

Despite such grounds for pessimism, the idea that principals *do* have the power to change school climate and school effectiveness has a multitude of advocates. Fred Hechinger, who wrote the foreword to a book by James Lipham, is characteristic:

> I have never seen a good school with a poor principal or a poor school with a good principal. I have seen unsuccessful schools turned around into successful ones and, regrettably, outstanding schools slide rapidly into decline. In each case, the rise or fall could readily be traced to the quality of the principal.

Whether the principal alone should carry the responsibility for creating an effective school or a healthy climate is open to debate. It is likely, though, that the actual power of the principal to influence the climate of a school lies somewhere between inefficacy and total responsibility. The principal is indeed subject to the norms and other socializing forces of the school; but the principal also holds more power than anyone in the school and can use that power to slowly work changes in the norms of the school.

THE PROCESS OF CHANGE

One promising system for eliciting change in school climate is that of organizational development (OD). "In essence," says D. D. Warrick, "OD changes the norms of an organization." Richard Schmuck, Philip Runkel, Jane Arends, and Richard Arends designed a text on OD in the schools "to help establish the organizational climates that nurture personal fulfillment" in the schools.

OD is basically a strategy for eliciting organizational change that utilizes — at least initially — an outside "cadre" of OD specialists. The specialists educate the members of the organization in such areas as communication skills, problem-solving, conflict resolution, decision-making, and goal identification. They attempt to get the members of the organization "to examine their communication patterns, their customary ways of working together in meetings, or the ways in which people are linked together to get their daily work done."

By the time an OD intervention is complete, state Schmuck and colleagues, "cognitive and affective change should have occurred; norms, roles, influence patterns, and communication networks should have become more receptive and responsive — indeed, the very culture of the school should have become different."

OD appears to be a powerful method for effecting change in organizational climate because it intervenes in the norm-behavior cycle and sets it on a new track. Although OD is best carried out with the help of specialists, many OD techniques and exercises (as found in Schmuck's book) can be used without special training.

Another approach to improving school climate utilizes "behavior modification" to break the norm-behavior cycle. Peter Mortimore, coauthor with Michael Rutter of *Fifteen Thousand Hours*, describes this approach in an interview in *Educational Leadership* (see "On School Effectiveness...").

Mortimore uses an example of a school in which the norm is for students to tear down student paperwork that is displayed on the walls. Mortimore emphasizes that changing such a norm would take time. If teachers wished to have work displayed on the walls, that would be a new departure, and students wouldn't be used to it. The teachers "would have to prepare the students beforehand, and they should expect some failure at first."

Eliciting change in norms is often a "two steps forward, one step back" proposition. It takes a constant emphasis on new behavior and a deemphasis on old. The new behavior must be "held in place" at first by special effort, until it becomes established and accepted. Once established, it will

181

begin to change the more stable and underlying norm of behavior. Eventually, the new norm will become the accepted norm.

When teachers first put work on the walls, the result is predictable: The work is torn down. But the teachers "insist" on the new behavior and monitor the halls to make sure it is not torn down. Less and less work is torn down, and more and more students see work displayed. The students get used to having the work on the walls, and used to getting punished, perhaps, for tearing down work.

More importantly, some students begin to recognize displayed work as a behavior associated with different norms or values. They begin to perceive a different value system beneath the patterns of behavior and interaction in the school. They then begin to behave in ways consistent with the new norm system.

Several principles for improving school climate can be derived from this example. First, the new norm system must be clearly conceived and communicated and then uniformly applied throughout the school. The principal should maintain high and consistent expectations for children's behavior and achievement and should make sure that everyone knows these expectations. "Assume," state Wilbur Brookover and his colleagues,

> that all children can and will learn whatever the school defines as desirable and appropriate. Expect all children to learn these patterns of behavior rather than differentiate among those who are expected and those who are not expected to learn. Have common norms that apply to all children so that all members of the school social system expect a high level of performance by all students.

Second, the new norm system should be consistently enforced. The new behaviors expected should be "held" in place until the new norm system takes root. Failure to behave properly "should be followed by immediate feedback and reinstruction rather than positive reinforcement," as Brookover states. Reinforcement and praise should be given when behavior is appropriate.

Third, the move toward the new norm system should be undertaken gradually. Too much change at once should not be expected. Insistence on too much too fast may provoke revolt.

"Most major change processes in education probably fail because they are too 'rushed'," states James Lipham. "Educational change is a time-consuming process; a major change takes many months, even years."

Fourth, the climate improvement program should be designed and implemented with the participation of others. Climate improvement must be a collective undertaking with staff members' full support and understanding. Goals should be clearly understood, and new patterns of behavior should be consistently enforced. By involving staff members in the decision-making process, as discussed in chapter 6, the school's personnel can approach the change process as a united, instead of a fragmented, group.

PRACTICAL SUGGESTIONS

Practicing educators and administrators tend to view school climate in terms different from those used by researchers such as Halpin and Croft. They are quite understandably more concerned with what to do to improve organizational climate than with precise measurement and description of climate.

The research, frankly, has yet to give practitioners concrete direction for administrative action. Classifying a school's climate as closed, for example, does not tell its principal how to make it more open. And it certainly cannot be very comforting to school administrators to learn that their impact on school climate is minimal, as a few researchers have suggested. School administrators, like everyone else, need to believe they can influence their environments in a positive and constructive manner.

As a result of researchers' seeming inability to tell practitioners what they need to know, a body of pragmatically oriented literature has evolved. School administrators have recounted their schools' successful efforts to improve "climate," though usually they use climate in a rather general way and frequently mean it to be analogous to morale.

These administrator-generated articles definitely accentuate the positive. The administrator, whether superintendent

183

or principal, is viewed as a leader whose actions can shape (and improve) the attitudes of staff, students, and community. The emphasis in most of this literature is on action rather than on analysis or reflection.

For example, Robert Lindstrom, a California superintendent, urges administrators to "Take some action!" as an antidote to "wringing hands" or "hopelessly staring out your window." Lindstrom follows his initial call to action by listing "six suggestions for developing a positive organizational climate," which he compiled from "activities that have worked for people in the field":

1. "Rebirth of the organization" — Let the staff know that organizational change is afoot by stating new goals and presenting a plan of action.
2. "Building a history" — Shared experiences among staff members (such as preschool retreats) can establish "a warm glow of camaraderie" that will boost morale.
3. "Building trust" — Lindstrom suggests management training exercises to help build trust.
4. "Communications" — Quality, not quantity, is important.
5. "Reinforcement" — Maintain group cohesion through staff meetings with informal, participant-generated agenda.
6. "Pride" — The administrator can involve each participant "in owning a piece of the action" by explicitly commending staff-developed innovations and improvements.

Some attempts have been made to synthesize a research approach to school climate (description, analysis) with the pragmatic, action-oriented approach. One notable example is CFK Ltd.'s School District Climate Profile and its accompanying recommendations, assembled by Thomas Shaheen and W. Roberts Pedrick. The Climate Profile is intended to provide administrators with "a convenient means of assessing the school district's climate factors and determinants."

The four components of the Climate Profile questionnaire are meant to measure general climate factors (such as "respect," "high morale," and "caring"), program determinants (such as "opportunities for active learning," "varied reward systems," and "varied learning environments"), process determinants (such as "improvement of school goals," "effective communication," and "involvement in decision making"), and material determinants ("adequate resources," "supportive and efficient logistical system," and "suitability of school plant").

Shaheen and Pedrick maintain that the superintendent is the most powerful person in the district when it comes to improving organizational climate. Here, as in Lindstrom's article, the administrator is viewed as having more influence over his or her environment than his environment has over him.

William Maynard has described efforts to improve school climate in Cleveland High School in Seattle. Like others on improving school climate, this article lacks a clear definition of what a good school climate is, but as evidence of improvement Maynard cites the pride that once alienated and apathetic students now have in their school and a significant fall in the absentee rate. Maynard began by selecting a school climate improvement team of students and faculty to develop projects and ideas to improve the school. Such ideas included a student "who's who" committee, hall murals painted by students and focusing on the theme "We've got pride," and an increase in shared decision-making in the school. It is of note that Maynard, unlike early researchers, sees student morale as a central determiner of school climate.

Frank Clark has listed "practical and specific suggestions" for improving school climate used by school districts. These include suggestions like forming a teacher advisory board, instituting a student forum, and issuing a variety of feedback forms for staff and students. An example of one feedback form is the "Quick Reply Form" on which a staff member is able to express an important concern that needs a reply within forty-eight hours. According to Clark, "When working smoothly, it's an excellent form, all but eliminating critical feelings from the staff." For Clark, school climate appears to mean everything from school morale to general school environment. It includes everything from "planning fun things to do at school" to generally "making things better."

Ways a school principal can begin to improve school

climate have been suggested by Phi Delta Kappa. Their publication sees the administrator's role as assessing needs, setting goals, and reducing goals to manageable projects. As an assessment instrument, the authors recommend and include the CFK Ltd. School Climate Profile.

It appears from the literature, then, that there are as many ideas on what a healthy school climate is and how to achieve it as there are ideas on what, in individuals, constitutes a healthy personality and how to achieve it. Yet the actual experiences of school leaders suggest that this lack of agreement and the lack of any hard data concerning the effectiveness of school climate improvement efforts may not be insurmountable problems. What seems to be true in practice is that almost any approach to climate improvement undertaken with energy and optimism helps enormously to improve school morale, communication, and relationships with staff, students, and community.

CONCLUSION

School climate is the feel an individual gets from his or her experiences within a school's social system. This feel or "subtle spirit" is the "global summation" of the individual's perceptions of how school personnel and students behave and interact. These behaviors, in turn, are largely determined by the underlying norms in the school, which dictate what kinds of behaviors and interactions are appropriate. Norms are largely self-perpetuating: the behaviors they define tend to reinforce and confirm the norms that gave rise to them.

Improving a school's climate depends on understanding the norm-behavior cycle and how to intervene in it properly with behavior modification or organizational development techniques. Numerous instruments for measuring school climate have been developed that can help administrators diagnose their climates before they attempt change. The experiences and suggestions of other administrators can also help school leaders understand climate and how it might be improved.

A healthy school climate is important because it is associated with higher student achievement, better behavior, and better attitudes. A large amount of recent research shows that the structures of social interaction and behavior in the school influence the student outcomes of the school. Thus, improving climate appears to be not only a worthwhile but an essential undertaking.

PART 3
THE SKILLS

PART 3: THE SKILLS
INTRODUCTION

Successful school leadership requires more than just an understanding of leadership and organizational structure. It also requires mastery of numerous "nuts-and-bolts" kinds of leadership and administrative skills. In this part of the book, some of these necessary administrative skills are explained and discussed. Attention is focused not so much on standard areas of administrative procedure but rather on some of the problem areas of modern school administration.

Chapter 8 begins by explaining the human communications process within the school and how it can be facilitated and improved. Such techniques as paraphrasing, behavior description, perception checking, and feedback are explained and illustrated, and exercises for improving communication are suggested.

The second half of this chapter deals with communications between the school and the outside world. An effective public relations program, the author emphasizes, doesn't just happen but is planned. School administrators should assess public opinions about the school, specify the objectives it wants its public relations program to meet, and then carefully plan what and how to communicate to the public. More specific PR suggestions for particular groups — parents, citizen groups, the media, and "key communicators" — are also given.

Chapter 9 discusses techniques a school leader can use to make meetings more effective. Before planning a meeting, the leader should decide what "leadership style" (as discussed in chapter 3) he or she will utilize. Then the leader should carefully consider the goals and purposes of the meeting, and whether a meeting is necessary at all.

Once these preliminaries are covered, the leader can get down to the basics of meeting planning. Chapter 9 discusses such considerations as the agenda, time allotments, who should attend, seating arrangements, and the meeting room. Next, the skills of human interaction necessary for successful meetings are discussed. Meeting leaders should be aware of the two distinct sets of activities that take place in every working discussion, the author emphasizes. First are "task" activities, which concern *what* the group is doing. Second are "maintenance" activities, which concern *how* the group is functioning.

A matter of personal interest to almost all school leaders is the problem of having too little time to do a job that by its nature entails considerable stress. The author of chapter 10, in a conversational style appropriate for her subject, distills from the available resources numerous practical insights and suggestions for managing time and stress. The best approach to time and stress management, advises the author, is a proactive one; the leader must take charge over time-and-stress problems with a positive attitude and a commitment to action.

Management of time and stress is an essential skill for any leader to master because time/stress problems are not merely personal but organizational in scope. The solution to those problems must involve both the leader and his or her support staff and colleagues. By initiating healthy time/stress management attitudes and practices, the leader helps set a positive tone for the entire organization.

Chapter 11 discusses an especially difficult leadership task — conflict management. Because conflicts often disrupt normal school operations and are costly in time and emotion, most administrators hold a negative image of conflict.

As the author of this chapter emphasizes, though, conflict is a two-sided coin. Conflict can indeed be disruptive and destructive, but it can also be a source of creativity and constructive action in the school. Thus, the astute administrator does not seek simply to resolve all conflict in the school; rather, he or she attempts to maximize constructive conflict and minimize destructive conflict.

Conflict has been defined, dissected, and classified in numerous ways. Several views of conflict are explained and discussed in chapter 11 to help administrators develop a better understanding of conflict. The final section of the chapter presents numerous techniques for managing conflict in the schools.

In chapter 12, three special problem-solving techniques are presented. The first — force-field analysis — is a means of dissecting complex problems into their major parts, or forces. Once a problem is broken down into its components, an administrator can more easily plot a course toward its solution.

Force-field analysis can also be used as a decision-making tool, particularly in situations in which the pros and cons of an issue seem evenly divided.

The nominal group technique — sometimes called "silent brainstorming" — is a means of generating alternative solutions to problems. Members of a group meet together but do not interact at first. They are asked to write down possible solutions to a stated problem. All proposed solutions are then compiled on a list in front of the group, clarified, and finally discussed. Proponents claim this technique has several advantages over brainstorming.

The Delphi technique is a now widely used technique for developing consensus on complex issues. It links minds together to do "collective figuring" yet avoids many of the disadvantages of group meetings. In Delphi, several experts on a subject are asked to respond to a series of questionnaires that usually funnel the group toward consensus on the issue being discussed. Delphi has a large number of variations and applications, several of which are discussed in chapter 12.

CHAPTER 8
COMMUNICATING
David Coursen

Good communication has always been an important part of effective school leadership. Whether educators have been outlining the rules to nineteenth-century children in a one-room school or explaining innovative teaching methods to contemporary parents, school teachers and administrators have always needed to be effective communicators.

In recent years, some fundamental changes in educational decision-making have made communications an even more essential part of the educator's repertoire of skills. Today it is no longer enough for school administrators simply to explain policies to parents or teachers; increasingly, by custom and by law, various groups are seeking to participate in the policy-making process. At the school site level, parents, other citizens, teachers, and even students may seek a voice in decision-making. It thus becomes the job of the administrator to work with such groups and to offer them appropriate forums for participation in school decision-making.

For the beleaguered school leader, communicating with all these groups, balancing their conflicting claims and interests, and still running the schools may seem like a task that would, as the old saw has it, tax the wisdom of Solomon. Fortunately, much of the king's proverbial wisdom was in his skill at communication — and listening — and in his ability to use simple common sense. These are skills school administrators, too, can exercise.

The following sections offer some suggestions for administrators who want to learn how to communicate more effectively with a variety of groups, both within and outside the school.

LEARNING TO COMMUNICATE

Communication is a human relations skill that is, in a sense, only half understood. Most people believe that if they speak or write clearly, or make gestures whose meanings can be clearly understood, they are communicating successfully. However, in a basic sense, communication is a two-way process, a sharing of information. This means that communication is listening as well as speaking, understanding as well as being understood.

HOW THE PROCESS WORKS

Jerry Pulley describes the communication process in general terms and identifies some of the points where problems can develop. Understanding these points of potential interference is essential to successful communication and to seeing why communications sometimes go awry. In the classical model of communication, there is a source, a message, a medium, a receiver, and a reaction. The following points are worth remembering about each:

- *Source.* How the source (in this case the principal) is seen is important; the principal should work to establish a positive image and an aura of credibility.
- *Message.* The message should be delivered in clear, grammatical language, free of jargon and loaded words; the principal should also be conscious of body language and other forms of nonverbal communication.
- *Medium.* A medium should be chosen that is effective and will reach the desired audience and get its attention. Face-to-face contact, which allows for direct feedback, can be ideal. It is sometimes a good idea to use several media simultaneously, so that the people missed by one will be reached by another.
- *Receiver.* People hear what they want to hear. The principal should try "to understand his receivers and to construct and transmit his messages as clearly and nonalienatingly as possible," as Pulley states.
- *Reactions.* Reactions are difficult to predict. Even if the first four parts of the model are carefully considered and appropriately handled, there may still be unexpected reactions.

Richard Schmuck, Philip Runkel, Jane Arends, and Richard Arends identify a number of elements of effective communication. These include openness, communication when emotions are high, offering personal responses, and trust. The last of these, trust, is particularly important, since there is always an element of risk in communicating openly. The authors therefore list a number of freeing responses that can increase trust:

- listening attentively rather than silently
- paraphrasing, checking impressions of the other's meaning
- seeking information to understand the other better
- offering relevant information
- describing observable behaviors that influence you
- directly reporting your own feelings
- offering opinions, stating your value position

On the other hand, there are also binding responses that can reduce trust:

- changing the subject without explanation
- focusing on and criticizing things that are unchangeable
- trying to advise and persuade
- vigorously agreeing or strongly objecting
- approving someone for conforming to your own standards
- commanding or demanding to be commanded

COMMUNICATION SKILLS

Charles Jung and his associates point out that there are no real tricks to good communication; the only secret is having a sincere interest in the other person. A number of skills, however, are important for the effective communicator to understand and master. The sections that follow on paraphrasing, behavior description, description of feelings, perception checking, and feedback are loosely adapted from the seminal work of Jung and his associates.

Paraphrasing

One of the oddities of modern life is that, if someone tells you his or her phone number, seven unambiguous pieces of information, you will probably repeat it to make sure you have it right, but if he or she makes a far more complex statement, you are likely to offer simple agreement or disagreement. In other words, as the possibilities for misunderstanding increase, our efforts to clarify messages generally decrease.

One way to remedy this situation is the use of paraphrasing to answer the question, "Am I understanding the other's idea as it was meant to be understood?" Paraphrasing is an effort to show other people what their words mean to you. Its goal is not only to clarify the message, but also to show your interest in the other person, an act that, in itself, can help improve communication.

What is most commonly meant by paraphrasing is simply putting a statement into different words. This does not always clarify things, as the following exchanges make clear:

One: "Jim should never have become a teacher."
"You mean teaching isn't the right job for him?"
"Exactly. Jim should never have become a teacher."
Two: "Jim should never have become a teacher."
"You mean he is too harsh with his students?"
"No. His tastes are too expensive for a teacher's salary."
"Oh. So he should have chosen a more lucrative profession."
"Exactly. Jim should never have become a teacher."

The communication in the first exchange is largely illusory since the "paraphrase" gives no real information about what the listener thinks the speaker meant. By contrast, in the second exchange even a "wrong" paraphrase that describes what the listener thought the speaker meant can lead to the exchange of more information and, thus, better communication.

The real purpose of paraphrasing is not to show what the other person actually meant (which would require mind-reading skills) but to show what it meant to *you*. This may mean restating the original statement in more specific terms, using an example to show what it meant to you, or restating it in more general terms.

It is possible, if somewhat unusual, to rely on paraphrasing excessively. When this happens, you avoid stating your own opinions, and the one-sidedness of the exchange may make the other person uncomfortable about giving information without receiving any in return. Extensive paraphrasing may be particularly important in situations where mistakes might be costly, or when strong feelings are present that might distort part of the message.

Behavior Description

When talking about what another person is doing, the communicator must recognize the difference between describing and evaluating. To be useful, behavior description, as Jung and his colleagues point out, should report

> specific, observable actions of others without placing a value on them as right or wrong, bad or good, and without making accusations or generalizations about the other's motives, attitudes or personality traits.

The communicator must tell people precisely what behavior he or she is responding to. For example, describing a specific set of actions ("You've disagreed with almost everything he's said") is very different from judging behavior ("You're being stubborn") or judging motivations ("You're trying to show him up"). Try to confine your remarks to things that are observable and stick to the facts without drawing conclusions about what they mean.

Practicing these rules can enhance communications and, at the same time, help reduce defensiveness and the problems that go with it. When someone feels threatened by a comment or an action, his or her defensiveness can become an end in itself and distract from the questions at hand. Types of supportive communication that can help reduce defensiveness include describing rather than evaluating, solving the problem rather than controlling the situation, being spontaneous rather than following a strategy, showing empathy for others rather than maintaining a posture of neutrality, relating to others as an equal rather than a superior or a subordinate, and approaching differences of opinion with openness to new perspectives rather than with certainty.

Description of Feelings

What someone else perceives you as feeling often has more to do with his or her own feelings than with yours. In addition, if you are like most people, you work harder at describing your ideas clearly than at describing your feelings. As a result, it is not always easy to describe or understand feelings.

The way to avoid misperception of feelings is to describe them as directly and vividly as possible. Attach the description to yourself by beginning it with the word "I," "me," or "my." Some ways to do this include referring directly to the feeling ("I'm angry"), using similes ("I feel like a fish out of water"), describing what the feeling makes you want to do ("I'd like to leave this room"), or using some other figure of speech.

Be precise and unambiguous in describing your feelings. Saying "Shut up!" vehemently may express strong feelings, but it does not identify what those feelings are. Instead, say something more informative like "It hurts me to hear this!" "Hearing this makes me angry with you," or "Hearing this makes me angry with myself"; any of these three statements explains *why* you want the other person to stop talking.

In this, as in most aspects of communication, it is crucial to be open and honest. Feelings should be offered as pieces of information, not used in an effort to make the other person act differently. Also, be sure to make your nonverbal cues (facial expression, tone of voice, body language) agree with your words.

Perception Checking

Just as paraphrasing is an effort to find out what another

person's words mean, so perception checking is an effort to understand the feelings behind the words. One way of checking perceptions is simply to describe your impressions of another person's feelings at a given time. This can help you to find out how well you are understanding the other person at the same time it shows the other person your interest in him or her. Perceptions should be shared in a way that avoids expression of approval or disapproval.

Feedback

One way to clarify communication is to ask people to give their reactions to the messages your behavior sends off about you. Feedback is a means to improve shared understanding about behavior, feelings, and motivations. In giving feedback, it is useful to describe observed behaviors as well as the reactions they have caused. There are a number of guidelines to follow in giving feedback:
- The receiver should be ready to receive feedback.
- Comments should describe, rather than interpret, action.
- Feedback should focus on things that have happened recently.
- Feedback should focus on things that can be changed.
- Feedback should not try to force people to change.
- Feedback should be offered out of a sincere interest in and concern for the other person.

There are also some guidelines for receiving feedback:
- State what you want feedback about.
- Check what you have heard.
- Share your reactions to the feedback.

EXERCISES FOR IMPROVEMENT

Richard Schmuck and his associates suggest a number of exercises that can be useful in clarifying and developing the skills described above. Some of their suggestions are as follows:

- *Paraphrasing.* Divide into small groups. One person asks a question; the next paraphrases before answering.
- *Impression Checking.* Divide into pairs; one person conveys feelings through gestures, expressions, nonsense language, while the other person tries to interpret these cues. The two then talk about how correct the interpretations were.
- *Behavior Description.* Describe the behavior observed during any nonverbal exercise.
- *Describing Feelings.* Each person is given a written list of statements and told to identify which describe feelings and which do not (e.g., "I feel angry" does, but "I feel it's going to rain" does not).
- *Giving and Receiving Feedback.* Divide into trios. One person describes two helpful and two unhelpful behaviors of the second, who paraphrases the descriptions; the third person acts as an observer, making sure the other two are using communication skills correctly.

The same authors also describe exercises that can be used to clarify communications in meetings. These include the following:

- *Right to Listen.* Each speaker is required to paraphrase the terms of the discussion up to that point before speaking.
- *Time Tokens.* Each person pays a poker chip each time he or she talks. This clarifies who talks how often; if it provokes long speeches, it will also illustrate their drawbacks.
- *High Talker Tap-out.* Signal when each speaker uses up an allotted amount of time; at the end, discuss the process and the reasons some people talk more than others.
- *Take a Survey.* Ask each person for an opinion about a certain question. Everyone contributes, if only to admit having nothing to say.

The authors also recommend that groups use circular seating, which has two advantages: nonverbal behaviors are most apparent when everyone can be clearly seen; equal participation is encouraged when there is no podium or head of the table to suggest that one person is in charge. They also suggest that, in certain circumstances, videotaping or audio recording may be useful if someone is available with the skills and knowledge to judge what to record and when to play it back.

Richard Gemmet stresses the importance of mastering the art of listening. One can become a good listener, according to Gemmet, by developing "the *attitude* of wanting to listen and the *skills* to help you express that attitude." Some of the best ways to communicate an interest in listening are nonverbal signals such as "eye contact, attentiveness, use of hands, facial expressions, and tone of voice." There are three essentials to good listening:

- Don't interrupt.
- Don't judge.
- Reflect before answering.

Gemmet also offers additional tips for listening:

- Face the speaker and be close enough to hear.
- Watch nonverbal behavior.
- Be aware of biases and values that may distort what you hear.
- Look for the basic assumptions underlying remarks.

At the same time, it is also important to keep in mind a number of things to *avoid* doing:

- thinking of other things while listening
- rehearsing an answer while the other person is still talking
- interrupting to correct a mistake or make a point
- tuning out and starting a silent combat when you hear certain "red-flag" words
- feeling compelled to have the last word

THE PRINCIPAL'S RESPONSIBILITY

Because of the principal's sizable influence on communication in the school, suggestions abound on how the principal can communicate most effectively. Jerry Valentine, Bradford Tate, Alan Seagren, and John Lammel found that certain types of principal behavior significantly affected school climate. Their main finding was that, "Generally speaking, the more direct the principal, the more positive the attitudes of teachers, students, and parents." In addition, they found that "the use of humor . . . indicated a significantly relaxed, positive human relations atmosphere."

An important element in good communications is a willingness to give strokes, to express appreciation for a job well done. Jodie King, principal of Vejas Elementary School, Walnut Valley, California, told the writer that the best way to do this is to

> offer positive reinforcement at all levels, focusing on the positive, letting people know what they are doing well — and praising them — and *then,* if necessary, suggesting things they need to do to improve.

One way King does this is by always leaving a note after she observes a class. She mentions only positive things in the note; if she has any criticisms to make, she asks the teacher to speak to her, so she can make them face-to-face.

Sandro Ingari suggests a number of things a principal can do to improve his or her relations with the school community. The most important thing is to be open and accessible, so that people will feel you are available and welcome personal contact with them. Spend time with various members of the faculty — over lunch, during coffee, in the faculty lounge, or at informal teacher "hang-outs." Add the personal touch by asking people about their families or calling them by their first names. Use a suggestion box.

COMMUNICATING IN SMALL GROUPS

Administrators have always had to communicate with groups of staff members, parents, and students. As shared decision-making has become more widespread, the importance of communicating effectively with groups such as these has increased significantly.

Facilitating the successful meshing of the various human participants in a group can be a difficult, delicate process. In a seminal work on the subject, Schutz argues that group members have three primary needs — for inclusion (belonging), control (power), and affection (friendship) — that must be satisfied if the group is to be successful. However, such satisfaction occurs only when these needs are met adequately but not excessively.

Inclusion is particularly important when a group is just starting. Introductions and biographical stories of each member can help meet this need; assigning a greeter at meetings, providing group members with name tags, and organizing get-acquainted activities and social events can also be useful. However, Schutz cautions against overinclusion, stressing the need for group members to "maintain some degree of distance from other group members and some individuality." This can typically be done by dividing labor or establishing subgroups.

Traditional techniques for providing group members with influence over decisions include the election of officers and the establishment of hierarchies. In addition, "in most groups, it is necessary to establish behavior patterns leading to a restriction of the amount of control some members have over others." Otherwise, a few individuals may dominate the group, restricting the influence of everyone else. Susan Sayers suggests studying and discussing the decision-making process and practicing role-switching (so that each group member has a dominant role at least part of the time) as ways to foster the equitable distribution of control.

Schutz maintains that group members must "relate to each other with sufficient warmth and closeness for group processes to proceed." Members must have freedom to express their feelings, to prevent energy being drained by "the suppression of hostile impulses." The need for affection is often satisfied by such activities as "side whispers, sub-grouping, after-meeting coffee, bringing food to meetings, and coffee breaks."

As with inclusion and control, affection is appropriate only in moderation. Too much closeness within a group can detract from the group's ability to meet its primary purposes and can lead to the personalizing of issues within the group. "Nepotism rules, fraternization rules, agenda and other procedural techniques, discipline and punishment for too much affectional play," are among the ways Schutz suggests for avoiding this problem.

REACHING THE PUBLIC

As important as it is for a school to have good internal communications, it is equally important to communicate effectively with the public outside. Administrators who believe that simply running their schools well makes a formal public relations effort unnecessary may be right, but their perspective overlooks the fact that every school has a public relations program — formal or not — operating whenever that school's staff or students communicate with the public. When a parent meets with a school official, when a child describes what went on in class during the day, or when a caller is greeted courteously — or inadvertently put on hold and forgotten — the school is communicating something to the public.

The question to ask about school public relations efforts is not, then, *whether* to develop a program, but *how* to develop a good one. Perhaps the ideal program is described in the National School Public Relations Association's definition of school public relations (quoted by Lew Armistead):

> a planned and systematic two-way process of communication between an education organization and its internal and external publics ... to stimulate a better understanding of the role, objectives, accomplishments, and needs of the organization.

School communications with the public can be divided into three classes: public and formal, private and formal, and private and informal. The first two types, which cover the school's "official" business, from report cards to press releases, are generally recognized as public relations concerns. The often-neglected third type, however, is by far the most common, the hardest to plan, and probably the most important.

Information communication takes place whenever anyone associated with a school gives the public any kind of message about that school. Such a message may be conveyed by a student, a volunteer, or an employee; many people see *all* school employees — custodians, secretaries, teachers, and administrators — as "insiders," with special knowledge about the school's operations. The message such persons convey may be verbal (a rumor or a comment about policy) or nonverbal (litter on a school neighbor's lawn or a group of students helping a motorist change a flat tire). Since many of these communications exchanges are beyond a principal's control, a well-run school with a satisfied, well-informed staff and student body is one essential element of any public relations effort.

PUBLIC RELATIONS STRATEGIES

The key to effective public relations is good planning; as Armistead notes, "constructive public relations is planned, while destructive public relations just happens." It is crucial to know whom you want to reach, what they know, and how you can get them information about what they don't know.

Don Bagin, Frank Grazian, and Charles Harrison emphasize the fact that school public relations, like all communication, must run in two directions; the school's job is both to inform the public about the school and to keep informed about what the public is thinking about the school. Thus it is important to assess the quality of current communications. Such an assessment includes analyzing what various groups and individuals think about the school, identifying major criticisms of the school, and evaluating the school's general reputation.

After carefully assessing the current status of a public relations program, the school should specify the objectives it wants that program to meet. Bagin and his colleagues cite as examples objectives drafted by Jane P. Braunstein of the Cherry Hill, New Jersey, Public Schools. Several of these objectives are abbreviated as follows:

- promote public interest in the school
- gather and report public attitudes about the school
- provide an honest, comprehensive flow of information
- use media effectively to reach each part of the public
- develop community confidence in the school
- integrate the home, school, and community to work cooperatively in comprehensively meeting children's educational needs
- anticipate and forestall problems caused by misunderstandings

Whatever the objectives, the school should plan its public relations carefully and work to define clearly what its publics are and how best to reach them. William Banach and Ann Barkelew suggest that brainstorming can be a useful technique in public relations planning. The authors claim that this method should make it possible to identify forty or fifty different groups worth reaching (from senior citizens and business organizations to religious groups) and generate perhaps a hundred public relations ideas (from writing without jargon to sending the school band to a convalescent home).

PARENTS

Probably the group most affected by what goes on in the school is parents. Besides concerns they share with many taxpayers about the quality of education the school is providing, parents are interested in such questions as what is being taught, what instructional methods are being used, and what special services the school offers. Of greatest interest to many parents, obviously, is how their own children are doing in school. For this reason schools should carefully consider how they are providing that information. Since praise is far more pleasant than criticism, schools might personally contact parents about the good things their children are doing, instead of reserving personal contact for discussing discipline problems or academic difficulties.

Much of what parents learn about schools comes directly from their children. One simple way to improve the quality of information children give their parents is to have students, particularly those in the lower grades, keep journals, making entries at the end of each day. Reviewing the day's activities in this way may help the child give clearer, more interesting answers to the familiar parental question, "What did you do in school today?"

When a parent — or anyone else — contacts the school, it is important to present a positive image. The main contact most people have with a school is over the phone. This makes it crucial that people who answer school phones understand the importance of being as friendly, courteous, and helpful as possible.

Schools should also try to be receptive to irate parents. Jodie King suggests that parents with complaints should know:

- that there will be a parking place for them when they arrive at the school
- that they will be greeted by the staff in a friendly manner
- that the principal will be available to speak to them within a reasonable time
- that some action (though not necessarily what they want) will be taken in response to their complaints

KEY COMMUNICATORS

Personal contact should not be directed only toward parents. School leaders obviously lack the avenues and time to make more than token contact with members of the public at large. What school leaders can do, however, is seek to identify and reach their community's "key communicators."

There are two types of key communicators. Some individuals are opinion leaders; they are respected and influential by virtue of their positions and reputations in the community. Other individuals occupy a key role in the community's communications network simply because they talk to a large number of people. Thus a key communicator can be a barber or beautician as well as a mayor or city councilor.

School officials would do well to cultivate good relations with both types of key communicator. This can be done informally — such as with periodic phone calls to discuss school affairs or by invitations to lunch at school — or by establishing a formal group of key communicators and meeting with it regularly.

Because of their ability to reach large numbers of people quickly, key communicators can be particularly helpful in clarifying misconceptions about the schools and dispelling rumors. Several writers suggest that timely contact with key communicators in potential crisis situations may be one way of defusing potential controversy and avoiding trouble based on false information.

Another valuable function of key influentials is their ability to provide schools with accurate and immediate feedback about how the public is responding to the school. Such feedback can offer administrators new perspectives on their schools and can make it easier to identify potential problems and areas of dissension. In addition, key communicators can sometimes function as sounding boards for testing public reaction to new ideas.

CITIZEN GROUPS

Another vehicle for direct contact between schools and the public is the citizens advisory committee. In many school districts, advisory councils are not an option but a necessity, as an increasing number of governmental programs require some form of community participation in school decision-making. Some such groups have an actual vote in policy-making, while others are strictly advisory. In either case, the introduction of citizen committees into the school's decision process represents a major change that may make administrators uncomfortable. Beyond the extra work and potential frustration an advisory council brings, however, are some clear benefits for administrators seeking public support for their schools.

As Richard Hofstrand and Lloyd Phipps point out, every community evaluates its schools; the advantage of a citizens advisory council is that it can channel the public's evaluation toward constructive ends. Public criticism based on vague or incomplete understanding of the schools can be reduced when administrators have a forum for giving clear facts about the school's strengths and weaknesses. Like key communicators, council members provided with such information can pass their knowledge along to the rest of the community.

But an advisory council or even a temporary group formed to deal with a single problem or issue can be much more than an arena for the dissemination of school policy. Don Bagin and his colleagues suggest that such groups can perform a wide range of functions, from determining and prioritizing a school's objectives and evaluating its progress toward meeting those objectives, to investigating facilities use and helping revise curriculum.

Advisory groups also provide a formal process by which opinions from the community can be incorporated into the school decision-making process. Schools are thus in a better position to reach decisions based on accurate information about the community's needs and expectations.

One of the more important factors in the success of an advisory council as a communications medium is its composition. Most councils should be made up primarily of parents but also represent a broad cross-section of the community. Diversity is essential. Jim Stanton and his colleagues report that most councils suffer from a shortage of "minority, low-income, student, non-parent, and except in leadership positions, male representation."

To fill these needs, active recruitment of members of these groups may be necessary. Title I mandates participation by lower-income persons and members of racial minorities, two groups that have traditionally been excluded from decision-making. The involvement of such persons is not always easy to bring about, since many have attitudes that make them reluctant to participate in school affairs. Often they are less favorable toward the schools, less patient in waiting for changes to take place, and less confident of their communications skills than the more affluent, well-educated persons who generally volunteer for school-related groups.

It is important to enlist the aid of individuals with special expertise in areas the council will be considering. Qualities to look for in all participants include interest, time, and an ability to get along with people.

The best way to attract and keep council members is to appeal to their self-interest, particularly by demonstrating that their actions can make a difference. Often, simply asking people to serve on a council or run for a position will be effective in convincing them that their services are valued. Nelson Price summarizes what is needed: "For citizen participation to be sustained, it must be a satisfying, rewarding, and productive experience."

The operation of an advisory council will surely test the leadership skills of the principal. C. C. Carpenter states that the principal's most important function is to make sure the advisory group is aware of its limits and responsibilities and the possibilities open before it. The principles and skills of leading meetings, managing conflict, sharing power, solving problems, and communicating effectively all apply to the process of governing a citizens advisory council.

THE MEDIA

Although personal contact is the long-range key to effective communication with the public, the best way to reach a large number of people in a short time can be through the news media, both print and broadcast. Reports in the media can have tremendous impact on the public's consciousness, because they are seen by large numbers of people almost simultaneously and because, as "news," they have a certain built-in aura of credibility.

Although media coverage offers school leaders an opportunity to tell their story to a large number of people, the fact that the form of that story is beyond the control of school administrators — that is, the coverage may be negative as well as positive — can be intimidating. Nevertheless, both the press's right to cover the news and the public's right to know dictate that newsworthy events in the schools will be reported. This makes it the administrator's job to learn to work with the media to see that coverage is as fair and factual as possible.

In working with the media, the biggest problem school leaders face may be the ease with which misunderstandings develop between the schools and the media. To a certain extent, this is inevitable, since there is an inherent tension between the objectives of the media and those of the school. Whereas the school wants reporting that promotes its objectives and doesn't cause trouble, the media seek stories of interest to their readers or viewers. Thus school officials are apt to see the media as distorting and sensationalizing events, taking comments out of context, and reporting events inaccurately. The media, on the other hand, may fault school officials for refusing to come clean, for limiting media access to information, and for offering the media material that is little more than puffery — enthusiastic but not newsworthy.

Don Bagin, Frank Grazian, and Charles Harrison suggest that striking the right balance between informing the public and helping the schools will be easier if schools are accessible to the media and accept the need for coverage of bad as well as good news. Schools need to recognize that the press has a legitimate function as the eyes, ears, and voice of the community it serves. Thus school personnel should treat reporters not as intruders but as trained professionals, with a right to keep the public informed. Since it is the press's function to report what it knows, school officials should take care to avoid saying anything they don't want to appear in print.

A working relationship based on trust and mutual understanding can be further promoted, according to Bagin and his colleagues, by a school's willingness to offer the press continuity (a steady diet of news on an ongoing basis, not just at budget time), candor (honesty and credibility), and consideration (respecting reporters' needs in areas like meeting deadlines). It can also be helpful for school personnel to get to know reporters personally. School officials should recognize, however, that reporters are paid to cover the news, and friendships will not prevent the reporting of unfavorable events. In addition, while most reporters are conscientious and careful, they can be so overworked and burdened with deadline pressures that occasional honest mistakes are almost inevitable. School leaders should try to avoid taking either negative coverage or mistakes personally.

In summarizing school-media relations, Bagin and his colleagues offer the following list of guidelines for schools to follow in working with the media:

- know a paper's policies and deadlines, and respect them in preparing or releasing material
- provide the media with calendars of newsworthy events, and agendas of meetings
- call press conferences when damaging events occur
- alert the press to potential stories
- deal with the press honestly, sincerely, and fairly
- send the press formal invitations to school functions
- cultivate relations with broadcast, as well as print, media

School-based media are another way of reaching various groups. These media allow school leaders to say exactly what they want in a form under their control. Those who develop such a publication should keep its purpose in mind, understand the audience it is intended to reach, and make sure the potential rewards justify the cost. All written material, from letters to publications, should strive for clarity in writing, in format and design, and in graphics. Printed material should be distributed by mail; sending it home with students may be cheaper, but even the U.S. Postal Service is far more reliable about delivering printed material than are most school children.

SURVEYS

One way of finding out what the public is thinking about, or what it wants from the schools, is to take an opinion survey. Before beginning a survey, the school leader should be aware of its cost and carefully determine what information is wanted and why. It may be possible to get the necessary information without taking a survey, by informally polling key communicators, for example.

Once a survey has been decided on, the next step is to clearly define whom to survey, what type of survey to use, and what types of questions to ask. It is important to realize in advance how reliable the survey will be and how quickly its results will become available. The best, most reliable, and most cost-effective survey is undoubtedly an ongoing two-way program of communication with the public that constantly keeps both the schools and the public informed about each other.

A TIME-SAVING SUGGESTION

An effective public relations program is essential to a school, but it takes time, one commodity no principal has enough of. One solution to this problem is to assess the situation, decide on a suitable public relations approach, and devote five minutes a day to implementing it. If the first day's task takes more than five minutes, the time can be credited to future days. As a result, there will be a systematic and ongoing effort to improve public relations that does not make unreasonable demands on the principal's time. Several writers suggest that it is surprising how much can be accomplished with even this modest investment of time.

CONCLUSION

As we have seen, communicating can be a complex, difficult, and occasionally frustrating business. The change in style from the paternalism of the fifties and sixties to the participation of today is not always an easy one for administrators to make, particularly since there are no secret formulas for communicating effectively in the new environment. In fact, good communication varies according to the needs of a situation; what works under one set of circumstances may be useless or even harmful under another.

Nevertheless, a few general guidelines have emerged from our discussion. The dominant theme is the need for clarity, which is at the heart of good communication, whether spoken or written. Parents, media representatives, and other citizens need to be kept informed, in the clearest possible terms, about what is happening in the schools.

Equally important, communication is a two-way process that involves listening as well as talking. There may be times when the best way to communicate — or to lead — is simply to listen to what others have to say.

CHAPTER 9
LEADING MEETINGS
John Lindelow

"Our meetings are so dull! And we never seem to get anything done."

"What few decisions we make are rarely carried through. Decisions are often forgotten, or no one remembers who was responsible for doing what."

"Most people just sit with blank faces and never get involved. The same few people seem to decide everything."

"The principal says he wants us to be involved in decision-making, but in the end he always has it his way."

How many times have you heard similar feelings expressed after supposedly productive meetings? So many meetings seem to be a waste of time for their participants. Besides being unproductive for the school, they give individual members little personal satisfaction.

So why are meetings usually so unproductive? Meetings, of course, are only a part of the total workings of the school organization. What goes on in a meeting is, in a way, simply a reflection of the attitudes, relationships, and organization of the larger school system. "Every meeting is a microcosm," says Richard Dunsing, "a condensed version of the values and style of the organization ... In working toward a change for the better ... meetings defy separate treatment because they are all contaminated by the organization's basic values and styles."

And just as the norms of the organization affect how meetings are run, what goes on in meetings generates a "ripple effect" on the rest of the organization. "A meeting of fifteen people," say Michael Doyle and David Straus, "can affect how 300 people work — or don't work — for the rest of the day or week or even permanently." Obviously, a poor meeting can have a debilitating effect on an entire organization. On the other hand, well-run meetings can rejuvenate an organization, leading to improved teamwork, communications, and morale on many levels.

Thus the problem of unproductive meetings is part of the larger problem of ineffective organization. Government and nonprofit organizations seem most prone to "sluggish" organizational functioning, one reason being the lack of direct personal reward for increasing efficiency. It is no accident that the great majority of literature on improving meetings comes from the profit- and survival-oriented business world.

Contributing to the problem of ineffective meetings is a simple lack of organizational and human-relations skills on the part of meeting participants. Many of these skills, though, are as old as meetings themselves, such as dealing with the long-winded participant, creating an agenda and sticking to it, and assuring that responsibilities are assigned and deadlines set.

Some other meeting techniques have been developed more recently. Social scientists in the field of group dynamics have been studying for decades the interactions of group members and how to improve the communications process. A more recent arrival is the behavioral science called organization development, which examines the whole of the communications structures of organizations. Both of these fields have shed new light on ways to make meetings more effective.

This chapter will present many suggestions aimed at helping educators improve their performance in meetings, both as group leaders and as participants. Before getting involved in the more practical aspects of meeting management, however, two important preliminaries will be examined: the leadership style you choose to use, and the importance of having clear-cut goals for your meetings.

CHOOSING A LEADERSHIP PATTERN

Ideas about leadership have been changing greatly in recent years. Earlier in this century, it was assumed that leaders should be autocratic, authoritative, and in full control of their organizations. Gradually, though, the idea surfaced that leadership could be a shared and democratic function. Social scientists began focusing on group members and their needs and found participative decision-making to be a workable alternative to traditional directive leadership.

Today's principals and administrators often find themselves torn between the two extremes of leadership behavior. The result is sometimes an uncertain compromise, with subordinates not quite knowing where the leader stands or what behavior would be considered "appropriate" in a given situation. Thus, before getting involved in the nuts and bolts of meeting management, it is helpful for the meeting leader or planner to give some thought to the kind of "leadership pattern" that is most comfortable for him or her.

In a classic article entitled "How to Choose a Leadership Pattern," Robert Tannenbaum and Warren H. Schmidt recognize the gamut of possible leadership styles, ranging from autocratic to democratic, and the importance for a leader to choose a leadership pattern compatible with his or her own personal needs, the needs of subordinates ("non-managers"), and the other "forces in the situation." They stress that no one style is necessarily right or wrong and that leadership behavior should be geared to the particular situation. Although the basic elements of Tannenbaum and Schmidt's ideas about leadership style were discussed in chapter 3, they are mentioned again here because they are particularly useful to those leading meetings, especially decision-making meetings.

At one extreme of the "continuum of leadership behavior" is the complete autocrat who makes all the decisions and simply announces these decisions to subordinates. A step away from the autocrat is the manager who "sells" decisions to group members. Here again, the manager identifies the problem and arrives at a decision, but "rather than simply announcing it, he takes the additional step of persuading his subordinates to accept it." Further along the continuum is the manager who presents his or her ideas and decision and then invites questions and comments from subordinates, so they might better understand what he or she is trying to accomplish. Next there is the leader who "presents a tentative decision subject to change," after input from subordinates.

Subordinates finally get a chance to suggest their own solutions at the next step on the continuum where the "manager presents the problem, gets suggestions, and then makes his decision." Near the democratic end of the spectrum is the manager who defines the problem and the limits within which the decisions must be made and then requests that the group make the decision. Finally, there is the leader who is primarily a team member and who imposes only those limits on the group that are specified by the organization or the immediate superior of the team leader.

In choosing a leadership style from this range of possibilities, a manager should consider three variables: his or her own personality, the characteristics of his or her subordinates, and the other factors in the situation, such as the norms of the organization. "Some managers," state Tannenbaum and Schmidt, "have a greater need than others for predictability and stability in their environment." Such managers would probably function better as more directive leaders. Other managers might have a greater "tolerance for ambiguity" that allows them to release some control over the decision-making process and thus over the predictability of the situation.

Subordinates, too, differ in their needs. Some enjoy clear-cut directives, while others have high needs for sharing in the decision-making process. Other factors influencing leadership style are the type of organization, the nature of the problem, and the pressures of time.

Even when the same group meets more than once, the leader may vary his or her style, depending on the type of meeting and its objectives. An autocratic style is appropriate when the meeting is mainly a briefing session, when the matters at hand are easy or routine, or when a crisis arises and decisions have to be made in a hurry. A democratic style is called for when decisions by consensus are necessary or desirable; when an informal atmosphere is needed, as in a brainstorming session, a gripe or rap session, or a creative problem-solving meeting; or when the acceptability of a decision is more important than its quality, as in a meeting held to resolve a conflict.

The effective meeting chairman, as summed up by Barry Maude, is one who, at the beginning of the meeting,

> sizes up the situation, decides what kind of leadership is required, then slips into the appropriate gear. So in one meeting he is an unassertive idea-eunuch: in the next, a tough, fast-talking overlord. Today he is a suction-pump drawing out people's ideas. Tomorrow he is a conveyor-belt, feeding the group with information, carrying them steadily and efficiently towards a

decision. The day after he becomes a spark-plug, showering the meeting with ideas. By discreet use of the loud and soft pedals he becomes a man for all meetings.

But simply varying style is not enough. It is incumbent on the meeting leader, say Len Chellew and Vern Trott, to tell "the staff or committee at the outset of the life of the group why his or her style of decision-making will be different in different situations. The designated leader who does not do this will create confusion, apathy, and lack of trust." Thus, leaders should clearly indicate the degree of decision-making power they have in a particular situation and then stick to that agreement.

When group members know clearly the structure of the decision-making process and the bounds of their power, they can begin to work within this structure toward group goals, without continual doubt or haggling over power. A known decision-making style, whether it be autocratic or democratic, lends a certain psychological solidity to meetings that can prevent many frustrations within a group. In a like way, meetings become more meaningful when they are called for specific purposes and have clearly defined goals.

GOALS AND VALUES OF MEETINGS

Before calling any meeting, the meeting planner should consider these few simple questions: What do I want to accomplish with this meeting? What goals and objectives do I wish to reach? Is a meeting the best route to my goal, or might some other form of communication be more efficient? Are there other values in meetings in addition to the obvious practical ends they achieve? These questions will be considered in turn.

MEETINGS WITH PURPOSE

"No wind favors him who has no destined port," goes the old saying. Yet how many meetings have you attended that have drifted pointlessly with no obvious goals or purposes to guide them? Every meeting needs one or more definite purposes that are known to all group membrs. Frank Snell emphasizes this point by defining a meeting as "a group talking together *with a clearly defined purpose in mind.*"

Most meetings take place for one or more of the following reasons:

- to receive or give information
- to make a decision
- to define, analyze, or solve a problem
- to reconcile conflicts
- to express feelings (for example, a gripe-session or rap-session)

Information

Some meetings are designed primarily for the exchange of information among participants. The meeting leader may want to simply brief members, or to instruct them, as in a training session. Conversely, the leader may want to receive reports from participants. In this type of meeting, a more autocratic leadership style is usually the most efficient.

One advantage of an information meeting over a memo or written report is that reaction and feedback can be immediate. Every member can hear in the short time of a meeting both the information presented and the reaction of all other members to it. Another advantage of an oral presentation, notes B.Y. Auger, is that it is often more effective and memorable than a written report. Furthermore, the nature of a group presentation often impels meeting participants to be more thoughtful in their preparation.

Decision-making

Decision-making style ranges from the autocratic to the truly democratic. An autocrat may simply wish to get some input from participants before making a decision. In meetings with a more democratic style of decision-making, everyone who has a critical stake in a decision is given a chance to be heard and to influence the final decision.

Problem-solving

Several heads are usually better than one, particularly for defining, analyzing, and solving problems. In a problem-solving session, the group brings together "the bits and pieces of experience and insight which may lead to common understanding," says Auger. "One person may describe an effect, while another suggests a plausible reason for it. Out of a pattern of this type of analysis, an acceptable cause-and-effect relationship may be discovered."

Another advantage of problem-solving sessions is that such meetings tend to correct for the flaws and idiosyncracies in the thinking of individuals. An effective group can be much more flexible and wide-ranging in its thought, but at the same time sift out impractical or far-flung ideas.

The style of leadership can vary widely in problem-solving meetings, depending on the nature of the problem, time limitations, and other variables. For example, a brainstorming session might be called to foster ideas for increasing community awareness of certain school programs. In such a session, a very informal, democratic atmosphere would be needed to stimulate a variety of ideas. If, on the other hand, the analysis of a problem calls for an orderly presentation of data and some hard thinking, a more leader-controlled meeting would be more efficient.

Reconciling conflicts

A meeting is often the only good place to explore sharp differences of opinion and to negotiate some kind of compromise. This type of meeting requires tight control so that tempers do not flare. When the conflict does not directly affect the group leader, he or she can work primarily as a facilitator, bringing out and clarifying the points of difference, making sure that each side's case is fully heard, and hammering out compromises. When the group leader is one of the principal contenders, it is necessary (and sometimes required by law) to appoint a neutral third party to manage the conflict.

Expressing feelings

It is sometimes wise to hold gripe-sessions or rap-sessions with staff members to sound out their feelings about the organization and its administration. Such meetings should be as permissive and unstructured as possible, for they are important steam valves for an organization. The leader, according to Barry Maude, should remain in the background and allow members to contribute spontaneously, for he or she recognizes "that any decision taken is less important than (a) providing a therapeutic opportunity for staff to express their feelings (b) ensuring that any decisions taken are acceptable to the participants."

The meeting planner should make sure that each agenda item has one or more of the above purposes and should clearly indicate the purpose on the agenda. For example, the agenda item "School lunch program" tells the meeting participant little about its purpose. A more complete description might be "Information on new school lunch program," or "Decision regarding continuance of lunch program," or "Defining possible nutritional problems in school lunch program." (More will be said about agendas in the next section.)

Some meetings have none of the above purposes, yet they may be very important to the health of an organization. These are meetings, say Ernest Bormann and his colleagues, that are used primarily as rituals. Ritualistic meetings, such as, for example, the presenting of the yearly budget, might seem to be only the rubber-stamping of decisions already made. Yet they have the value of "adding to the cohesiveness of the organization," and sometimes such meetings assure "that hurt feelings do not impede efficiency." For example, a person in a position of authority might be invited to attend a meeting in which he or she has little active interest. "But the very fact that he was invited to attend," say these authors, "communicates to him that the people calling the meeting recognize his importance within the organization." If the proponents of policy or proposals fail to have a ritualistic meeting in which all people of authority are informed about developments, they may "suddenly find many roadblocks in their way."

IS A MEETING NECESSARY?

The first step in reducing the huge amount of time wasted in meetings is to ask the simple question of whether the goals of a meeting might be reached in some other, more efficient way. Too many meetings are called simply because it's that time of the week or month. Often, memos or telephone calls (individual or conference) can accomplish the communication desired without the time and expense of a meeting.

A general rule of thumb is that meetings should not be called when an individual decision-maker can get better results. Meetings are often of value even for deciding simple matters, however. As Antony Jay has observed,

> Real opposition to decisions within organizations usually consists of one part disagreement with the decision to nine parts resentment at not being consulted before the decision. For most people on most issues, it is enough to know that their views were heard and considered. They may regret that they were not followed, but they accept the outcome.

Individuals are more efficient when the matters to be decided are routine and, surprisingly, when the decision depends on the use of subtle, hard-to-explain reasoning that cannot be done spontaneously. "Research indicates that subtle reasoning problems are generally performed more accurately by individuals than by meetings," reports Maude. "The great danger of presenting difficult reasoning problems to meetings to solve is that the competent members (those who know how to solve the problem) may be out-voted or even convinced by the rest."

However true this may be with some decision-makers, one should remember that meetings often serve as a valuable check on the errors in reasoning of some members. In the broad area between very simple and very complex reasoning tasks, research shows, again according to Maude, that group decisions are more likely to be on target than individual decisions. And in this era of increasing accountability, more and more decisions must be made in which the reasoning process is open to public scrutiny.

HIDDEN VALUES OF MEETINGS

Most meetings have value beyond the achievement of obvious organizational goals. Meetings satisfy, or can satisfy, the personal and emotional needs of individual members, such as needs for participation, belonging, achievement, and power. Participants interact, develop roles, and share their experiences, problems, and successes.

Meetings also have value in building the cohesiveness of an organization. "In the simplest and most basic way," says Jay, "a meeting defines the team, the group, or the unit. Those present belong to it; those absent do not. Everyone is able to look around and perceive the whole group and sense the collective identity of which he or she forms a part."

Richard Schmuck and his colleagues sum up the values of meetings as follows:

> While all channels of communication in a school can be useful, meetings are singularly important in providing a setting in which school members can communicate and coordinate information about problems and decisions and at the same time satisfy emotional needs for activity, achievement, affiliation, and power. Meetings provide an opportunity for participation not found in memos, newsletters, loudspeaker announcements, and the like. They enable an immediate check of reactions to what another person has just said and to one's own immediate utterances as well. If managed effectively, meetings can be the principal channel for bringing staff members into collaboration to reach common understandings and for that reason can be highly productive and satisfying events in the life of an organization.

BASICS OF MEETING PLANNING

"Conducting a meeting without a plan," states Jack Parker, "is much like trying to build a house without blueprints. It can be done, of course, but the end result is likely to be less than desirable and the process can be expensive and nerve-wracking."

A good part of the planning is already done once the purpose of the meeting is decided. This immediately gives a preliminary idea of who will be attending and what might transpire.

But engineering a successful meeting usually requires some careful strategic planning. The meeting planner should try to imagine what is likely to happen in the meeting from beginning to end, and especially what barriers to accomplishment might spring up. The planner might ask himself or herself questions such as the following: Who will be the meeting participants, and what stakes do they have in the matters to be discussed? What are their personalities and their stances on meeting issues? What conflicts are likely to develop among participants? Who will be asked to change or adjust, and how might they react?

What skills will be required to deal with problems facing the meeting, and are these skills available within the organization? If not, what experts can be invited? What are the critical issues on which a decision might hinge? What is the range of possible compromises that might be reached? What can and cannot be traded off?

Other important facets of meeting planning, to be considered in the following pages, include writing up the agenda and allotting time for each item, deciding who will attend, arranging the seating, and selecting the meeting room.

THE AGENDA AND TIME CONSIDERATIONS

The heart of the organizational structure of a meeting is the agenda. "Without an agenda, the most skilled meeting leader might not be able to bring off a meeting successfully," says B.Y. Auger.

> With an agenda, however, he is able to devote his talents to managing the interplay of personalities in the meeting room. He can do this more effectively because he knows what he wants to achieve. With this general strategy mapped out in the agenda, he can concentrate on the more fluid tactics of the meeting room.

Before a meeting, it is wise to consult with meeting

participants to determine what topics need to be on the agenda. Sometimes a premeeting discussion can eliminate the need to put a topic on the agenda, saving everyone's time. And often it can stimulate participants to properly prepare for the meeting. Don Halverson suggests that this participant input can be achieved by "circulating a skeletal or blank agenda and asking for agenda items."

Once the agenda is drawn up, it should be distributed to meeting participants. The optimum time to distribute the agenda for most meetings is one to three days before the meeting. If the agenda is circulated too far in advance, some participants may forget it or lose it. But at least twenty-four hours should be allowed so participants can give some careful thought to meeting topics.

If the meeting is called on short notice, advance distribution of the agenda may be impossible. On the other hand, very early distribution of an agenda may be necessary for an elaborate meeting or one requiring a lot of advance preparation.

Along with the agenda, any necessary background information should be distributed to participants before the meeting. "High-quality information leads to high-quality decisions," says Barry Maude, and prevents a discussion from becoming "a mere pooling of ignorance." Supplying background information can allow participants to consider matters carefully in advance and formulate useful questions. "But the whole idea is sabotaged once the papers get too long"; says Antony Jay, "They should be brief or provide a short summary."

One useful approach is to ask the person who will be making a presentation to provide the meeting planner with the necessary background information. The planner or a staff member can then write up a short summary of important points and distribute the summary to participants with the agenda.

The agenda should include both the starting and ending times of the meeting. Having a definite ending time is important, for participants have other responsibilities and appointments to attend to, and it is only common courtesy that they know when the meeting will be over. "If meetings have a tendency to go on too long," suggests Jay, "the chairman should arrange to start them one hour before lunch or one hour before the end of work." Other authors warn, however, that meetings at these times may be less productive because of low blood sugars and general weariness.

In addition to definite starting and ending times, meetings should have an internal structuring of time. Each agenda item should be allotted a certain amount of time, depending on its importance. For a productive meeting, these time constraints must be held to, or at least closely approximated. Of course, the amount of time each topic will need is an extremely unpredictable quantity. With experience, however, the meeting planner will be able to better estimate the time needed for particular kinds of topics. Until then, it may be wise to follow the system that Maude wryly suggests for working through a particular agenda:

1. Estimate the time required to deal with each item.
2. Calculate the total time required.
3. Double this figure.

While working on a particular agenda item, the trick is to get all the necessary information out in the open, but to cut off any superfluous additions. This is truly an art, but a chairman skilled in discussion techniques (discussed in the next section) can approach this efficiency ideal.

Another aspect of meeting design that can be altered to achieve desired ends is the order of agenda items. Naturally, urgent items need to come before those that can wait. But if some items might divide members, and others might unite them, the meeting planner can vary their order to produce, hopefully, a smoother meeting. In any case, it is always a good idea to end each meeting with a unifying item. Jay makes these suggestions concerning the order of agenda items:

> The early part of a meeting tends to be more lively and creative than the end of it, so if an item needs mental energy, bright ideas, and clear heads, it may be better to put it high up on the list. Equally, if there is one item of great interest and concern to everyone, it may be a good idea to hold it back for a while and get some other useful work done first. Then the star item can be introduced to carry the meeting over the attention lag that sets in after the first 15 to 20 minutes of the meeting.

If there is a large number of topics to discuss, it may be best to hold two or more separate meetings. Similar topics can be clustered in each meeting allowing a smaller number of participants.

It is very rare for meetings to remain productive after two hours. As Frank Snell points out, "Clear thinking falters as the clock goes round, and in turn, emotions take over. Weariness breeds dissension and contrariness." The ideal length seems to be from an hour to an hour and a half. If the meetings must be held for longer periods, be sure to provide coffee and fresh air breaks.

In addition to the meeting date, starting and ending

TABLE 1: SAMPLE AGENDA

District C Managers' Conference
December 17, 1979, 9:00-10:45 A.M.
Central Meeting Room
AGENDA

Topic	Person Responsible	Objective	Time
1. Approval of Agenda	Al Herbert	Decision	5 minutes
2. Discussion of possible state funding decrease for 1981-82.	Al Herbert	Discussion	10 minutes
3. Shall district lunch program be contracted out next year?	Ed Freemont	Decision	20 minutes
4. Discussion of new district information packet.	Al Herbert	Information	5 minutes
5. Discussion of proposed 1981-84 contract.	All	Discussion	30 minutes
6. New requirements for parental advisory groups.	John Nelson	Information	10 minutes
7. Cutting energy consumption to meet federal guidelines.	Ed Freemont	Problem-solution	20 minutes

times, and the place where the meeting is to be held, the agenda should contain a brief description of each topic, the objective desired for each topic (for example, decision, discussion, information), the name of the person responsible for each topic (who should introduce the item at the meeting), and the time allotment for that item. A sample agenda is presented in table 1. (A variation of this agenda is to simply head each agenda item with "For discussion," "For information," or "For decison.")

Although a firm structure is desirable for effective meetings, the planner should not "overstructure" the meeting. As Auger puts it, "One must not create the impression among the participants that the meeting has been so finally and rigidly preplanned that they are merely assembling to hear a proclamation." Participants should be left with the impression "that there is a legitimate need for the meeting and that their views, information and problem-solving talents can be considered." So within the structure of the agenda, a good bit of flexibility is advised.

WHO SHALL ATTEND?

Once you decide what you want to accomplish in a meeting, the question of whom to invite will be half answered. For starters, you will need those who are most affected by the issues to be discussed, those who have to give or receive information at the meeting, and those whose presence is necessary or desirable for decision-making purposes.

Maude stresses that meeting participants be chosen from the organizational level most appropriate to deal with the problem. Long-term policy issues, for example, should be decided by experienced, upper-level administrators who "have the experience and the over-view to grasp the financial implications of a particular decision and to overcome the inherent uncertainty of this kind of long-term decision-making."

In the same manner, middle-level managerial decisions and day-to-day operating decisions should be made at the appropriate level. Maude warns against "inviting people to meetings simply because of their high status in the organisation." One secret of making meetings more efficient, he states, is to "push decision-making as far down the organisation as it will go, i.e. to the lowest level competent to handle the problem."

Depending on the goals of your meeting, you can invite either a group with diverse personalities, or a more like-minded group. Maude quotes research that has "found that meetings made up of people of unlike personality often produce better solutions than like-minded groups. The reason may be the wide range of ideas that is likely; or simply that different-minded people tend to disagree and this prevents over-hasty decisions being made." So for creative problem-solving sessions, it may pay to invite a range of people from different levels and backgrounds, perhaps even some "outsiders."

Now that everyone who might either do the meeting some good or gain something from it has been identified, the next step for the meeting planner, and a very important step, is to pare down the attendee list so it includes only those members whose presence is absolutely necessary. There is universal agreement among meeting-improvement experts that a major reason for poor meetings is that too many people have been invited.

"Large, unwieldy meetings seem to be especially common in the public sector," says Maude, "perhaps because of legal and representational considerations." The philosophy of "participative management" is one of the reasons for ineffective meetings, according to Richard Dunsing. "In line with a tradition of 'touching base with everyone', some groups that are supposed to be working groups grow to assemblies of 20, 30, or even 40 people. But though they're billed as 'working' meetings, their size alone makes them barely able to function at all."

Dunsing states that the working meeting should rarely consist of more than 8 to 10 people. Jay states that "between 4 and 7 is generally ideal, 10 is tolerable, and 12 is the outside limit." Maude prefers 5 to 9, and Snell sets a limit at 15. If you must hold a meeting with a large number of participants, it may be desirable to create committees or subgroups to work on particular topics.

Small groups of four or less are more prone to biased decisions, and they lack the "breadth of experience and thinking to deal adequately with complex problems," says Maude. On the other hand, when groups grow to over ten, "an increasing number of people are scared into silence" and "intimate face-to-face contact between all members becomes impossible, so the meeting tends to split into cliques."

The optimum number for a particular working group is best found by experimentation. The ideal size is one that is large enough to provide the needed expertise for solving a problem, yet is small enough to prevent communications and control problems.

SEATING ARRANGEMENTS

Yet another factor that the astute meeting planner can vary in designing a successful meeting is the arrangement of attendees in the meeting room. Again, the type of seating arrangements will depend on the objective of the meeting and the kind of leadership style the meeting leader chooses. In addition, it will depend on whether the meeting planner wishes to promote or prevent conflict among individuals or factions in a meeting.

A "democratic" seating arrangement is one that emphasizes the equality of members, for example, a round or square table. A variation is to use low coffee tables, or no tables at all, as might be done in an informal rap-session.

The leader becomes more central when he or she sits at the middle of a U-shaped arrangement. This "leader-centered" symbolism becomes stronger still when the leader sits at the head of a long, narrow table. With the traditional rectangular table, says Maude, "you talk either to the chairman or to the people opposite and you respond to comments by the people opposite more than to comments made by people alongside you." Particularly if the table is narrow, participants are forced into uncomfortable direct visual contact with the people sitting opposite, and they have to crane their necks to see the leader. The result is that "this kind of meeting often turns into a kind of verbal tennis match, with contributions flying to and fro across the table rather than around it."

Another way to minimize social contact is to place the leader at the front of the room with all other chairs facing the front. "The easiest way to maintain a group as strangers," says William Spaulding, "is to seat them theater-style so that except for those on either side, they never become acquainted with anything other than the backs of their colleagues' heads." However, this may well be a good set-up if your primary objective is to give information to participants.

In general, the meeting planner will want to increase interaction and eye contact among meeting participants. When participants can see each other's faces and read the body language of other members, their understanding of each other will be maximized. For greatest eye contact, use a U-shaped or circular table.

If there are two conflicting groups, and you wish to minimize tension, be sure to break up the groups. In particular, do not put opposing camps on opposite sides of a rectangular table. Likewise, keep individuals who are antagonistic a good distance apart. As Snell observes, "Distance will definitely make the hearts of two opposites grow fonder!"

THE MEETING ROOM

"Surroundings tend to affect the way we think and act," states Auger, "and a poorly arranged and uncomfortable room is not likely to produce positive meeting results." Common sense, you say, yet how many meetings have you attended where something disturbed your concentration, such as an uncomfortable chair, a burnt-out projector bulb, a hot, overcrowded room, or a dance class meeting on the floor directly above? Attention to the physical setting of a meeting can't guarantee a good meeting, but it can prevent a bad one.

The location of your meeting depends on its purpose. If it is an instructional meeting, a classroom may be the best place. If it is a "ritualistic" meeting, it should probably be held in the best conference room available. And if it is a problem-solving or decision-making meeting, a simple meeting room is best. But "do not hold a decision-making meeting in the office of a high status member," caution Bormann and his colleagues — the surrounding symbolism is bound to inhibit free communication.

The size of the meeting room should match the size of the group. Maude reports that "the size of the room preferred by most participants is one that gives the impression of being comfortably full — not crowded — when everyone is present and sitting around the table."

Chairs should be comfortable, but not so comfortable that participants are prone to doze off. There should be ample electrical sockets for projectors, recorders, and so forth, and the meeting planner should make sure that the correct audio-visual equipment will be available and serviceable. Paper and pencils should be in ample supply, and a coffee pot should be nearby.

Good acoustics, lighting, and ventilation are other common-sense necessities for a good meeting. A room with poor acoustics is apt to lull participants to sleep, or frustrate them. Poor lighting and ventilation can also make group members irritable.

If there is antagonism between the smoking and non-smoking factions of the meeting, try to put the smokers together in the best ventilated area of the room. An increasingly popular remedy is to restrict smoking during the meeting altogether.

Meeting distractions come in the form of incoming telephone calls, late-comers, and outside noises. All calls to meeting participants should be held unless there is an emergency. If there are two or more entrances to the meeting room, only one should be used to minimize interruption by late-comers. And the meeting should be held in a room that is not usually subject to outside noises.

Of course, it is impossible to meet in an "ideal" room every time, but with judicious attention to environmental factors that can be altered, the meeting planner can most often ensure that the meeting environment will be comfortable and conducive to good communication.

THE ART OF LEADING THE MEETING

Good meeting planning is essential for having consistently good meetings. Yet even with the best planning, meetings can go awry. The other half of the meeting leader's art consists of successfully managing the "human energy" *during* the meeting.

An influencing factor, as always, is the style of leadership that the leader chooses. Do you want to run your meetings in traditional fashion, like a captain running his ship, giving orders and taking full command? Or do you prefer to view yourself as a subtle facilitator who is *at the service* of the group?

The concept of leadership, as noted earlier, has been changing rapidly in recent decades. Earlier meeting manuals stress the importance of a strong leader who is the master and controller of the group. More recent publications portray the meeting leader as a manager and facilitator whose primary function is to foster a democratic and cooperative group process among participants. In keeping with the spirit of the times, the suggestions in this section are designed more for the "leader as facilitator" and less for the "leader as captain."

THE WHAT AND HOW OF MEETING MANAGEMENT

A trained meeting observer or a perceptive meeting participant will be aware of two distinct sets of activities that take place in every working discussion. The first set, called the "task" or "content" activities of the group, has to do with *what* the group is doing. The second set, called "maintenance" or "process" activities, has to do with *how* the group is doing it. The effective group leader should be aware of and facilitate both activities.

Task activities, says Richard Dunsing, are "rational, systematic, cognitive efforts of the kind we typically expend in talking about and working on a problem." The goals of task activities are the stated goals of the meeting: to make a decision, to solve a problem, to plan a budget, to exchange information. Examples of task activities are setting goals, listing priorities, using background and history, examining consequences, linking with other issues, setting assignments, and agreeing on time limits.

Maintenance activities (also called human relations activities), continues Dunsing, concern "the way people think, act, and feel while they're immersed in the task." The goals of maintenance activities are the personal, usually unstated goals of each member: to feel acceptance and affiliation, to achieve, to have power. Things to watch for in assessing process activities include the eruption of conflict and how it is handled, body language, the relevance of inputs from each participant, the expression of emotion by participants (such as anger, irritation, resentment, apathy, boredom, warmth and appreciation, or satisfaction), and the mixture of seriousness and playfulness in the group.

Barry Maude has observed that "meetings oscillate between intellectual and emotional activity as the pressures of decision-making arouse emotions in people."

When emotions start surfacing, it is time for the group leader and other sensitive meeting participants to start "maintaining" the human relations in the group. When the "meeting machine" is back in smooth working order, the meeting leader should guide the group back into task activities.

TASK FUNCTIONS

The primary tool the group leader has to help a group toward its goals is the agenda. The agenda defines the topics and objectives of the meeting and structures the time within the meeting. It is the backbone of the meeting, the roadmap to its goals.

The first topic on the agenda should be the approval of the agenda itself. This activity allows participants to review the "meeting menu" and suggest changes if they feel they are necessary. For example, some members might think that the time allotment for a topic should be greater in light of recent events, or that a certain topic should be talked about first thing. Even if no changes are made, the agenda review and approval are valuable for setting the stage for the meeting and allow members to get into the right "mental set."

The meeting leader should constantly monitor the meeting in relation to its plan, the agenda. When the conversation gets off track, the leader should correct the direction of the meeting. Questions are a useful way to do this; for example, the leader may ask: "Just a moment, please. How does this relate to the point Janet made earlier?" A more direct approach is sometimes needed: "This is interesting, but we're getting off the subject. Let's get back to the main topic."

The leader should watch for signs that the topic has been discussed enough — such as the repetition of ideas or loss of interest — and move the group on to the next topic. But the leader should also be flexible and not hurry the meeting along too fast in the interest of sticking to the agenda. Says Maude, "Meetings need time to deal with complex problems: under pressure, they settle for quick but unsound decisions."

A good way to round off the discussion of a topic is to summarize the main points brought up. An added benefit is that the leader can gracefully move into the next topic after summing up. Another simple approach is to ask participants if they think enough time has been devoted to the topic, and whether they would like to move on.

Just as the leader helps the group round off its discussion of one topic, he or she helps the group begin discussion of the next. The leader may simply indicate the group member responsible for the next topic, as indicated on the agenda. Or the leader may give background information on the topic and then "immediately encourage the contribution of opinions and information by group members," says Leland Bradford. "If the leader fails to promote initiation by all members, the group can quickly become passive and uninvolved."

At times it may become obvious that a different approach is needed to solve a problem. The leader can stop discussion, suggest the new strategy, and ask what the group thinks about the change. Such "restructurings" of the group process can both save time and prevent unnecessary conflict.

In most meetings, there are some members who are more aggressive than others in their presentation of ideas. More timid members may have good ideas, but their ideas may only get half-stated or half-heard. It is up to the meeting leader to draw out the idea, particularly if it is a good one, and elaborate it for the group. This prevents the loss of good ideas and prevents the timid group members from withdrawing from active participation to the detriment of the whole group.

When the desired end-product of a discussion is a decision, the leader should step in when he or she senses there may be a consensus and ask if the group is in substantial agreement. If no consensus is in sight and the discussion seems to be going nowhere, the leader can call for a vote. If consensus is required or desired, however, the leader may have to be imaginative and think of a new method for resolving the remaining conflicts.

When a decision is made, the meeting leader should make clear just what the decision is and how it will be implemented. Responsibilities should be assigned and deadlines for action set. This solid information should be entered at once into the minutes of the meeting.

Even if there was substantial disagreement during a meeting, the leader should attempt to end on a positive note. A good means of doing this is to save for last an agenda item that everyone can agree on.

Finally, the meeting leader should briefly sum up the entire meeting and restate its decisions and the assignments of responsibility. Just before the meeting adjourns, it may be a good time to arrange the next meeting time with group members.

MAINTENANCE FUNCTIONS

Properly maintaining the human relationships in a group is somewhat like properly maintaining the machines in a factory, says Bradford. "The effective group ... learns that consistent maintenance not only resolves problems; it makes working together a rewarding experience." But "without attention to moods, feelings, and interpersonal relationships, a group chokes its lifeline of energy and motivation to complete the task."

Other authors address the task/maintenance issue in terms of a balance between effort and reward. According to Michael Burgoon and his coauthors, the amount of personal reward members receive influences both "the willingness of group members to participate and their satisfaction with group outcomes."

> Individuals bring to the group their personal anticipations of the amount of effort they will expend compared to the amount of reward they will receive. If the amount of effort required becomes disproportionate to the amount of reward received, willingness to be involved in the group decreases .... The group must, therefore, select its responsibilities and design its activities so that the members are collectively and individually satisfied with the relationship.

The goal of the leader's maintenance activities, then, is to create a group in which members feel involved, nonthreatened, and satisfied in their personal needs. Such a group can reach its maximum productivity as negative interpersonal conflicts fade out and the natural tendencies of humans to cooperate and solve mutual problems emerge.

One maintenance function already mentioned is that of drawing out and encouraging the more timid members of a group. Not only does this increase the "idea pool" of the group, it prevents the withdrawal of timid members from active participation in the group. The danger of withdrawn members is double: first, they are "dead weight" on the group's shoulders, contributing little to the group's productivity; second, out of feelings of resentment, they may sabotage group decisions by "forgetting" to do things or by working actively against implementation of the decisions in which they "really had no say."

Group members who feel that they and their ideas are valuable to the group will work for the group instead of against it, because they will have gotten something positive from the group: acceptance, identity, and a feeling of belonging. Thus, the group leader should encourage participation from all members and make sure that the "smaller voices" are not overwhelmed.

When conflict breaks out in a meeting, as it inevitably will, the role of the leader becomes that of harmonizer. "Harmonizing," says Bradford, "is negotiation between opposing sides in which one member serves as a third-party peacemaker, trying to retrieve the best ideas of both sides." However, Bradford warns, "When overdone, harmonizing dulls the flash of creativity that confrontation can produce."

So a certain degree of conflict is part of a healthy group process. But when conflict is extreme, and egos are involved, the progress of the group toward its goals often comes to a complete standstill.

One useful technique for decreasing personal conflicts in meetings is to distinguish clearly between ideas and individuals. Ideas, *not* individuals, should be evaluated by the group, stresses Bradford. "An individual may feel that a critical evaluation of his contribution is a rejection of himself. Such individuals, unable to separate their ideas from themselves, may withdraw. Others may fight, creating polarization and conflict in the group."

Of course, it is no easy trick getting participants to keep their minds on ideas instead of individuals. Certainly, reminders from the leader at critical times can help. A useful exercise for helping members learn the distinction is this: Have members write down their ideas for the solution of a problem. Collect the ideas and emphasize that they are now "group property." Then have the group evaluate the ideas one by one.

The leader should not, if at all possible, take sides in an argument. If questioned about his or her opinion, the leader can relay the question back to the group: "That is a tough problem. Does anyone have any ideas?" If the leader does answer questions about substantive measures, warn Bormann and his associates, "he is quite likely to be drawn into the conflict. Once a part of the fight, he loses control of the meeting. It is difficult to lead and take an active part. The man who does both may monopolize the meeting."

Indeed, monopolizing the meeting is usually what a traditional-style leader does when conflict is brewing. Yet how can you both lead a meeting in which you have a critical stake and facilitate the meeting, as if you didn't? One approach is to have several or all members trained in facilitating meetings. Then when conflict erupts, the person most neutral on the issue can "referee." Another approach, to be discussed later in this chapter, is to have a neutral person from outside the group facilitate the entire meeting (see the Interaction Method).

YOU AS A PARTICIPANT

A meeting's success should not, of course, be solely dependent on the leader's capabilities. Participants, too, have responsibilities for making meetings work.

The first rule for meeting participation is to come prepared. Read the agenda and think about the topics to be discussed. Make sure you understand the issues. Read the background information provided with the agenda, if any. Formulate your own views and questions, and imagine what other points of view might be presented.

When you have a presentation to make at a meeting, prepare yourself fully: make an outline, prepare any visual aids you need, and rehearse your presentation. When your proposals may be controversial, discuss them with key people before the meeting.

When in the meeting, use good manners: try not to shuffle papers or engage in side conversations. Listen carefully to what others say and try to see the issue from their viewpoints. Speak up when you have knowledge or an opinion to share, but don't overparticipate — try to get an active group process going. Ask clarifying questions when there appears to be confusion.

Help the leader by sticking to agenda topics and time limits, drawing out the ideas of others, facilitating the resolution of conflicts, and criticizing ideas instead of people. And . . . please arrive on time.

UTILIZING MINUTES

Memory is as fleeting as time itself. How much do you remember, for example, about your day just one week ago? We begin forgetting events immediately after they occur, and even when we do think we recall something, we are often incorrect in our recollections.

Auger brings this point home by summarizing the results of a memory-retention study, conducted on the attendees of a psychological society meeting. Two weeks after the meeting, the average attendee could recall "only 8.4 per cent of all points actually covered in the meeting." Worse yet, "forty-two per cent of what they thought they remembered was incorrectly recalled."

Thus, a very important principle for making meetings more effective is to *document the results* of the meeting. Promptly getting the decisions made and actions required onto paper will help ensure that they are both remembered and implemented properly.

The amount of detail you put in your minutes depends on the situation. Sometimes a detailed transcript or tape recording may be desirable or required. More frequently, a group will wish to have a simple record of the main points made in a meeting, including, perhaps, the reasoning used to come to conclusions. "Even when a proposal is rejected, it may be useful to keep a record of the argument," says Maude, "so that if ever the issue is raised again the committee will be able to refer back to the report and see what its thinking and its reasons for rejection were last time."

Even if your minutes consist of a few simple statements outlining the major decisions of the meeting, they should contain a certain minimal amount of information: What is going to be done, and how will it be done? Who is going to do what? When should these actions be completed? It is important that these details be written down to avoid the common after-meeting syndromes of forgetfulness, procrastination, and confusion about what is required or who is responsible.

Minutes that are limited to key decisions can often be taken by a group member, or the group leader. When a decision is reached, the minute taker should record the decision and all its details and immediately read it back to the group for confirmation.

When more detailed minutes are desired, a formal minute taker from outside the group is usually needed; a group member taking detailed minutes cannot actively participate in discussions, because he or she is busy writing. In addition, an external notetaker is less likely to be biased in recording the proceedings. On the other hand, the notetaker may have difficulty understanding what is going on in the meeting and may consequently make recording errors.

A disadvantage of taking minutes on the traditional notepad, says Richard Dunsing, is that "the course of events is hidden from view on the note paper. Others at the table cannot refer to past key points." A method growing in popularity is to have the proceedings of a meeting recorded on large pieces of paper taped to the wall, or on large pads on an easel.

With this form of minutes, participants can see the past flow of ideas in the meeting and won't feel the necessity of repeating their ideas as much because others in the group have forgotten them. Another advantage, says Don Halverson, is that "it serves to depersonalize the ideas — they become 'the group's' ."

When the meeting is over, copies of the minutes should be made and distributed to group members within forty-eight hours of the meeting, and preferably sooner. B.Y. Auger even suggests that, given a nearby secretary and copying machine, the minutes can be handed to group members as they leave the room.

If more detailed minutes are taken, it may be desirable to

write up a summary of the meeting's major decisions. The summary should be distributed to participants and the original detailed minutes kept on file.

THE INTERACTION METHOD

One way to solve the leader/facilitator conflict mentioned earlier is to have a person from outside the group do the facilitating. The leader is then free to concentrate on the "what" of the meeting (the task functions), while the facilitator takes care of the "how" (the maintenance functions). This is the approach proposed by Michael Doyle and David Straus in *How to Make Meetings Work*.

The "Interaction Method," as Doyle and Straus call their approach, actually defines four separate roles "which collectively form a self-correcting system of checks and balances." The *facilitator* is "a neutral servant of the group and does not evaluate or contribute ideas." The facilitator suggests methods and procedures for the meeting, protects members of the group from personal attack, and assures that everyone has an opportunity to speak. In short, "the facilitator serves as a combination of tool guide, traffic officer, and meeting chauffeur."

The *recorder*, or minute taker, is also neutral and nonevaluating. The recorder writes down the group's ideas on large sheets of paper on the walls, using, whenever possible, the actual words of each speaker. The advantages of this approach, according to the authors, are that "the act of recording does not significantly slow down the progress of the meeting," and the written record (called the "group memory") serves as "an accepted record of what is happening as it is happening."

The *group maker* is one of the active participants in the meeting. The group members "keep the facilitator and recorder in their neutral roles" and "make sure that ideas are recorded accurately." Group members can also "make procedural suggestions" and "overrule the suggestions of the facilitator." Other than these functions, their main focus is on the agenda and the tasks to be accomplished.

The fourth and final role is that of the *manager/chairperson*, who becomes an active participant in the group, yet retains the powers and responsibilities of the traditional leadership position. The manager "makes all final decisions; has the power to set constraints and regain control if not satisfied by the progress of the meeting; sets the agenda; argues actively for his or her points of view"; and "urges group members to accept tasks and deadlines." (Although the Interaction Method is built around this fairly autocratic leadership style, there seems to be no reason why it could not be adjusted to a more democratic style, or even to a leaderless group.)

Doyle and Straus, who run a "consulting and training firm with expertise in problem-solving" (Interaction Associates Inc.), claim wide success with their method in education, business, and government meetings. Their book contains a complete description of the Interaction Method and a wealth of meeting improvement techniques.

TOOLS FOR EVALUATING AND IMPROVING MEETINGS

The literature on group dynamics and organizational development is replete with exercises, techniques, and "structured experiences" for evaluating and improving meetings. Some can be implemented quite easily and do not require special training. Many others take a fair amount of preparation and followup and work best with a meeting consultant.

As an example of the former, Ernest and Nancy Bormann provide three checklists for meeting improvement. The first is a planning checklist that asks critical questions of the meeting planner, such as "What is the purpose of the meeting?"; "Who will participate?"; and "Will the room be ready and open?" The second checklist is designed for evaluating a meeting by a participant or observer. Questions include, "Was the preparation for the meeting adequate?"; "Was a permissive social climate established?"; and "Did the leader exercise the right amount of control?" The final checklist is designed for the leader to evaluate how well he or she led the meeting: "Did you 'loosen up' the group before plunging into discussion?"; "Did you pose a challenging question to start the discussion?"

Leland Bradford provides six other brief meeting evaluation forms that are designed for recording participant reaction at meeting's end. The group can use the resulting data in several ways: a summary of the results can be announced at the next meeting; the leader can select themes from the forms and ask for discussion on those topics only; or the group can devote a whole meeting to the maintenance issues that surfaced via the evaluation forms.

Some of the evaluation forms Bradford provides are taken from University Associates' *The 1979 Annual Handbook for Group Facilitators,* edited by John Jones and William Pfeiffer, a much wider source of evaluation and group-process awareness exercises. Each *Annual* "is intended to make widely available to group facilitators an up-to-date repository of information, techniques, methods, and 'tools of the trade' (structured experiences and instruments)." University Associates encourages users to duplicate and adapt the materials for their own educational and training needs.

Don Halverson describes several simple techniques for improving meetings. In "Going Around the Room," each participant in turn is asked to state his or her position at that moment. This method is useful "when the group is hung up around the views of those who are dominating the conversation," says Halverson, as well as "when the group seems to have run out of solutions." It is also useful for quickly evaluating a meeting and for winding up a meeting.

In "Subgrouping," the group is temporarily divided into smaller groups of from two to six people to discuss either the same or different topics. Subgrouping is useful in larger groups because it keeps members involved, allows every participant to be heard, and permits more than one topic to be discussed at once. (A legislature with its committee system is the epitome of subgrouping.) Jack Fordyce and Raymond Weil report the success of subgrouping in a meeting that included both professional and clerical workers: "To surface underlying issues for the agenda, the group was divided into homogeneous subgroups. Each subgroup reported its proposed agenda items. For the first time, the voices of the clerical staff were clearly heard."

Another series of exercises and evaluation instruments are presented in *The Second Handbook of Organization Development in Schools* by Richard Schmuck and his associates. Although designed for organization development consultants, many of the exercises are easily implemented without specialized knowledge.

Other publications containing some evaluation tools are *Taking Your Meetings Out of the Doldrums* by Eva Schindler-Rainman and her colleagues, *You and I Have Simply Got to Stop Meeting This Way* by Richard Dunsing, and *The Small Meeting Planner* by Leslie This.

CONCLUSION

As educators are burdened with an ever-increasing number of duties and responsibilities, effective meeting techniques become more and more important. No longer can education afford the price of unproductive and unsatisfying meetings. Each meeting must become more effective at grappling with the future, more effective as an arena of controlled change. At the same time, the meeting must serve to satisfy personal needs for affiliation, achievement, activity, and power, for the long-term benefit of both the organization and society.

Briefly, this chapter has outlined the process of successful meeting management as follows:

At the beginning of the meeting process, the meeting leader decides on a compatible leadership style after considering his or her own nature, the needs and desires of group members, and the characteristics of the organization and situation. In planning the meeting, the leader's first guides are the goals and purposes he or she wishes to accomplish. Next, the meeting planner draws up the blueprint for the meeting's actions — the agenda. The framework of the meeting takes form as the participants are invited, the seating arrangements are decided on, the meeting room is arranged, and background information and agendas are distributed to participants.

Finally, the meeting opens and the interpersonal and discussion skills of the chairperson come to the fore. Using the agenda as a road map, the leader skillfully guides the group through the chaos of problem-solving and decision-making. At the same time, the leader is alert for the surfacing of negative emotions and maintains the human relations in the group as needed. When decisions are reached, the leader makes sure that responsibilities are clearly designated and that deadlines for action are set. After the meeting, the leader distributes the minutes, follows up on the decisions made, and evaluates the effectiveness of the meeting.

When meetings are run in this way, they can actually become both productive and satisfying! With some thought given to leadership style, purpose, planning, and the personal needs of participants, your meetings, too, can become more effective.

CHAPTER 10
MANAGING TIME AND STRESS
Sandra Huffstutter

Office graffiti. You find it in virtually every workplace and the subject is virtually always the same: stress arising from work and the lack of time to do work right. Coffee mugs, plastic plaques, and tacky statuary communicate the wit and wisdom of these occupational plagues.

"As soon as the rush is over I'm going to have a nervous breakdown."

"My cup runneth amuk."

"Why is there never enough time to do the job right, but always enough time to do it over?"

"Worker's Dilemma:
1. No matter how much you do, you'll never do enough.
2. What you don't do is always more important than what you do do."

Folk wisdom aside, it is no secret that the management of time and stress in the workplace has become a major concern to employee and employer alike. In a recent article, John Ivancevich and Michael Matteson cite estimates of a seventeen billion dollar loss in industrial productivity within the past few years, due to stress-related dysfunctions.

Furthermore, occupational stress and pressures posed by constraints exacerbate worker's stress, and unremitting stress reduces the worker's capacity for intelligently managing his or her time.

This true "Worker's Dilemma" has definitely not by-passed the schools, as evidenced by the recent mushrooming of articles in educational journals on the subject of time and stress management. Everyone seems to be aware of the problems, but few seem to do anything constructive (aside from the therapeutic posting of graffiti) about them.

Why is this the case? Let's take a look at two kinds of mental sets: those that block and those that boost the effective management of time and stress.

BLOCKS TO TIME/STRESS MANAGEMENT

One reason for resistance to a change in work habits is rooted in our national character. The Protestant Work Ethic dictates that we labor ceaselessly — or, at least, appear to do so. Any change in work habits that would provide worker "down-time" would therefore be morally suspect, to say the least.

Another set of values that conflicts with effective office management includes those oriented against any form of regimentation. "Go with the flow" and "hang loose" attitudes accentuate the value of spontaneity at the expense of productivity and the mental ease provided by stable routine.

A major block to the effective management of time and stress is the employee's actual cherishing of time/stress pressures. In many organizations, excessive busyness is a sign of status — the mark of being indispensable — and stress is the "designer label" of that status. Excessive busyness is also cherished as a respectable form of procrastination — of avoiding important tasks due to preoccupation with innumerable trivial tasks. Thus Alan Lakein, a popular advocate of time management, describes the "Overdoer" as someone who is "so busy doing things that he has no time to assess their true value."

The laughable excesses of some time management advocates also constitute a block to serious consideration of their programs. Suggestions for solving problems while you sleep, practicing isometrics whenever placed "on hold," and listening to language tapes while commuting all seem excessive. Such time management zealots probably need to be reminded of Bunuel's Law (quoted from Block): "Overdoing things is harmful in all cases, even when it comes to efficiency."

A final and more serious impediment to time/stress management is the "It won't work here" attitude. It's human nature to feel that one's own business, staff, service, whatever, is unique and not reducible to generalized precepts. This attitude is particularly tempting in a "people business" like education. However, Lee Smith, president of Southwest Texas State University, asserts unequivocally that "there is a great similarity among time problems at all levels and in all organizations."

By way of further support, Gilbert Weldy, in his highly readable monograph on time management for the school administrator, agrees that difficulties in the management of time cut through distinctions between education and industry. Principals, he says, face the same kinds of problems with effective time management and to the same degree as do business managers. He cites a 1965 study of high school principals in which 86 percent of the respondents indicated that "lack of time" was their greatest obstacle to adequate job performance.

The primary challenge, then, is this: to *unblock* the route to effective time/stress management by recognizing unproductive values and attitudes (like those just described) and then to make a commitment to replace any unproductive values with productive ones. Time and stress management is primarily a challenge to your values and attitudes and only secondarily a challenge to your skills.

BOOSTS TO TIME/STRESS MANAGEMENT

Management consultants are given to speaking in aphorisms. Peter Drucker, whose management expertise has made him the patron saint of both MBA students and executives of multinational corporations, says, "Time is the scarcest resource, and unless it is managed, nothing else can be managed." Alan Lakein opens his best-selling *How to Get Control of Your Time and Your Life* with the words: "Time is life. It is irreversible and irreplaceable. To waste your time is to waste your life, but to master your time is to master your life and make the most of it."

These eminently quotable consultants developed their aphoristic style out of a need to motivate — to motivate their clients to value those character traits, attitudes, and concepts that facilitate effective management. These facilitators can be grouped into two broad categories: "self-control" and "job-control." Let's take a brief look at each before turning to practical skills and strategies for improved management of time and stress.

SELF-CONTROL

Fundamental to self-control is self-knowledge. What are your strengths, your weaknesses, your skills? What is your personality type, your physiological type? Are you a detail person or a "big picture" person? Are you a reader or a listener? A participant or an observer? A morning person or an evening person? What forces shaped your past? What do you project to be the shape of your future?

As Hamlet has taught us, knowledge of self is unproductive unless coupled with discipline in action and behavior. Alan Lakein devotes whole chapters to the subjects of self-discipline and willpower and how to bolster both. Like the ancient Greek's ideal of the "Golden Mean" and the Bible's exhortation that "to everything there is a season," Lakein's book espouses balance and control: a time for work and a time for relaxation, a time for working together and a time for working alone.

Another sort of balance and control is discussed by management consultant and writer W. A. Mambert. Linking time management directly to self-knowledge and maturity, Mambert issues a caveat against "excess emotional and mental baggage," including "compulsive talking, over-defensiveness, over-explaining, self-justification, fear, guilt, worry, gossip, office politics, over-sensitivity, and similar subjective activities related to being a basically immature person."

Self-knowledge plus self-discipline equals maturity, and maturity boosts one's potential for effective management of time and stress.

JOB-CONTROL

Like self-control, job-control requires knowledge — knowledge of the primary purpose of your organization and of your own specific role therein. In *Executive Time Management,* Helen Reynolds and Mary Tramel assert that the employee's "raison d'être" is to further the organization's "primary purpose" (for instance, to give all students access to a quality education), not merely to perform the functions listed in the employee's job description. The authors warn against confusing your "functions" (developing curriculum, attending school board meetings, supervising teachers, disciplining students, and so forth) with your primary purpose, since

> your value as an executive is measured in degrees of effectiveness. It is not so much how efficiently you perform your function as it is how effectively you move toward the attainment of the organization's primary goal.

With your overall purpose firmly in mind, you will find it easier to clarify your role and its functions, objectives, and areas of responsibility. Such a clarification requires precise communication between yourself, your staff, and your superiors, but will pay off in reduced stress and reduced time misuse caused by excessive, ambiguous, or conflicting responsibilities. Role clarification as a technique for stress management will be discussed in greater detail later. Here the emphasis is on its importance as a *facilitator* for the initiation of time/stress management strategies within your office.

In addition to knowledge of your school district's primary purpose and knowledge of your own role within the district, job control also requires knowledge of various leadership styles for executing your role. This, in turn, implies the mature recognition that different leadership styles are appropriate for different occasions. A thorough discussion of this subject can be found in chapter 3; once again, the main point here is that the knowledge and use of varied administrative styles is one more boost toward effective time/stress management. And now, keeping in mind the importance of commitment and control, let's turn to practical procedures for improved management of time and stress.

TIME MANAGEMENT STRATEGIES

If time management was a mystery ten years ago, it certainly is not today — as a quick check of your library's journal indexes and card catalogue will confirm. The variety of titles are strikingly unvaried in content, so much so that one can speak of a "classical" approach to time management — a four-part, rather circular process that includes the following:

1. goal-setting, which leads to prioritizing

2. keeping a daily time log, which leads to the identification of time-wasters
3. management of time-wasters, which leads to increased discretionary time
4. wise use of discretionary time, which leads to the accomplishment of those goals identified in step one

GOAL-SETTING AND PRIORITIZING

Just as the smart shopper does not shop without a grocery list, and the smart teacher does not teach without a course outline, so the smart administrator needs a written list or outline of professional goals to administer effectively. The operative word here is "effectively." When Reynolds and Tramel asserted that "your value as an executive is measured in degrees of effectiveness," they were reiterating a key distinction made by Peter Drucker: the distinction between effectiveness and efficiency. Drucker insists that "the executive's job is to be effective," not efficient — which means getting "the right things done," rather than merely doing things right. And those "right things" relate directly to advancing the organization's primary purpose, as discussed earlier.

While your goals list will help you to identify those crucial "right things," the list itself can take any number of forms. Lakein recommends identification of lifetime goals, three-year goals, and six-month goals. The Colorado State Department of Education's *School Improvement-Accountability Process Kit* on "Managing Time" recommends ranking, in order of importance to you, the six main life-roles you enact: professional, family, community, social-cultural-recreational, personal, and self-service (that is, physical maintenance activities).

More to the point, perhaps, is the Association of California School Administrators' *Project Leadership* component entitled "Personal Activity Plan" (as shown in their 1979 notebook, *An Update on Time Management*). This activity plan addresses job-specific priorities. It involves written goal statements with specific activities and specific professional growth requirements (new skills) to meet those goals; it also involves descriptors of concrete, accomplished tasks and assessment mechanisms for final evaluations.

Regardless of the form in which you put your goals statements, the important thing is that you put them in writing. List them, chart them, diagram them, or index-card them, but above all, *write them*! Write them because, as any four-year-old knows who has just penciled her own name for the first time: writing makes it real.

After listing your goals, the next step is to prioritize them. Not all goals or values are equally important, nor are they of the same importance at all times. Prioritize based on your point of view of right *now*. You can (and should) upate your goals and priorities when your point of view changes — as it inevitably will.

Once you've prioritized, you're ready to select your two or three most important goals and to list specific, short-term activities that will further those goals. For example, if one of your goals is to initiate a program of gifted education in your school, your activities list might include checking with the school district to see what state and local funds are available; forming a committee of parents, teachers, and administrators to investigate various kinds of existing gifted programs; and so forth.

Finally, after listing activities for your three most important goals, prioritize again. This should result in your "A-1" goal and your "A-1" activity to further that goal, as Lakein would say. This activity constitutes your foremost "right thing": your most valuable, potential contribution to your school district, your primary leadership responsibility.

Now the overriding question becomes: how you are going to find the time — in an already overburdened workday — to pursue this priority activity. The answer is simple: you identify time-wasters with the use of a daily time log and learn to manage those that are within your control.

THE DAILY TIME LOG

When Peter Drucker listed five characteristic practices that distinguished the effective executive, the one that topped his list was the fact that "effective executives know where their time goes." To know for certain where your time goes, most management consultants recommend that you keep some kind of *written* daily log for at least a week. Once again, the kind of log you use is less important than that you (or your secretary or assistant) track your time. You can track fifteen-minute segments, one-hour segments, or simply note the time whenever you change activities. You can track each distinct activity or only the main activity in the specified time block, or you can track only certain kinds of activities that concern you for some reason or another (telephone calls, drop-in visitors, scheduled meetings, whatever).

As you track your activities, or perhaps at the end of each day, try to evaluate each activity on the basis of its significance. Michael Sexton and Karen Switzer recommend the following rating system:

#1 = Professional Goal Functions (long-range planning and leadership activities; curriculum planning, for example)

#2 = Critical/Crisis Functions (immediate, situational concerns; a student-teacher conflict, for example)

#3 = Maintenance Functions (routine administrative tasks; fire drills for example)

P = Personal Activities (calling home, going to the dentist)

While your primary responsibility as a leader is to engage in #1s, your time log will probably reveal that your workday is consumed entirely by #2s and #3s. Patrick Duignan found that the school superintendent is precluded from long-range planning and other leadership functions by virtue of the incredibly interruptive and discontinuous nature of his or her workday. Duignan observes that, within the superintendent's typical 8.2 hour, work-through-lunch workday, he or she engages in about thirty-eight disparate activities, nearly 40 percent of which "lasted less than five minutes each."

Moreover, the author found that fully 25 percent of the superintendent's day is spent in unscheduled meetings (drop-in visitors are included here), and nearly 25 percent more is spent in scheduled meetings. Rather than acting as a decision-maker, then, the superintendent acts as a contact-person, an "information broker," who spends three-quarters of the day in verbal contacts for the purpose of receiving or dispensing information.

Does this sound familiar? Does your time log coincide with Duignan's observations? If so, then, like so many other leaders, you are working in the "reactive" mode, rather than in a self-directed "active" mode. Your response time (time spent responding to people, mail, and situations) far outweighs your discretionary time (time spent in A-1 activities). To put your workday into a more productive balance, you now need to recognize and manage time-wasters. Or, as Sexton and Switzer advise, you need to learn how to do the #2s and #3s *efficiently*, so that you will have time to do the #1s *effectively*.

MANAGING TIME WASTERS

The time-waster is a two-headed dragon. External time-wasters wear the face of "the other": visitors, telephone calls, meetings, paperwork, coworker's needs. Internal time-wasters wear the face of the self: inability to say "no," inability to schedule and prioritize, inability to delegate, tendency to procrastinate. Let's look at these one at a time, with an eye toward specific, dragon-slaying strategies.

Visitors and Telephone Calls

Telephone and visitor interruptions are two of the three worst daily time-wasters (meetings being the third). Because they act as interruptors, they destroy concentration and momentum — the twins of productivity. Management of these time-wasters is, as always, first a matter of attitude and only then a matter of skill. Administrators must recognize that total accessibility (the "open-door" policy), while subjectively gratifying, is professionally counterproductive. It follows that administrators must value their own time before expecting others to do the same.

Most time management experts recommend reducing visitor and telephone interruptions through the use of "buffering" and "limiting" techniques. That is, they suggest you should buffer (insulate) yourself from excessive or unproductive personal contacts and consciously limit the time spent on each necessary or unavoidable contact.

Translated into office procedure, buffering is primarily accomplished by the secretary — who screens all calls and visitors — while limiting is accomplished by the development of some rather brusque habits, such as not offering coffee and tea to visitors, not offering your visitors a chair, not socializing excessively, and so forth.

However, these standard recommendations may be inappropriate in the educational setting. As educational managers, democratic and open communications with students, parents, colleagues, and staff probably constitute some of the highest and best uses of your time. Therefore, the conventional wisdom of business-oriented time management consultants requires some tempering here.

Perhaps the most productive strategy for harried educational administrators is the scheduling of regular blocks of time during which you are inaccessible to visitors and telephone calls. Because it is commonly accepted that one is unavailable when involved in a scheduled meeting, consider this block of time to be a "meeting with yourself" — as it certainly is.

During this time, have your calls intercepted by your secretary or your switchboard. Close the door to your office. Place bookshelves and files with often-needed information adjacent to your desk, so that such information is readily available. Strive to make yourself highly invisible during periods of inaccessibility, just as you strive to make yourself highly visible (in the staff lounge at lunch time, in the halls before school, in the meeting room before board meetings) during periods of accessibility.

Above all, train your staff and colleagues to respect this quiet time, because studies show that it will likely be the *only* productive work time available to you during the entire day.

The next major external time-waster — meetings — is covered at length in chapter 9. The strategies discussed there for holding efficient, productive meetings will inevitably cut down on time wasted in inefficient, unproductive meetings. Note particularly the time-wise advice on scheduling, agendas, and limiting attendees.

Paperwork

After drop-ins, the telephone, and meetings, paperwork ranks as the next most frustrating external time-waster. Donna Douglass and Merrill Douglass assert that "there are only three kinds of paper": action items, information items, and throw away items. After your secretary screens, categorizes, and prioritizes your mail accordingly, try some of these methods for effectively dealing with action and information items:

Action items ☐ One of Lakein's laws prescribes that you "handle each piece of paper only once." In support, Donna and Merrill Douglass estimate that "at least 80 percent of the mail could be answered immediately when read." Don't let those action items pile up. Handle them quickly, in order of priority, at a scheduled time of the day.

☐ Action items with a low priority may not need doing at all. Lakein suggests a procrastination drawer: dump low priority items into it and see if they're ever missed.

☐ Weldy suggests that you categorize your action items into separately labelled manila folders: "urgent," "dictate," "to do," "for Faculty Bulletin," and so forth.

☐ Delegate paperwork to your secretary. Pencil a brief note of response in the margin of incoming correspondence, letting your secretary draft the formal response from that.

☐ Whenever possible, use time-saving paperwork expediters: routing slips, attachment slips, form letters, form paragraphs, handwritten responses, and the telephone.

☐ Learn to use a dictating machine. You will save not only your own time (since one can dictate at sixty words per minute as opposed to writing longhand at ten words per minute), but your secretary's time as well (since transcribing by dictaphone is faster than either taking shorthand or reading longhand).

☐ Initiate a "tickler" or "suspense" filing system. Manila folders or accordion files labelled one through thirty-one and January through December will permit you to keep track of upcoming tasks, commitments, or annual responsibilities. For example, if annual budget estimates are due each May, "tickle" a reminder in April's file that it is time to begin gathering the appropriate data. Use the daily tickler files in the same way.

257

Information Items ☐ Use a variety of filing systems: desk top files and ticklers, desk files that include most-often-needed items of information, and cabinet files that are systematically arranged in a way that is clear to both yourself and your closest staffpersons.

☐ Recognize this: Some studies estimate that fully 95 percent of all papers filed are never retrieved again. Donna and Merrill Douglass recommend the following steps for determining whether an item is worth keeping:
1. Have your secretary keep a log, for several months, of items retrieved from files. These items will comprise your "useful filing" list.
2. Before filing an item, ask yourself: "Does this item fit in the 'useful filing' category?" "Could I retrieve this information from someone else's files, if needed?" "What use shall I make of this item within the next year?"

☐ Schedule an annual Spring cleaning of the files, with an eye toward tossing as much as possible.

☐ Learn to skim reading matter or train your secretary to skim, highlight, and digest. Redirect reading matter to your subordinates and colleagues.

☐ Keep journals, articles, and updates in one section of your shelves, ready for availability when heading out to dentists' appointments or business trips.

Before moving from "external" to "internal" time-wasters, mention should be made of one time displacer that actually straddles the two categories. This time waster is what Oncken and Wass (as described by Carol Giesecke and others) have termed "monkeys": those demands inappropriately placed on the administrator by subordinates. Whereas the administrator generally *must* respond to demands made by superiors, and whereas he or she generally *chooses* to respond to demands made by peers, the administrator needs to perceive demands made by subordinates as an often inappropriate use of his or her time and an example of "passing the buck upwards."

For example, a recently hired administrative assistant inquires about the district's pension plan. Rather than accepting the "monkey" and rifling among the files for explanatory documents, the time-wise administrator should briefly refer the new employee to the personnel department. Learning to shrug off "monkeys" is akin to learning to say "no" — the first internal time waster we will consider.

Internal time wasters are both the easiest and the hardest to control, and for the same reason: their control lies exclusively within yourself. Your success at managing them is entirely up to you, but, as always, awareness and attitude will take you halfway there.

Inability to Say "No"

Let's begin with learning to say "no." In this regard, Lakein advises that "you must set priorities based on the importance to you of the person doing the asking and the consequences if you don't do what's being asked." If you subsequently decide that the task is not a priority item, you simply and courteously refuse, with perhaps a brief explanation of your time constraints.

Peter Drucker suggests that you review your daily time log with a view toward asking yourself, "What would happen if this were not done at all?" He goes on to say that "all one has to do is to learn to say 'no' if an activity contributes nothing to one's own organization, to oneself, or to the organization for which it is to be performed." He concludes by asserting that you can thus dispose of one quarter of your time demands with no significant effect.

Similarly, W. A. Mambert recommends the "Wash Decision" — a decision to not proceed with a project when complications begin to outweigh the value of the final result. The fundamental principle implied in all these recommendations is that of the "primary purpose." With your chief contribution to the school district's primary purpose firmly in mind, deciding whether to say "yes" or "no" to any activity should be simplifed.

Inability to Schedule

Consciousness of your primary purpose will also help to eliminate another internal time waster: the inability to schedule. Scheduling is actually a multifaceted gem that includes planning, prioritizing, clustering, and delegating. All are essential to managing time effectively.

You began to plan when you accomplished your prioritized list of goal statements and activities. Now you need to narrow your focus, to make the best use of the days that will carry you toward your goals.

Daily planning can be done first thing in the morning or last thing in the evening — whenever you have fifteen minutes of quiet time. Make a "to do" list that includes the day's chief tasks, including some steps toward accomplishment of your A-1 activity. Then systematically prioritize those tasks (using Sexton and Switzer's #1, #2, #3 system or Lakein's A, B, C system).

Prioritizing is greatly aided by knowledge of the 80/20 rule, Lakein's definition of which seems to be the most explicit:

> The 80/20 rule suggests that in a list of ten items, doing two of them will yield most (80 percent) of the value. Find these two, label them A, get them done. Leave most of the other eight undone, because the value you'll get from them will be significantly less than that of the two highest-value items.... It's important to remind yourself again and again not to get bogged down on low-value activities but to focus on the 20 percent where the high value is.

Next, coordinate your "to dos" with your scheduled appointments, remembering to schedule a block of quiet time for work on your A-1. While most management consultants recommend blocking out one to two hours for this leadership activity, Weldy estimates that the educational administrator can probably wrest only half an hour of such time from daily demands. Above all, schedule this time realistically. A glance at your daily time log should reveal peaks and lulls in external activities and in your own internal energy level. Common sense dictates, then, that you schedule your leadership time as close as possible to the intersection of peak energy and low activity levels.

After scheduling, attack your "to dos" in order of priority. Do the important tasks first, delegate whatever you can, and don't fret if the #3s have to wait for another day. It is not important to do everything — just the important things. Cluster similar activities (for example, all call-backs, all paperwork) whenever possible and steel yourself to finish each task before going on to the next, because clustering and completion eliminate wasteful transition time.

Inability to Delegate

For a variety of reasons, many of which are purely and emotionally subjective, most administrators find it difficult to delegate. Again, an attitudinal change must precede the learning of new skills. People tend to perceive delegation as a thrusting of one's "dirty work" onto others. Instead, the leader should distinguish between work that advances one's contribution to the organization's primary purpose and work that does not.

Once that distinction is made, the leader should retain the former and delegate the latter, in addition to delegating routine tasks, tasks at which others are more skilled, tasks at which the leader is already skilled, and tasks that the leader actively dislikes.

A quick review of your daily time log should raise your consciousness in regard to delegating. Assess each activity in terms of whether it could have been delegated and then commit yourself to better manipulation of this time displacer.

Both the ACSA Update and Helen Reynolds and Mary Tramel offer useful lists of practical tips for delegating. Suffice it to say here that effective delegation requires clear communication with the delegatee, assignment of authority and decision-making capability to the delegatee, a system for monitoring and followup, and a relaxed attitude toward the delegatee's work procedures (since, as W. Michael Born points out, the secret to delegating is "to hold (the delegatee) . . . more accountable for results than methods").

Gilbert Weldy says that it helps to perceive delegation as an investment in time that accrues long-term benefits. One of those benefits is invaluable on-the-job training for your staff, whose expertise reflects directly on you, their leader. Moreover, your ability to rise to a more challenging position hinges directly on the knowledgeability and effectiveness of those you have trained in your current position.

Procrastination

Finally, the last internal time waster that deserves mention here is a demon with whom we are all familiar: procrastination. Procrastination is professionally debilitating in that we tend to procrastinate precisely those difficult, challenging A-1 activities with which we should be most integrally involved. Low priority tasks, on the other hand, are quickly accomplished, provide instant gratification, and are therefore completed with much more regularity.

Allen Lakein's advice on this subject is both practical and persuasive. In eight key chapters, he suggests a variety of tactics, including the following: recognizing the consequences of delay and the advantages of action; reducing a large task to small subtasks; working at the task for five minutes per day to initiate involvement; gathering additional data; performing a subtask of the A-1 that coincides with your current mood; setting deadlines and announcing your deadline to someone else; taking rest breaks; and rewarding yourself as subtasks are accomplished.

Of the four-part process to time management, this completes part three: subduing the doubleheaded dragon of external and internal time wasters. At this point a warning must be sounded. Incorporating any of the preceding strategies into your office routine may require uncomfortable changes in comfortable habits. For this reason, and because he is convinced that "evolutionary changes of style are more profitable than revolutionary changes," Ray Cross recommends adopting time management strategies gradually, one at a time. In other words, instead of quickly slaying the two-headed dragon, you should actually try starving it to death. Once you have successfully internalized a new strategy and made that new strategy a comfortable habit, you can then add another, and another, to your repertoire.

And to what end? Darrell Lewis and Tor Dahl state that "It is generally accepted that most managers should be able to clear about 25 percent of their time with little or no drop in current output" — which leads us to part four. Thus cleared, that time becomes discretionary time, leadership time, time for planning and executing Drucker's "right things."

Weldy closes his monograph with a shopping list of

suggested leadership activities that includes detailing a "great idea" for your school, making fresh contacts with students and parents, planning the next year's chief objectives, and writing an article. At this point we shift our attention to another leadership activity worthy of addition to Weldy's list. Having begun the management of time, why not research and implement a program for its corollary — the management of stress?

STRESS MANAGEMENT

Previously it was noted that time and stress management are two strands of the same braid. Not only does mismanagement of the one exacerbate mismanagement of the other, but also specific problem areas in the management of both are identical. For instance, paperwork, telephone and visitor interruptions, excessive meetings, lack of planning time, and procrastination are both timewasters *and* stress producers.

The correlations between time and stress management suggest that the strategies for attacking both would also correlate. And so they do. Like time management, the management of stress requires the following: (1) a shift in attitudes and level of awareness, (2) self-analysis and identification of stressors via the daily stress log, and (3) practical techniques for the management of those stressors identified. As always, awareness and attitude come first.

What precisely is stress? Among the myriad of definitions in print, that advanced by Donald Dudley and Elton Welke is exceptional for its simplicity: stress is "an adaptive response in which your body prepares, or adjusts, to a threatening situation."

Such preparation manifests itself in a host of symptoms, both physiological (increase in heart rate, blood pressure, respiration, and levels of adrenalin) and psychological (irritability, depression, anxiety, withdrawal). Further, stress is integrally related to control: the greater one's sense of powerlessness over the stressor, the greater the stress.

Because one's perception of a "threatening situation" is

often highly subjective (discounting obvious physical calamities), stress itself is a highly subjective phenomenon; it truly is "all in the mind." Consequently, intellectual awareness of and proper emotional attitudes toward stress are even more important than a similar enlightenment toward time, which is a highly objective phenomenon.

One instructive orientation into common stressors and their relative magnitudes is Holmes and Rahe's Social Readjustment Rating Scale. The scale lists forty-three different "life events," ranging from "Death of Spouse" to "Minor Violations of the Law" and assigns each event a numerical value (from a high of 100 to a low of 11) that correlates to the stressfulness of the event. To use the scale, one need merely note which "life events" occurred to him or her during the previous two years and tally the associated numerical values. The significance of the scale lies in the fact that studies have shown a positive correlation between degrees of stress and the probability of incipient illness or accidents, as Dudley and Welke explain:

> Should you accumulate 150 points on the Social Readjustment Rating Scale within a period of two years, there is a 33 per cent probability for you to contract an illness or suffer an accident. When 300 points are accumulated, the probability soars to 66 per cent. At 450 points the probability is almost certain — in the 90 per cent range.

While a personal tally on the rating scale will certainly prove revealing, Walter Gmelch, in his lucid article entitled, "The Principal's Next Challenge: The Twentieth Century Art of Managing Stress," issues this caveat against an overly literal reading of the scale:

> A few points should be kept in mind: first, both pleasant (marriage) and unpleasant (divorce) life events can cause harmful stress; second, no one can escape, nor does anyone necessarily want to escape all these crises, since to some degree stress *is* life; and, third, due to differing abilities to cope, the same event does not have the same impact on all individuals.

The ability to cope is a learned set of skills and is central to the understanding and management of stress. How well do you cope? Dudley and Welke offer a coping quiz that asks questions ranging from "Do people who know you well think

TABLE 1: SOCIAL READJUSTMENT RATING SCALE

Rank	Life Event	Mean Value
1	Death of a Spouse	100
2	Divorce	73
3	Marital Separation	65
4	Jail Term	63
5	Death of Close Family Member	63
6	Personal Injury or Illness	53
7	Marriage	50
8	Fired at Work	47
9	Marital Reconciliation	45
10	Retirement	45
11	Change in Health of Family Member	44
12	Pregnancy	40
13	Sex Difficulties	39
14	Gain of New Family Member	39
15	Business Readjustment	39
16	Change in Financial State	38
17	Death of Close Friend	37
18	Change to Different Line of Work	36
19	Change in Number of Arguments with Spouse	35
20	Mortgage over $10,000	31
21	Foreclosure of Mortgage or Loan	30
22	Change in Responsibilities at Work	29
23	Son or Daughter Leaving Home	29
24	Trouble with In-Laws	29
25	Outstanding Personal Achievement	28
26	Wife Begins or Stops Work	26
27	Begin or End School	26
28	Change in Living Conditions	25
29	Revision of Personal Habits	24
30	Trouble with Boss	23
31	Change in Work Hours or Conditions	20
32	Change in Residence	20
33	Change in Schools	20
34	Change in Recreation	19
35	Change in Church Activities	19
36	Change in Social Activities	18
37	Mortgage or Loan Less than $10,000	17
38	Change in Sleeping Habits	16
39	Change in Number of Family Get-Togethers	15
40	Change in Eating Habits	15
41	Vacation	13
42	Christmas	12
43	Minor Violations of the Law	11

Reprinted with permission from *Journal of Psychosomatic Research*, vol. II, T. H. Holmes, R. H. Rahe, 1967, p. 216, table III, Pergamon Press, Ltd.

you get upset easily?" to "Have you set goals for the future that satisfy you and are realistic?" Your answers should prove as revealing as your tally on the Social Readjustment Rating Scale.

Another instructive exercise is the "Type 'A' Behaving" questionnaire included by Michael Giammatteo and Delores Giammatteo. A high proportion of yes answers to such questions as "I'm frequently in a hurry," "I really enjoy winning and hate to lose" and "my job is the most important thing in my life" indicates the probability of a "Type A" personality, defined by Michael and Delores Giammatteo as "one who is always pushing, doing, creating, initiating, and who may be headed toward an early death or heart attack."

After orienting yourself to the subject of stress in general and personal stress factors in particular, you'll want to take stock of the attitudes with which you confront your working day. Constructive attitudes for the management of stress will be discussed later. For now, be aware of the following attitudes that have been variously identified (by Michael and Delores Giammatteo, Ari Kiev, and C. Eugene Walker) as promoters of stress: authoritarianism, intolerance, being overly concerned with what "should be" rather than with what "is," indecisiveness, worry, perfectionism and searching for the one "perfect" solution to every problem, "stockpiling hurts," magnifying minor irritants, failure to communicate feelings, believing that you are a victim of fate and of your feelings, and needing and seeking love and approval from everyone.

Although this list of negative attitudes is by no means a definitive one, familiarity with these provides one more orientation into the subject of stress and one more preparation for self-analysis and the identification of specific stressors via the daily stress log.

DAILY STRESS LOG

The purpose of tracking sources of stress for several weeks is the same as that for tracking time: to become aware of specific problem areas and their patterns of reoccurrence. The stress log suggested by Gmelch in *Release from Stress* is reprinted here as a suggested format (see exercise 1) but, as with

EXERCISE 1: STRESS LOG

Stress can come from a single dramatic incident (Isolated Stress), or from a cumulation of less dramatic related incidents (Synergetic Stress). For one week, at the end of each working day, describe:

1. The most stressful single incident that occurred on your job (confronting a staff member, etc.)
2. The most stressful series of related incidents that occurred on your job (frequent telephone interruptions, etc.)
3. How your day went. Indicate from "one" (not very stressful) to "ten" (very stressful) the approximate level of your stress for each day.

1) Single Incident	2) Series of Related Incidents	3) Daily Stress Level

Monday
Date:

Tuesday
Date:

Wednesday
Date:

Thursday
Date:

Friday
Date:

From *Beyond Stress to Effective Management* by Walter Gmelch. To be published in Spring 1982 by John Wiley & Sons. Used by permission.

the daily time log, the form is less important than that you do this preliminary exercise and do it in writing.

After keeping a stress log for several weeks, you might want to compare your stressors with Gmelch's administrative stress index — a list of thirty-five typical stressors identified by educational administrators, including "preparing and allocating budget resources," "trying to resolve differences between/among students," and "being involved in the collective bargaining process." Of these thirty-five stressors, Gmelch identified and ranked the following top ten:

1. Complying with state, federal, and organizational rules and policies
2. Feeling that meetings take up too much time
3. Trying to complete reports and other paperwork on time
4. Trying to gain financial support for programs
5. Trying to resolve personnel conflicts
6. Evaluating staff members' performance
7. Having to make decisions that affect the lives of individual people that I know (colleagues, staff members)
8. Feelings that I have too heavy a workload, one that I cannot possibly finish during the normal work day
9. Imposing excessively high expectations on myself
10. Being interrupted frequently by telephone calls

The results of Gmelch's study correspond to those derived from a stress survey of principals in a large Canadian city. As reported by Kenneth Washington, the survey "placed demands by central administration in first place, followed by supervision of teachers . . . relationships with parents, government regulations, student problems, and instructional problems."

A third study, by Robert Koff and his colleagues, reinforces and refines those presented by Gmelch and Washington. Using methodology similar to that of the Social Readjustment Rating Scale, the study factored and weighted four areas of stress for elementary, middle, and secondary school principals. Conflicts with teachers were consistently ranked as the highest stressor. Irregular events with severe consequences — events in which the administrators felt threatened and powerless — were rated the next most stressful. (Examples include teacher strikes, involuntary transfers, bad publicity, threats and assaults, and legal actions against the school.) Student conflicts were rated below these, though the stress therein increased significantly from elementary to high school. Finally, routine management tasks were consistently ranked as the lowest, most manageable stressor.

Both Gmelch and Koff and his colleagues echoed what was noted earlier, that stress is integrally related to feelings of powerlessness — feeling out of control. Successful stress management requires not just the identification of your stressors but also the categorizing of them into those that are within your control and those that are not. The distinction will determine your strategy for attacking the stressor, though *all* the various strategies share one trait in common: all return a measure of control to their user.

MANAGING CONTROLLABLE STRESSORS

In any discussion of stress management, one strategy always highlighted is that of time management. Properly executed, time management creates the balance and control in one's life that Alan Lakein repeatedly emphasizes.

But time management can be subsumed by a larger, more generalized concept, that of "pacing," of consciously regulating the ebb and flow of your life. Time management will help you to do that. So will familiarity with and proper use of the Social Readjustment Rating Scale; for instance, if you are aware that you've recently experienced a high number of life change events, you should consider consciously forgoing another controllable change — moving to a new neighborhood, for example, or taking classes toward your Ph.D.

You can also pace yourself by regulating what Donald Dudley and Elton Welke refer to as naturally occurring cycles of "activation and withdrawal." While it is normal to alternate between periods of outward-reaching activity and periods of quiet renewal, the authors caution against abrupt swings between either extreme:

If your customary manner is type A, fast-paced, try to slow down by mild degrees in a uniform way rather than suddenly embracing total relaxation between outbursts of activity. In the same way, if you are a classic type B, relaxed and calm, try to modestly pick up your life tempo uniformly across periods of both work and play.

Another strategy for managing stress — problem-solving — is discussed at length in chapter 12. The applicability of problem-solving to stress management lies in the fact that delays in confronting problems inevitably tend to magnify them. Such procrastination not only allows the problem situation to deteriorate, but also allows mental mushrooming of the problem — mental exaggeration that is disproportionate to the problem's actual severity.

A third strategy in the management of stress — control of communications — is also allotted a full chapter elsewhere. The importance of skillful communication to stress management becomes clearer as one recalls that authoritarianism (excessively directive communications), intolerance (excessively negative communications), and failure to express feelings (excessively repressive communications) are three key promoters of stress. It's important to recognize that the words you use — and choose not to use — don't merely describe reality; they create it.

Additionally, you may want to consult the list of fourteen "Questions for Accepting and Clarifying" offered by Michael and Delores Giammatteo. Designed to facilitate open communications in even the most problematical situation, these questions ("What do you mean when you say that ...?" "Have you been feeling this way long?" "What would be examples of your idea?" "What other possibilities are there?") are open-ended, problem-oriented, and promote active listening — a primary comunication skill.

Job and role clarification also contribute significantly to the management of stress. A job can be inherently stressful (hence worsening each daily occasion of stress) if one's role is unclear or subject to conflicting expectations, or if the job involves too much work, too little work, too little opportunity for achievement, and/or inadequate performance evaluation.

"Preventive management," assert James Quick and

Jonathan Quick, is the key to reducing this kind of stress. While the authors recommend several specific management tools for the clarification and restructuring of jobs/roles, any process that analyzes and sets out, in writing, the expectations inherent to each job is useful. Peter Drucker's well-known system of "Management by Objectives" is a prime example.

Finally, controllable stressors can be confronted one at a time via formalized methods of frontal attack. Walter Gmelch, in *Release from Stress*, offers the following systematic procedure:

1. Identify your most bothersome stressors and select *one* to resolve
2. Search for the causes of this stressful event
3. Generate a set of possible solutions to remedy the causes
4. Specify a plan of action you will take to alleviate one cause
5. Develop a timetable to implement your plan of action
6. Set a date and method for how you will follow up and evaluate the effectiveness of your plan
7. Investigate the potential problems or unintended consequences (additional stress) your action plan may have created

Similar to Gmelch's seven steps is the ten-point process outlined by Michael and Delores Giammatteo for the management of a specific category of stressor — the interpersonal conflict. The methods differ in that the latter authors ask that you consider your antagonist's "probable reaction" to each of the various solutions that you generate, and then that you select one or two solutions that would be mutually acceptable.

At the risk of belaboring the obvious, one last management strategy for controllable stressors is worthy of mention before moving on to the subject of uncontrollable stressors: that strategy is simply to ask for help. Management consultants, self-help books, professional associations, central administration, your professional peer group, the school advisory council or other parent committees, and professional analysts can all help to generate solutions to stressful situations. Don't suffer in silence. Use them.

MANAGING UNCONTROLLABLE STRESSORS

When stressors are beyond your personal control (for example, statewide budget cuts, a personality conflict with your immediate superior), you must seek to reduce stress in the one area left to you: within yourself. This is accomplished through a series of strategies that build up your resistance to stress — that innoculate you, so to speak, and increase your level of tolerance.

General physical health and well-being are fundamental here. The importance of regular exercise, good eating habits, and periods of recreation are clichés that nevertheless merit repeating.

Because stress is such a subjective phenomenon, a variety of mental skills work to fight stress on its home ground — in the mind. Many of these skills — meditation, biofeedback, yoga, the relaxation response — increase one's inner sense of calm well-being. Additionally, C. Eugene Walker suggests self-hypnosis, both to produce a state of calmness and to creatively work out problems while relaxed. "Mental imagery" — the conscious production of positive mental scenes — is also often suggested as a means of manipulating one's sympathetic nervous system into a state of relaxation.

James Manuso recommends the learning of a "quieting response" — a reaction to minor daily irritations in which "one takes two deliberate deep breaths, paying attention to relaxing the jaw, the shoulders and tongue, and one tells himself he will not permit his body to get involved in this. This breaks the sequence of the stress reponse."

Similarly, Walker recommends "thought stopping" as a means of quieting internal anxiety. In thought stopping, one learns to banish obsessive or worrisome thoughts by mentally shouting "Stop!" and then insisting to oneself that "I'm not going to think about that now." After this mental interruption, the individual then consciously seeks an alternative thought or activity with which to become involved.

"Systematic desensitization," a formalized method of dealing with anxiety-producing situations developed by Dr. Joseph Wolpe, is discussed at length by Walker. Briefly, this process involves the indentification of a habitually stressful situation (confronting a hostile antagonist, for example, or taking a test) and then the listing of specific instances or variants of this stressful situation. Next, one practices the relaxation response or some other method of inducing total relaxation and, thus composed, exposes himself to the previously identified stressors, one at a time, beginning with the least stressful variant and gradually working toward the most stressful. While reading the descriptions, the subject visualizes them carefully and does not proceed to the next until each instance is visualized *without* an accompanying physiological stress response (increased heartbeat, flushing, nausea). This process is repeated regularly until the subject's habitual response to the stressful situation is successfully unlearned. Of this procedure, Walker claims that "if done properly, it works almost every time."

Since we began by discussing attitudes, it's appropriate that we circle back as we approach our close. The attitude most relevant to this section is *tolerance* — tolerance of individuals unlike ourselves and of situations unlike those we desire. In support, Michael and Delores Giammatteo state that "tolerance demands serenity on our part to become aware and then to make decisions about our response to the environment, people, and philosophies in it."

Walker goes beyond attitudes to the affirmation that relaxed living requires a healthy, thoughtful development of personal values — values that are oriented toward an enriched, contributing, and accepting lifestyle. Echoing the philosophy of Viktor Frankl, Walker affirms the necessity for a meaningful life: "This is what separates man from other animals. The animal seeks pleasure and conquest, but meaning is unknown to him. The essence of man is meaning."

CONCLUSION

The successful management of time and stress cannot be exercised in a vacuum. Nearly all the strategies, and even some of the attitudes, require a team approach. Minimally, that team consists of you and your secretary, since the secretary is the administrator's partner in production or, as Weldy intones, "his ever-present time guardian, his reminder of things to do, his appointment maker, his interceptor of interruptors, his buffer and protector."

Programs for time and stress management should encompass the leader's support staff and colleagues and, better yet, even filter upwards. Many of the time/stress management strategies discussed — delegation, role clarification and restructuring, rejecting monkeys, communication skills — are dependent upon contact with and cooperation from the leader's colleagues.

But more significantly, these programs involve your coworkers because you are in a leadership role and are therefore — for better or for worse — a role model whose attitudes and practices set the tone for the entire office. And as a role model, your staff can perceive you in one of three ways: passively ineffectual in the management of time and stress; actively detrimental in the management of time and stress (a time-waster and stress-carrier); or worthy of emulation in the management of time and stress — a true leader.

Managing time. Managing stress. Concentrating on effectiveness, contribution, and purpose. What results from accepting these challenges? As usual, Peter Drucker says it well:

> What is being developed here is not information, but character: foresight, self-reliance, courage. What is being developed here, in other words, is leadership — not the leadership of brilliance and genuis, to be sure, but the much more modest yet more enduring leadership of dedication, determination, and serious purpose.

CHAPTER 11
MANAGING CONFLICT
John Lindelow

Conflict is an inevitable and natural part of human existence. It is as surely a companion of life as change, death, and taxes.

Conflict exists on many levels and takes many different forms. Within society, there are focal points of conflict, where numerous "forces" seem to clash time and again. One of these focal points is the public school principalship. As James Lipham and James Hoeh, Jr. state, "All institutional roles, particularly those in public institutions, are subject to numerous sources and types of disagreement or conflict. But few seem so fraught with conflict potential as that of the public school principal."

Because conflict is such a pervasive and unavoidable part of the principal's role, it is important that the principal learn to manage conflict effectively and turn it toward constructive ends. To do this, principals must understand conflict — what it is, where it comes from, and how it develops and dissipates. They must, in addition, possess the skills necessary to manage conflict effectively.

THE VALUE OF CONFLICT

As Stephen Robbins notes, the word *conflict* has a negative connotation for most individuals. Indeed, many if not most conflict situations are disturbing to participants and observers alike, and many conflicts lead to destructive ends.

But as Robbins and numerous other authors emphasize, conflict is a two-sided coin. Conflict can indeed be disruptive and destructive. But it can also be a source of creativity and constructive action. Many thoughtful writers even consider conflict to be "the Mother of creativity."

Warren Schmidt and Robert Tannenbaum stress that "differences among people should not be regarded as inherently 'good' or 'bad'." Sometimes conflicts produce important benefits for an organization, and sometimes they disrupt an organization.

"Until quite recently," Stephen Bailey observes, "western man has suffered a kind of Hobbesian anxiety: a concatenation of beliefs that all conflicts are bad." In recent years, however, conflict has been recognized as a valuable source of organizational renewal. Thus, "some conflicts are resolved only at the price of mildew," Bailey wryly notes. "But other conflicts," he warns, "unless quickly resolved in some fundamental sense, can destroy an organization."

Writers in the field of organizational development also recognize the potential value of conflict. According to Richard Schmuck, Philip Runkel, Jane Arends, and Richard Arends, for example, "some conflicts are natural and inevitable and may even provide a creative tension that has the effect of improving school performance." Other conflicts, these authors are quick to add, can seriously weaken a school's instructional program and should be resolved promptly.

Stephen Robbins — a strong believer in the value of conflict — has even included in his book a chapter on stimulating conflict within organizations by disrupting communications and altering organizational structure. "Organizations that do not stimulate conflict," he states, "increase the probability of stagnant thinking, inadequate decisions, and at the extreme, organizational demise." Research support for this contention comes from Jay Hall and Martha Williams (quoted by Robbins), who found that "established groups tended to improve more when there was conflict among members than when there was fairly close agreement."

Thus, the effective school administrator should not seek simply to *resolve* all conflicts that arise in the school; rather, he or she should attempt to *manage* conflict by maximizing constructive conflict and minimizing destructive conflict.

In the next section, the nature of conflict will be described and explored. With a better understanding of conflict, the reader can move on to the final section, which describes a variety of conflict management techniques.

UNDERSTANDING CONFLICT

Just what is conflict? Webster's Third New International Dictionary defines it as the "clash, competition, or mutual interference of opposing or incompatible forces or qualities (as ideas, interests, wills)." A similar definition is provided by Robbins, who describes conflict as "all kinds of opposition or antagonistic interaction."

Conflict according to these general definitions can thus include disharmony within a single individual, interpersonal conflict, intergroup conflict (including international conflict), conflicts between philosophies or ideas, conflicts between people and external forces, and so forth. Such a broad view of conflict illustrates how all-pervasive conflict is, but here a narrower definition of conflict is called for.

The main focus in this chapter will be on social conflict — conflict between individuals and conflict between groups common to the school environment. Discussion of intrapersonal conflict and of larger forms of societal and political conflict will be excluded. Of course, these kinds of conflicts can, at times, have significant influences on a school's operation; but the management of conflict within the school is obviously of more immediate interest to educational administrators.

Numerous writers have gone beyond simple definitions of conflict and have sought to more fully characterize conflict by identifying *types* of conflict, *sources* of conflict, and *stages* of conflict. These three views of conflict — discussed in turn below — are valuable for gaining a better understanding of conflict and conflict management in school settings.

TYPES OF CONFLICT

One typology of conflict already mentioned is that of constructive and destructive conflict. Constructive or "functional" conflicts, as Robbins states, "support the goals of the organization and improve performance." Destructive or "dysfunctional" conflicts, on the other hand, hinder organizational performance and should be "eradicated."

"The demarcation between functional dysfunctional is neither clear nor precise," Robbins continues.

> No level of conflict can be adopted at face value as acceptable or unacceptable....The level that creates healthy and positive involvement towards one group's

277

goals, may in another group or in the same group at another time, be highly dysfunctional, requiring immediate conciliatory attention by the administrator.

Schmidt and Tannenbaum classify conflict according to the four kinds of issues over which people can disagree. First, disagreement can occur over *facts,* as when two parties "are aware of different pieces of relevant information, accept or reject different information as factual, or have differing impressions of their respective power and authority."

Second, disagreement can occur over *goals* — "the desirable objectives of a department, division, section, or of a specific position within the organization." Third, people can disagree over *methods* — the procedures and strategies for getting from here to there. And fourth, disagreement can occur over *values* or *ethics* — the "way power should be exercised."

Schmuck and his colleagues explain a similar conflict classification system that they call the "S-T-P" typology. The S refers to the *situation* or the "realities of a current situation." The T refers to *target,* which includes goals and objectives as well as values. And the P refers to *proposals,* the strategies for moving from the present situation to a desired future situation.

Another way of classifying conflict is by its severity or quality, as Bailey suggests. At the first level of conflict severity, there is "an endless simmer of petty personality conflicts reflecting the chemistry and foibles of interacting humans." The administrator can control these conflicts with such techniques as separating antagonists, redefining roles, expressing confidence in both antagonists in each other's presence, and appealing "to the maturity, good sense, and common organizational goals of everyone concerned." Ultimately, says Bailey, the wise administrator "settles for a low hum of contentiousness as a necessary — and at times healthy — noise of the human condition."

The second level of conflict severity involves differences over program and budget matters. "These are the daily-diet conflicts that most educational administrators spend the overwhelming part of their time adjudicating and managing," states Bailey. At this level, the conflict management tools of the behavioral sciences (many of which are discussed in the next section) are most useful.

Level three of conflict severity is that of "revolutionary" conflict, which involves "the legitimacy of regime" rather than program priorities. The wisest course in such crisis situations, Bailey offers, is to redress the grievances that are stimulating the revolution. Techniques useful at level two are less likely to be of value at level three:

> At the height of a battle over the legitimacy of the system, even sensitivity groups or face-to-face problem-solving sessions are unlikely to pacify militant blacks, apoplectic Birchers, relentless liberated women, striking teachers, or draft-defying young men.

SOURCES OF CONFLICT

A fuller understanding of conflict can be gained by considering conflict's origins. Three primary sources within the school can be identified: comunications problems, organizational structure, and "human" factors, such as personality.

One common communications model, outlined by Robbins, has six parts: the communication source, encoder, message, channel, decoder, and receiver. "The message is encoded (conversion of an idea or thought to symbolic form), passed by way of some medium (channel) to the receiver who retranslates (decodes) the message initiated by the sender." Distortion or miscommunication can occur at any point in this process, leading, at times, to conflict.

Two conflicting parties may have access to different information or different forms of the "same" information (for example, the first and second drafts of a report). One or both parties may have incomplete or distorted information on an issue. If both have the same information, each may be interpreting it differently because of different backgrounds or philosophies. Semantic problems may also exist.

One party might assume that he or she knows what the other has said, because "I've heard it before." One or both parties may be filtering out important statements and hearing only what he or she wants to hear. Each party may hold assumptions about the other's ulterior motives, or may be emotionally upset at the time of communication.

In cases where communications problems appear to be

the source of conflict, simply bringing the conflicting parties together in a problem-solving session (as discussed in the next section) can often resolve the conflict.

At times, however, it may be very difficult for one party to "hear" what the other is saying, even if repeated numerous times. In such cases, communications exercises such as paraphrasing (as discussed in chapter 8) may be of help.

The structure of the organization is another possible source of conflict. For example, size "has been found to correlate with amounts of conflict," according to Nebgen. "The larger the school, the greater the number of conflicts and the higher the rate of conflict intensity."

Robbins, however, reports on a comprehensive study of 250 separate organizational units that "could not support the size-conflict relationship." He concludes that size may indeed stimulate conflict, but the seriousness and intensity of conflict are also affected by many other variables.

The argument that size does make a difference, however, appears sound, as Robbins explains:

> Size alone would restrict communication, impede interaction and foster separateness. Therefore, it can be generalized that as a structure increases in size, goals will become less clear, relationships will by necessity become more formal, specialization will create increased pressure to protect one's bailiwick, and more opportunities for distortion will occur as information must be passed through a greater number of levels.

Bureaucratic qualities can also affect climate. One study reported by Robbins found that less job routinization increased the likelihood of conflict. "As job structure is reduced," states Robbins, "the probability of conflict would increase as the job becomes less programmed and surrounded by greater uncertainty." Higher levels of specialization also appear to correlate with increased conflicts.

Other research reported by Robbins indicates that established groups "develop more constructive conflict than ad hoc formations." The same research showed that established group members more frequently attacked the *ideas* of their colleagues, whereas ad hoc group members more often attacked each other as *persons*.

Several studies reported by Robbins show that the rate of conflict increases with increased participation in decision-making. Although the overall number of conflicts went up with participation, however, the number of major incidents of conflict went down. Participation in decision-making, Robbins suggests, "permits a greater opportunity for the expression of existing disputes and allows more occasions for disagreements to arise." The same opportunity to express minor conflicts, however, may "prevent minor irritations from developing into major incidents."

Another study discussed by Robbins indicates that "power can facilitate coordination and concurrently reduce conflict." Up to a certain limit, increasing a school principal's formal authority can reduce conflict between the principal and staff.

On the other hand, conflict does arise in organizations in which a less powerful group attempts to force more powerful members to give up power. "Imbalances of organizational power by themselves may not initiate conflict," Robbins concludes, "but when attempts are made to correct perceived inequities, hostility is apparently stimulated."

In addition to communications and structural sources, conflict can arise from "human factors" within an organization. Communications and structural factors can, in part, be controlled by an administrator. Human factors, however, are largely beyond the administrator's control.

According to Robbins, three personality traits correlate with increased conflict: high authoritarianism, high dogmatism, and low self-esteem. Organizational members' dissatisfaction with role requirements is also a source of conflict. Finally, one of the most powerful "human" sources of conflict is differing value or goal systems, which are quite often impossible to change and can only be "managed."

STAGES OF CONFLICT

Another means of diagnosing conflict is by examining its dynamics. Schmidt and Tannenbaum identify the following five stages of conflict development:

1. *The phase of anticipation,* in which, for example, a manager knows of an impending change and projects its consequences.

2. *The phase of conscious, but unexpressed, difference.* Word leaks out about the change, and a feeling of tension begins to build in the organization.
3. *The phase of discussion.* Information is formally presented about the change. Differing opinions begin to emerge.
4. *The phase of open dispute.* Differences become more sharply and explicitly defined.
5. *The phase of open conflict.* Each disputant tries to force his or her view on the others. The only possible outcomes now are win, lose, or compromise.

Other authors dissect the dynamics of conflict differently, and most include a stage of "relaxation" after the conflict has peaked.

Conflict management is usually more effective when the administrator intervenes in the early stages of conflict. As the conflict develops through different stages, different management techniques become useful. "Techniques of prevention and resolution adequate for the incipient stages of conflict are unlikely to be useful during the crisis stage," states Bailey, "and they tend to be irrelevant at the stage of relaxation."

> When conflict is incipient, or in early stages of virulence, a sensitive administrator may release dangerous tension with a special meeting or a joke. When the storm is raging, certain types of meetings become impossible, and the very notion of jokes becomes obscene. When exhaustion is followed by a new-found harmony, the administrator's best therapy may be "natural healing," rather than any conscious strategy.

TECHNIQUES FOR MANAGING CONFLICT

According to Stephen Robbins, there are three primary philosophies of conflict management. The first, which Robbins calls the traditional philosophy, prevailed from the late nineteenth century and into the 1940s. In this philosophy, "*all* conflicts were seen as destructive and it was management's role to rid the organization of them."

The second philosophy, the "behavioral" view, started to take hold a few decades ago, and, says Robbins, "unfortunately is still the generally accepted approach to managing conflict in the majority of organizations." In the behavioral view, conflict is accepted as a normal part of an organization's functioning. The problem, says Robbins, is that conflict is still viewed in a negative light, and thus the behavioralists concentrate almost solely on finding ways of resolving conflict.

A more positive approach, says Robbins, is the "interactionist" philosophy, which "recognizes the absolute necessity of conflict," explicitly encourages conflict at times, "defines conflict management to include stimulation as well as resolution methods," and "considers the management of conflict as a major responsibility of all administrators." Indeed, an increase in constructive conflict may be called for in some organizations that have lost their spark of creativity or in which apathy has reached epidemic proportions.

The preponderance of conflict management techniques discussed in this section, however, deal either with resolving conflict or with channeling potentially destructive conflict into constructive conflict. This emphasis on conflict resolution recognizes that the public schools are already in a state of rapid change, with concomitant conflict; that few administrators feel the need to stimulate more conflict, since there is already an overabundance in the schools; and that most administrators are more interested in learning how to manage the conflict that already exists in the schools. There may be times, however, when "stirring the pot" may be the best remedy for an ailing school or district.

Administrators should use a variety of approaches and techniques for managing conflict. "No one method or outcome should be considered to be automatically 'best' for every situation," as Edgar Kelly states. "The resolution of conflict is always unique to the setting in which conflict occurs."

Any administrator who attempts to use the same techniques for different kinds of conflicts, says Bailey,

> is either a genius or a fool. For example, assume that a superintendent observes a raging conflict within his board of education. Quiet catalysis in the form of friendly visits to the homes of contending leaders may be the most useful approach. If the conflict is between

two subordinate principals arguing about bus routes, a structured confrontation may be desirable. If the struggle is between the local John Birch Society and the local chapter of the American Association of University Women over sex education, public rhetoric and careful and elaborate coalition building may be the superintendent's most effective tactic. The point is that such stratagems are not usually interchangeable. Conflict-resolution styles and techniques useful in one context may be quite disastrous in another.

When a conflict occurs, state Diane Frey and Joseph Young, "most people are impulsive about their manner of resolving it. They usually choose a method learned at an early age from significant others in their environment." Administrators, Frey and Young advise, should develop an awareness of the conflict management styles they habitually use and then broaden their repertoire to include other techniques.

Even a thorough knowledge of the techniques outlined here is not enough, though. The administrator must ultimately master the "art of conflict management" in the field, as Bailey rightly observes.

AVOIDING CONFLICT

"The most natural manner in which all animals, including man, eliminate conflict is to avoid it," states Robbins. Avoidance techniques include ignoring conflict, procrastination, isolation, withholding feelings or beliefs, staffing with like-minded people, and smoothing. Although avoiding conflict may seem like "the wrong thing to do," it is often a valuable short-term alternative.

Whenever possible, humans withdraw from conflict and ignore the situation if they can. This instinctive response, however, is not always in need of correction. Often, events will reach their own state of equilibrium, and intervention may be either unnecessary or counterproductive.

A variation of ignoring is procrastination, or "deciding not to decide," which may, at times, also be a valuable short-term management strategy. The administrator may need more information or time to understand a situation or may be waiting for the situation to take clearer form before taking action.

Taking a "wait and see" attitude may be the best strategy in these cases.

Deciding when to intervene and "uncover" conflict can be difficult. The administrator must decide whether bringing out a conflict will have destructive or constructive consequences. Low levels of communications and problem-solving skills and low levels of trust among school staff may well engender destructive outcomes. "Uncovering conflict, then, involves a certain risk," as Schmuck and his colleagues note.

A manager can avoid conflict between two potentially explosive individuals by isolating them in the organization so that they seldom interact. Two individuals may do this themselves, as Robbins notes, and stake out distinct, nonoverlapping territories for themselves. Often, an administrator and subordinate will use this technique. "In those cases where the employee sees no other viable alternative to his present job and his superior finds the employee's performance to be satisfactory, we can expect this avoidance technique to be effective," states Robbins.

In cases where two individuals find it impossible to avoid each other, they may withhold stating their feelings or beliefs in the presence of the other. Such mutual ignoring, of course, only conceals differences, but as Herbert Shepard (quoted by Robbins) has observed, this technique is probably "society's chief instrument for handling conflict." Despite its drawbacks, it does avoid overt confrontation.

Another means of avoiding conflict is to staff the school with like-minded people. This approach may be appropriate in schools that are extremely conflict torn because of diverse viewpoints. But "the manager who uses this approach consistently runs the risk of reducing the total creativity of his staff," state Schmidt and Tannenbaum. "When everyone in the room thinks the same thing, no one is thinking very much."

"Smoothing" is the process of playing down differences between conflicting parties while emphasizing their common interests. Issues about which there are differences are not discussed, while areas of agreement are stressed. Although smoothing is often relied on, says Robbins, it is "only a superficial resolution. The differences, which are not explicitly confronted, still remain, and it becomes only a matter of time before these dissimilarities arise again."

Avoiding conflicts in the ways outlined above can be valuable for managing conflict in some situations. "As a general rule, however, a conflict avoided, regardless of its cause, is only temporarily resolved," as Nebgen states.

SUPERORDINATE GOALS

A superordinate goal is a highly valued goal that two conflicting parties can reach only by cooperating with each other. "The cooperative environment grows as effort is directed away from concern with separate and independent units to recognition that the conflicting units are part of a larger group," Robbins explains. Superordinate goals are quite popular in the applied conflict management literature, Robbins adds, because of their promise of "win-win" solutions.

Several difficulties exist, however. First, actual superordinate goals that supersede the conflicting parties' individual goals are difficult to create. Second, the mutual trust and confidence needed for conflicting parties to work together is often absent. Finally, says Robbins, the effectiveness of superordinate goals may be severely limited in cases where conflict originates from personal-behavior differences. Nevertheless, this technique can be useful in some instances.

CREATIVE PROBLEM-SOLVING

> Had the six blind men who came into contact with different parts of the same elephant pooled their information, they would have arrived at a more accurate description of the animal. In the same way, many problems can be seen clearly, wholly, and in perspective only if the individuals who see different aspects can come together and pool their information.
>
> Schmidt and Tannenbaum

Mutual problem-solving, some writers suggest, is often the best means for resolving social conflict. Conflicts often exist because of a lack of or problems in communicating.

Bringing conflicting parties together to discuss their differences can, if properly managed, lead to increased understanding, clarification of differences, and constructive collaboration.

Schmidt and Tannenbaum provide several guidelines for conducting an effective problem-solving session. Many of these suggestions are discussed more fully in chapters 8 and 9. The administrator should:

- Welcome the existence of differences within the organization as a valuable resource
- Listen with understanding rather than evaluation
- Recognize and accept the feelings of the individuals involved
- Clarify the nature of the conflict
- Indicate who will make the decision being discussed
- Suggest procedures and ground rules for resolving the differences
- Create appropriate vehicles for communication among the disputing parties
- Encourage the separation of ideas from the people who propose them

Problem-solving is especially valuable for resolving conflicts that arise from communications problems. In a problem-solving session, a great deal of communication takes place. Facts, goals, and strategies are discussed and clarified. Positions become understood. Areas for potential compromise are discovered. Faulty perceptions are corrected.

When group members have varied opinions on some issue yet are not entrenched in their positions, problem-solving sessions can be used to channel the energy generated by conflict into creative solution making. As Robbins notes, however, "problem solving is inherently weak in regard to conflicts based on differing value systems — one of the primary sources of conflict." Problem-solving can elucidate the differences in two value systems, but argument can rarely alter deeply held beliefs. Forced problem-solving between two parties with incompatible value systems, Robbins observes, "only widens the differences and entrenches each of the participants deeper into his position — for all intents and purposes probably increasing, and certainly not lessening, the level of conflict."

287

COMPROMISE AND USE OF A THIRD PARTY

Compromise techniques, states Robbins, "make up the major portion of resolution methods developed in the literature." Compromise can be generated internally as in a problem-solving session, or it can be externally generated by a third-party mediator or arbitrator.

Compromise does not result in clear winners and losers, and it requires each conflicting party to give up something. "The idea is that it is better to have half a loaf than none at all," says Nebgen. Compromise is the norm in legislative decision-making. And unlike avoidance techniques, Robbins states, "it does result in a decision, though not an optimum one for either party."

Compromise works best, states Nebgen, when "the cooperative interests of the bargainers are stronger than their competitive interests" and when both parties have ample resources with which to bargain.

Often, a building administrator will find himself or herself in the position of a third-party arbitrator or mediator. Two individuals or groups will present the principal with conflicting ideas or requests. The groups may ask the principal to make a decision, or the principal — exercising his or her positional power — may decide to make the decision. The principal can act as a mediator, clarifying and facilitating communication between the two parties, or can act as an arbitrator, making the final decision after both sides have presented their claims. And if the principal is one of the conflicting parties, he or she may call for a neutral third party to help settle the dispute.

AUTHORITATIVE COMMAND

In hierarchical organizational structures, states Robbins, "the authority of a higher-ranking individual is the most frequent resolvent of interpersonal or intergroup conflict." In using authoritative command for intergroup conflicts, the principal is, in effect, deciding to be the third-party arbitrator. When the principal uses authority to settle disputes with subordinates, he or she is simply using the traditional power of position to overrule the subordinate.

"Individuals in organizations, with rare exceptions, recognize and accept the authority of their superiors," states Robbins. "Though they may not be in agreement with these decisions, they will almost always abide by them."

Authoritative command can solve conflicts quickly and neatly. The overuse or misuse of authoritative command, without meaningful input from subordinates, can foment a more serious kind of conflict — challenge to the legitimacy of authority.

The use of force to settle disputes, states Nebgen, "may be most usefully applied to conflicts which arise out of differing goals or values of special interest groups and interpersonal provocation." If the opposing parties are firmly entrenched in their positions and there is little chance for compromise, "only forcing the issue will settle the problem."

As emphasized throughout this handbook, the effective leader utilizes a variety of leadership styles in managing the school, including, at times, an authoritative style. And when the leader decides to settle an issue through authoritative command, or by any other means for that matter, he or she should clearly communicate how the matter will be settled *before* the process begins.

ALTERING ORGANIZATIONAL STRUCTURE

Conflicts can often be successfully managed by making changes in the structure of the organization. Group members can be transferred or exchanged, special coordinating or conflict management positions can be created, the communications process can be facilitated with interlocking team structures, grievance and appeal systems can be created, and the number of subunits in the organization can be altered.

Separating conflicting parties, as discussed earlier, is one means of reducing conflict. In some cases, however — as when two departments or other subunits are in conflict — it may make more sense to *increase* contact between the conflicting parties. When this is done, barriers to communication are often reduced.

Robbins cites the example of a major company in which two departments were in continual conflict. The management had the two supervisors switch jobs for six months, a move that "promoted greater understanding and reduced intergroup conflict as the modified views filtered down" through each department.

Another means of enhancing communication between conflicting departments is to create a position of "coordinator" of the two groups. The coordinator would perform functions in both departments and integrate their functions.

Improved intraorganizational communication can also be gained by creating a system of interlocking management teams in the school or district, as Schmuck and his colleagues suggest. The advantage of such a "multiunit school," state these authors, "is that it offers a communicative link between each hierarchical level and each formal subsystem." In such schools, everyone "knows someone who can communicate directly with the leadership team, and this arrangement permits direct managerial contact with those who may be in conflict."

Small organizations, such as elementary schools, may deal with conflict through regular administrative channels. But more complex organizations, such as school districts, "should have special formal structures alongside the regular managerial hierarchy for this purpose," state Schmuck and cowriters.

Special grievance and appeal systems can be designed to allow organizational members to challenge the rulings of superiors. "By giving the subordinate an alternative to unsatisfactory directives of his superior," states Robbins, this technique "can act to reduce conflict by requiring the superior to rethink the legitimacy of the demands he makes upon his subordinates."

Some research has shown that as organizations become more complex, more conflict occurs. Thus, minimizing the number of administrative subunits may serve to reduce conflict. This approach, however, may be overly simplistic; a complex organization may well function smoothly if designed appropriately.

Too much stress on unity and common organizational goals may also be a source of conflict, state Schmuck and colleagues, especially "when the philosophies and instructional styles of faculty members are highly varied." Conflict in such schools may be successfully managed "by allowing for planned pluralism or school structures in which there are several teams, houses within schools, even schools within schools."

PREPARING FOR CONFLICT MANAGEMENT

An early step in learning to manage conflict, Frey and Young point out, is for the individual to become aware of what conflict management styles he or she already uses. Next, the administrator should increase his or her awareness of other possible management techniques.

Numerous exercises have been designed by organizational development specialists (see Schmuck and colleagues) and others interested in the communications process (see chapter 8) to help breed an awareness of communications and conflict management processes. Exercises of this sort, says Bailey, "are useful in sensitizing the uninitiated to the varied worlds of conflict management."

"But alas," Bailey continues, "most are as effective as learning to swim on the sand. And many lessons learned in sociodramas are forgotten in the heat and confusion of reality."

Bailey believes that field experience is the best way to develop conflict management skills. Thus, many successful administrators of tomorrow, he states, may come from large families "where from infancy they have participated in bouncing ego brawls and have learned the hard way the value not of unanimity" but of "multanimity" — the "philosophical acceptance and delight in variety."

In preparing administrators for conflict management, Bailey adds, "it can be said that case studies, sensitivity training, and simulation are better than formal theory, that novels and plays are better than textbooks, and that apprenticeships and direct responsibility are better than anything else." In short, says Bailey, in the field of conflict management "we learn by doing."

SOME FINAL ADVICE

Bailey, in the final section of his excellent essay on conflict management, offers additional valuable suggestions for successfully managing conflict. First, the administrator should breed an awareness of what is "bugging" colleagues, teachers, and students. The administrator's ability "to recognize legitimate grievances and patent injustices and his willingness to respond to new hungers, new values, and new norms by reasonableness and open-mindedness are essential if conflicts are to be precluded and ultimately resolved in any basic sense."

Second, collective judgment should be substituted wherever possible for personal discretion. "The wise administrator knows how to create baffles and buffers to buy time, to absorb heat, to promote collective wisdom, to insure a maximum sense of legitimacy for final decisions."

Bailey's third piece of advice is valuable in those conflict situations that have gone beyond a state of rational negotiation. Essentially, the administrator adopts Harry Truman's five-point strategy: estimate your own resources, estimate your enemy's resources, form a judgment about what is to be done, implement your judgment with a plan, and, finally, persuade your leaders of the value of that plan and mass your forces for the attack.

Finally, the administrator should be "harshly realistic" about his or her limitations in managing conflict. "There are times in a year, in a career, in a life when cyclonic winds and waves will roll over everything in sight and when the skill of the ablest mariner is probably less effective than his praying on his knees — if for no other reason than that he has thereby lowered the ship's center of gravity."

CONCLUSION

Conflict is a constant companion of all human undertakings and should be considered a natural, not an anomalous, phenomenon. For most observers and participants, conflict invokes negative feelings, for it often leads to destructive ends. But conflict can also be a constructive force in organizations, leading to increased creativity and adaptability.

The art of conflict management involves maximizing constructive conflict and minimizing destructive conflict. To achieve mastery of this art, the educational administrator must understand conflict — its types, sources, and dynamics — and must be familiar with numerous techniques for managing conflict.

But knowledge alone is not enough; ultimately, administrators must hone their conflict management skills in the field, in their day-to-day dealings with conflict.

CHAPTER 12
SOLVING PROBLEMS
Norman Hale and John Lindelow

The information explosion, technological advances, and the sheer complexity of the school district and its services have combined to create complicated management systems. Tools like PERT (program evaluation and review technique) and PPBS (program, planning, budgeting systems) are only two examples of districtwide technological systems that evolved in the sixties. Other computerized methodologies can be used for projecting enrollments, scheduling the use of facilities, writing student schedules, and computing the costs of contracts; these are now commonplace in large school districts.

One effect of such systems has been to require that educational planners and decision-makers possess much greater knowledge and expertise than traditional management methods required. As Stanley Sanders notes, this "specialized knowledge and skill . . . is not possessed by many of the administrators and leaders who are truly responsible for policies and planning." Consequently, more decisions are left to the "educational technologist," who has acquired a greater role in decision-making. As more problems come to be defined in technological terms, people who are not information specialists may be edged out of the policy processes. Either decisions will be increasingly left to the technologists or, worse, problems may simply be ignored.

While many of the problems of the school district are amenable to technological solutions, many are not. Questions of creating new programs, cancelling old ones, changing the curriculum, implementing regulations, providing community services, and locating new facilities are nonrecurring situations that require one-of-a-kind programs or decisions. They require a problem-solving flexibility that technological systems do not provide.

Where does the administrator turn when he or she needs to make decisions in these areas?

Unfortunately, much of the literature on problem-solving and decision-making is either diffuse and mathematical or too abstract for practical use. The theories are not often translated into easily understandable and applicable formulas. And non-technological systems are especially difficult to formalize.

As an attempt to bridge the gap between a pure theory of decision-making and a theory of decision-making as an intuitive, unstructured process, we offer three nontechnological models from current educational literature. The models have been chosen for specific reasons. First, they present current alternatives to technological systems. They are inexpensive: they require no equipment more sophisticated than a hand calculator. Second, each model has several variant forms and can be applied to many different kinds of problems. Third, each has been chosen because it reflects a belief that consultation and group effort are preferable to individuals acting unilaterally.

Most important of all, each model has a specific strength. The value of force-field analysis is its ability to visualize and analyze the elements of a problem. The nominal group technique is a means of polling constituent or client preferences concerning both problems and solutions. The strength of the Delphi forecasting model is its ability to create consensus.

Like other management techniques, these problem-solving models yield their greatest value when the user is aware of their limitations as well as strengths. Although the techniques are useful in organizing data and in guiding the decision-making process, they are designed to inform and not replace the administrator's intuition. They do not replace subjectivity in the decision-making process despite their appearance of objectivity. The leader still has to decide on what data and information to include, how it is to be arranged, and most importantly, what it means.

With this qualification in mind, these models should aid school leaders who are faced with the problem of evaluating a new program or an old one, working with a community group, or deliberating on new policy. Used imaginatively, these models provide attractive, simple alternatives to more complex procedures. Their use will also encourage participation by more people in all areas of district decision-making.

UNDERSTANDING A SITUATION: FORCE-FIELD ANALYSIS

Force-field analysis is an especially useful technique in the early stages of problem-solving. It provides a graphic means for either one person working alone or many people working together to dissect a problem into its major parts (forces). It can also be used to help make decisions in situations where the pros and cons of a particular action seem evenly divided.

According to force-field theory, every situation is in a state of "quasi-stationary equilibrium" as the result of a "complex field of forces" that work in "varying directions, at differing strengths. The existing situation, or status quo, is the result of the combination of these forces.

Force-field's view of any situation as a conglomeration of poised forces makes itself especially useful in the analysis of problems. Before making any decision on a course of action, decision-makers must be able to enumerate the various forces, both driving and restraining. Stanley Sanders notes that this rigorous analysis reveals that problems are composed of "complex fields of forces and myriad influences rather than single or isolated factors." It helps the administrator to recognize that a single hasty action as the result of a premature decision may have no effect on the complex of forces.

The following hypothetical example, which appears in a report by William Gaskell, is only one of many applications of the technique. In this situation, a teacher feels a lack of communication in the classroom. The teacher has a goal he defines as the "Open and Active Criticism of Ideas between Us." In an analysis of the situation, the teacher draws a diagram and lists the forces pressing for open criticism and those pushing against it (see figure 1). The forces on the left, if allowed to become dominant, would push toward the goal of open and active criticism between students and instructor. The forces on the right are those that inhibit the attaining of the goal and could result in the complete absence of criticism.

With the "identification of forces," we have completed the first of what Sanders sees as the four steps in any kind of "decision making, problem solving, change, or program plan-

THE SKILLS: SOLVING PROBLEMS

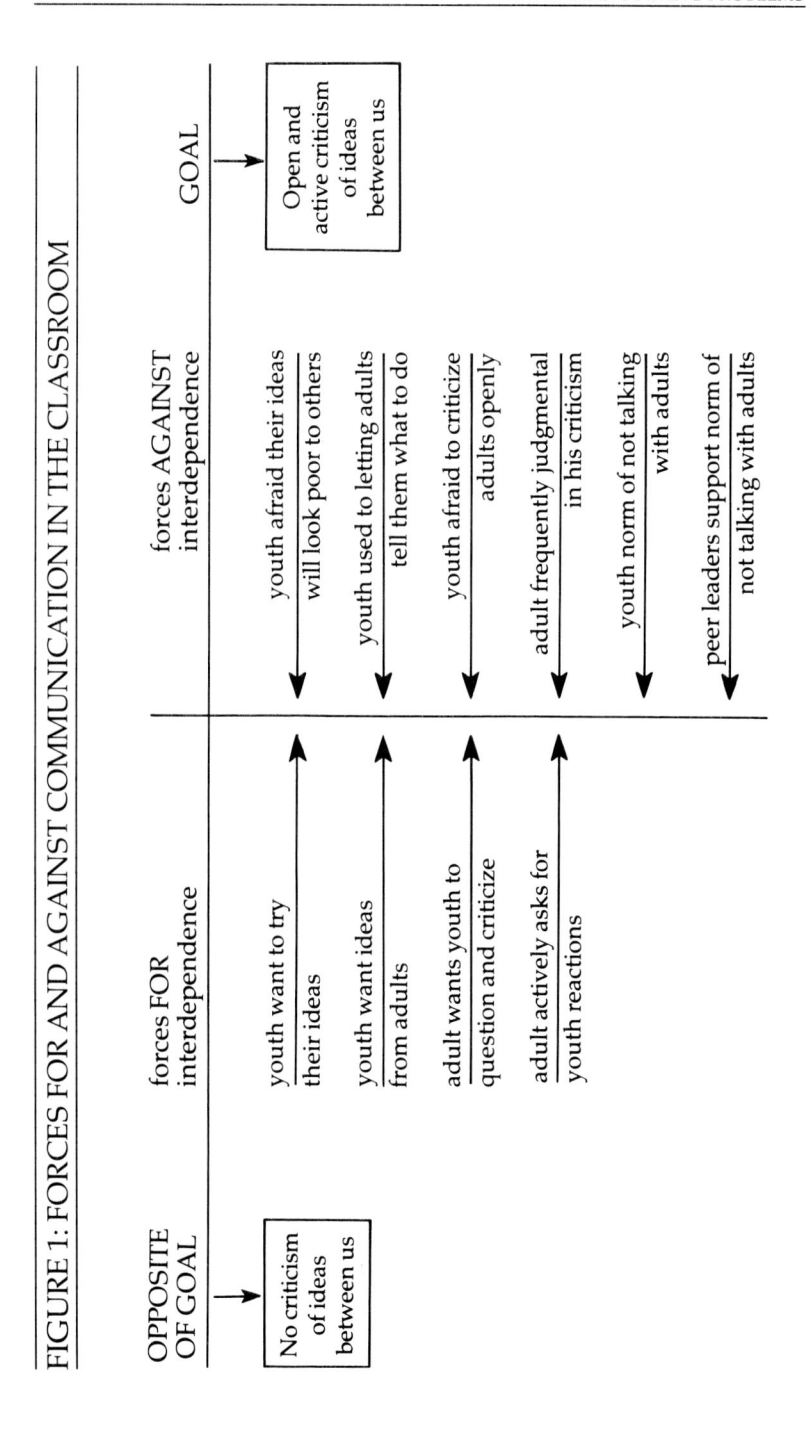

FIGURE 1: FORCES FOR AND AGAINST COMMUNICATION IN THE CLASSROOM

OPPOSITE OF GOAL	forces FOR interdependence	forces AGAINST interdependence	GOAL
No criticism of ideas between us →	youth want to try their ideas ↑	↓ youth afraid their ideas will look poor to others	→ Open and active criticism of ideas between us
	youth want ideas from adults ↑	↓ youth used to letting adults tell them what to do	
	adult wants youth to question and criticize ↑	↓ youth afraid to criticize adults openly	
	adult actively asks for youth reactions ↑	↓ adult frequently judgmental in his criticism	
		↓ youth norm of not talking with adults	
		↓ peer leaders support norm of not talking with adults	

From *The Development of a Leadership Training Process for Principals. Final Report* by William G. Gaskell. Central Washington State College, 1973.

ning." The second step involves choosing an entry point or "unfreezing" the current situation. A decision is made to strengthen a driving force or to weaken a restraining force in order to move the program in the desired direction. Sanders disagrees with many of the authorities in change strategy who "suggest that a strong unsettling experience is necessary to destroy the equilibrium of the status quo." Sanders believes it is preferable to weaken a restraining force, thereby avoiding severe reaction and disruption.

Step three involves "moving to the new level." This movement is the result of a planned combination of strengthening and weakening forces. When the program reaches its new level, it undergoes "refreezing," the fourth step, which requires "planned and organized evaluation and monitoring of the new process." This monitoring assures that inertia will not drag the program back to its old level.

Gaskell recommends that the compilers of the field analysis rate the driving forces on a simple numerical scale in terms of their importance and their ease or difficulty of change. Such a ranking system might be of help when making a decision about the entry point.

When used as Sanders and Gaskell suggest, force-field analysis can help educators diagnose complex problems and then plot a course toward a solution. Because of its power to reveal the many forces in a situation, however, the technique can also be used as a simple decision-making tool, particularly in cases where the pros and cons of an issue are many and seem evenly divided.

A publication of the Massachusetts State Department of Education shows how force-field analysis can be used in this way. First, all the forces for and against a decision are listed and then inversely ranked according to their importance, so the most important force has the highest number. Importance is defined as the degree to which change of a particular force would cause the situation to move most toward or away from the goal.

Next, each force is rated in terms of "clarity," which is defined as "having objective data with which you could stand up in court and prove your case beyond a shadow of a doubt." The clarity rating, then, is essentially a correction factor for subjective yet unsupported belief. Forces are given a clarity rating of three for "clear," two for "partly clear," and one for "unclear."

Finally, the inverse rank of each force and its clarity rating are multiplied to give a final score for each force. The totals for and against a decision are then computed and compared.

To illustrate this technique, the authors of the Massachusetts publication ask the reader to imagine himself or herself as a chemistry teacher in a high school with an A to F grading system. A senior girl from a low-income family has earned a D in chemistry, yet needs a C to receive financial aid at the only college that has offered her aid. Without the aid she will probably not be able to go on to college.

As her teacher, what do you do? Change the grade and thus allow the student to attend college, or stick with a D and cut off her financial aid and her college chances?

One teacher's force-field analysis is shown in figure 2. Clearly, for this teacher, the "forces against" are more powerful than the "forces for" in this case.

Of course, the ratings given for the importance and clarity of each force are critical in determining the final scores and, thus, the final decision. When force-field analysis is used by groups as a decision-making tool, there will likely be significant differences among group members concerning the ratings given each force. The search for clarity does not eliminate subjectivity. Nevertheless, the technique is a valuable means of stimulating thought about all the forces influencing a particular decision.

Force-field's great advantage, in both problem analysis and decision-making, is its simplicity. The technique can be learned in a single sitting. Yet, as simple as the procedure is, it nonetheless provides an alternative to other "oversimplified systems which see only a single cause and effect." Sanders also points out that it can be used in conjunction with statistics to "any degree of sophistication which may be considered desirable."

FINDING SOLUTIONS: THE NOMINAL GROUP TECHNIQUE

Force-field analysis is quite useful for characterizing and

FIGURE 2: A TEACHER'S SAMPLE FORCE-FIELD ANALYSIS

Goal: To change the girl's grade to a C to provide her with an opportunity to continue her education.

Importance	Clarity	Score	FORCES FOR	FORCES AGAINST	Importance	Clarity	Score
4	3	12	The girl should have the opportunity to continue her education.	The girl earned a D in chemistry.	8	3	24
3	3	9	She would probably be unable to go to college without financial assistance.	Standards of performance should not exist if they are not adhered to.	9	3	27
2	1	2	The A through F grading system is not an equitable measure of student performance.	It would be unfair to the other students to change her grade.	6	3	18
1	2	2	Everyone should have the opportunity to go to college.	The girl might not be "college material."	5	1	5
				It would violate the teacher's personal value system to change the grade.	7	3	21
		25	TOTALS				95

Adopted from *Force Field Analysis* by Massachusetts State Department of Education, 1976.

analyzing problem situations. Although it prescribes change through the weakening or strengthening of particular forces in a situation, it does not identify how these changes might best be made. Thus, the leader needs some sort of method for generating alternative solutions to problems. One such method is the nominal group technique.

AN ALTERNATIVE TO BRAINSTORMING

The nominal group technique is sometimes called "silent brainstorming." Brainstorming — often cited as a model of democratic procedure — is characterized by an open exchange among group members in which everyone is encouraged to participate freely. Some writers, however, believe that brainstorming has some serious drawbacks. Brooke Collison and Suzanne Dunlap, for example, believe that brainstorming is a valuable process but "does not always provide participants with sufficient time to organize their thoughts and express their ideas."

Andrew Van de Ven and Andre Delbecq contend that interacting groups often get stuck on a single topic and merely elaborate on it. Interacting groups reach for decisions before problems are fully aired and are more geared to problem disposal than problem understanding. Such groups also have a regrettable tendency to reinforce certain human weaknesses: people are more comfortable responding to ideas already proposed than they are coming up with new ideas. Verbally proficient members dominate the interacting group. Divergent opinions are often ignored.

To combat these weaknesses, Delbecq and Van de Ven have described a group process model in which "individuals work in the presence of each other but do not interact."

> Instead, each individual is writing ideas on a pad of paper in front of him. At the end of 10 to 20 minutes, a very structured sharing of ideas takes place. Each individual in round-robin fashion provides one idea from his private list which is written on a flip-chart by a recorder in full view of other members. There is still no discussion, only the recording of privately generated ideas. This round-robin listing continues until each

member indicates that he has no further ideas to share. The output of this nominal process is the total set created by this structured process.

After all aspects of the problem have been explored, the ideas are discussed and then ranked in order of their importance to the group.

A similar explanation of the nominal group technique (NGT) process has been outlined by Collison and Dunlap. First, the group's task is explicitly defined to avoid confusion and ambiguity during the process. Next, the time limits for the NGT process are announced by the group leader (or they may be posted in advance). Specifying a particular time for completion of the task, state Collison and Dunlap, lends "emphasis to the feeling of accomplishment within a certain time period."

Third, members are asked to write down their personal responses to the defined task. During this period, "silence is important in order to ensure maximum individuality of lists." Next, the group's ideas are placed via a round-robin process on a master list in front of the group. Items on this list should be unedited and "there should be no discussion of the merit or appropriateness of an item" at this time.

In the fifth step, the group discusses each item on the list with the purpose of clarifying the meaning of each item. Only after the items are clearly defined are they finally discussed and evaluated by the group. Following discussion, the group members can rank or rate the ideas if they wish, or can decide on a course of action if this is called for.

Because NGT is a flexible method for generating ideas, it can be used to identify both problems and possible solutions. In an initial round, for example, group members could be asked to concentrate on identifying the problems at hand. In a subsequent round, they could be asked to generate solutions. Van de Ven and Delbecq suggest that the two different aspects might be approached either in different sessions or by different groups.

How effective is the nominal group? Van de Ven and Delbecq cite studies showing that in terms of the "mean number of ideas," "the mean total number of ideas produced," and the "quality of ideas produced," the nominal groups were found to be "significantly superior to brainstorming in generating information relevant to a problem."

THE NOMINAL GROUP AS AN INTERVENTION TECHNIQUE

Donald Mosley and Thad Green report success in applying nominal group procedures in all areas of problem diagnosis, planning, and evaluation and in institutions as diverse as business organizations, churches, and a university. The members of the organization constitute the membership of the nominal group. Employees work together to identify the organization's problems and to suggest solutions.

For interventions of this sort, Mosley and Green recommend a different problem-identification procedure. They suggest that the participants list the organization's strengths before they list problems: "Changing this one-sided, negative focus into a two-dimensional perspective which includes organizational strengths often has a dramatic, positive effect on the general receptiveness of the entire OD (organizational development) effort, most of which still lies in the future." They also recommend that when intervention in a hierarchical structure becomes necessary, persons of similar rank should be grouped together to prevent a potential influencing of subordinates.

Another, quite different, application of the nominal group is cited by Charles Zastrow and Ralphe Navarre. They used the technique to poll a university social work class to discover student preferences for course content. By means of the technique, Zastrow and Navarre report they were able to understand the students' interests and were better able to serve those interests.

PLANNING NEW PROGRAMS

Because of its ability to generate problem descriptions from a client population, the nominal group technique is especially suited to the early stages of program planning. It is especially useful in cases where a "variety of groups, fragmented in terms of vested interests, rhetorical and ideological concepts, and differential expertise, need to be brought together for a program to emerge or for change to take place" (Delbecq and Van de Ven).

This description would seem to apply to community

service programs in the public schools or any service program designed for the benefit of clients of the school district. These might include programs designed to reach disadvantaged students (special skills programs for minority or handicapped students), programs to implement busing, vocational guidance programs, and counseling and testing programs. Within the district itself, the technique can be used to gather information and ideas about curricular change, policy changes, and program implementation.

Delbecq and Van de Ven have described a program planning model that makes use of these nominal group techniques. The first step of the model is called the problem exploration phase. A target group of participants is identified in terms of their involvement either as potential clients of the new program or as people responsible for implementing it. Which individuals are included in this group depends on the degree to which the program will affect them. Once this group is assembled, members are asked to identify problems this new program must solve.

Delbecq and Van de Ven have discovered that the enumerating of problems often involves a revelation of personal details. For example, a program being set up to help handicapped students will probably require the sharing of considerable personal information by the handicapped members of the nominal group. The authors feel that the nominal technique provides a way for the participants to gradually volunteer these "personal dimensions a little at a time."

The actual machinery for running the group will vary from case to case. In large groups, William Vroman recommends that satellite groups of from ten to fifteen members be used. The display of written materials will also depend on the number of participants involved. Some commentators recommend listing all materials on a large board in front of an assembled group. Often a break in the proceedings will be necessary to compile and display the list of problems. Some groups will choose to vote on and display only the most significant problems uncovered. In some cases it may be more advantageous to display *all* ideas to the group.

Knowledge exploration, the second phase of the model, brings together a selected group of clients from phase one and a group of resource experts. This new group is presented with the list of problems resulting from the first meeting. Using nominal group technique again, this group responds to two questions: "What existing resources can be used to solve these problems?" and "What new resources will have to be created to solve these problems?" Respondents list their answers, which are again collected and displayed round-robin fashion. From these answers, a list of existing resources and a list of new resources will be developed.

The final phases of the program do not utilize nominal group procedures. The actual writing of the program description must be accomplished by technicians who match needs with resources. However, the very last phase of the program involves reporting back to the participants in phase one an explanation of the final content of the program.

Thorough information gathering and analysis are important parts of decision-making. The nominal group technique presents an easy, convenient method of gathering information and ideas on a variety of topics from the clients or constituents of an institution.

ACHIEVING CONSENSUS: THE DELPHI TECHNIQUE

As experienced leaders know, reaching consensus on complex issues can be a frustrating process. Committee meetings — the traditional forum for decision-making — have numerous disadvantages. Group members, as Lewis Thomas notes, are often more involved in such ego-based activities as "winning points, leading the discussion, protecting one's face, gaining applause, shouting down opposition," or "scaring opponents" than they are in actually thinking about the problems at hand.

In the past twenty years, however, a new "meeting" technique has been developed that links minds together to do "collective figuring," yet avoids most of the disadvantages of group meetings noted above. This new consensus-producing tool is commonly called the Delphi technique.

HISTORY AND ASSUMPTIONS OF DELPHI

As Norman Dalkey and Olaf Helmer report, Delphi was originally conceived by the Rand Corporation as a method of obtaining "the most reliable consensus of opinion of a group of experts." The general procedure for the Delphi forecast is quite simple. A number of experts on the subject under examination are selected. They agree to respond to a series of questionnaires to be mailed to them. On the first questionnaire, the experts answer questions and make predictions about the matter under study. The questionnaires are returned by mail, the results are collated, and a second questionnaire is returned to each participant.

On this second questionnaire, some means of reporting the group consensus is employed. The individual's score is also reported. Each participant whose answer lies outside the group consensus (usually defined by a modal or median score) is asked to reconsider his or her original prediction. Any respondent who wishes to remain outside the group consensus is asked to justify that position. A third round of questionnaires reports the new consensus and may also include a minority report of the general reasons participants chose to stay outside the consensus. The original Delphi consisted of five rounds.

What Delphi amounts to, then, is "a really quiet, thoughtful conversation, in which everyone gets a chance to *listen*," as Thomas notes. "The background noise of small talk, and the recurrent sonic booms of vanity, are eliminated at the outset, and there is time to think."

Rand researchers discovered that the "controlled opinion feedback" that Delphi provided was successful in shaping diverse thoughts into meaningful consensus. It was extremely successful in answering almanac-like questions and producing consensus predictions about future technologies. The first Delphi attempted to gather opinion about the amount of nuclear firepower that would have to be directed at United States industrial targets to reduce munitions output by a certain amount. Since then, Delphis have been used to predict energy demands, growth trends, and the depletion of resources. Not surprisingly, when social scientists saw the success of Delphi they were attracted by both its consensus-producing powers and its future-predicting qualities. They wanted to use it in their own research.

But as W. Timothy Weaver points out, the kinds of questions Delphi was most successful in answering had objective, "knowable" technological factors to them. The social sciences do not yet include such factors. It cannot be determined, for example, when "alienation and impersonality of urban living will reach its maximum." In fact, says Weaver, we do not even know "what it means to speak of a maximum in this case." Because the data base for the social sciences is so much less developed than it is for the hard sciences, and because of differing interpretations of social indicators, Delphi forecasts have been less successful when dealing with social issues.

THE NEW FORMS OF DELPHI

Although the Delphi cannot be used to predict the "likelihood of a certain future," Weaver believes we can use the Delphi to talk in terms of what the future "can be made to be." The technique can be used to help define and create a consensus about social and institutional goals. When used in this way to project a set of values and goals, Delphi is an important tool in futures planning.

The traditional forecasting Delphi has given way in education to the "normative" Delphi where the goal is to probe values and preferences rather than future events. Richard Weatherman and Karen Swenson analyze two forms of Delphi that have the greatest applicability in school districts: the "strategy probe" and the "preference probe." The strategy probe might be employed by a school district that has mandated a new program and wants to poll opinion on the choice of a strategy to implement it. The first questionnaire might be open-ended and simply ask respondents to suggest alternatives. Subsequent questionnaires would ask respondents to narrow their choices and compare the alternatives in terms of cost, ease of implementation, and so forth. In consecutive rounds, a consensus toward a single strategy will emerge. If the respondents themselves are the persons responsible for implementing the program, the move toward consensus will further guarantee the program's success.

The preference probe is used in cases when a school district wants to poll its clients or constituents about its priorities. This probe reveals essential information about the participants themselves and their preferences, which the district takes into account when setting its goals.

Both these probes differ significantly from traditional Delphis in that they do not depend on expert opinion. When comparing two studies, Gordon Welty discovered that in the area of values forecasting laymen and experts produced roughly the same results. There is no need, then, especially in the area of values forecasting, for a selected panel.

SAMPLE APPLICATIONS

Delphi has many variations. The following applications exemplify some of the situations to which the method has been applied.

Paramus, New Jersey, Public Schools

Arlene Hartman describes how the Delphi technique was modified in one school district for use as a "short-term decision making and conflict resolution" tool.

In the Paramus Public Schools, curriculum development is carried out by committees appointed by a broad-based Curriculum Council. The Administrative Council — consisting of all principals in the district — has the right to review proposals from the Curriculum Council before they are sent to the school board for approval.

In one instance, a committee composed of teachers, parents, and students was established by the Curriculum Council to review the curriculum for gifted and talented students. The committee sought representation from the principals, but none was able to serve. When the committee later presented its proposals to the principals, however, several major points of disagreement emerged. Meetings between the two groups only heightened and polarized the differences.

The groups then asked Hartman — the district's Curriculum Coordinator — to resolve the conflicts without further joint meetings. "Given the need to reach consensus without common meetings," states Hartman, "I felt a variation on the Delphi Technique would be the best tool for resolving the conflict."

Hartman composed a list of twenty policy statements that represented key issues between the two groups and then sent the list to committee members and principals. Individuals could respond in one of three ways to each of the statements: they could agree with it, they could indicate that they were uncertain but willing to try it for a year, or they could disagree with it. If they disagreed, they were asked to indicate how they would amend the statement to make it acceptable.

After the results were compiled, Hartman sent revised lists back to the respondents. Each individual's "phase two" list indicated the number of respondents who had selected each choice, the individual's initial choice "as a reminder of his or her original decision," and, below each statement, a suggested change or addition. "In this phase, the respondents were to check their preference again, whether the same or different, and indicate whether or not they would accept the modification statements."

After phase two, not more than one person disagreed with each of eighteen of the twenty amended statements. Of the remaining two statements, two respondents still disagreed with each. Since these results showed a near consensus on the policy statements, the statements were amended to the curriculum committee's original report and sent to the school board, which approved the report.

Hartman believes that this modification of Delphi has many advantages over normal group processes. Every individual must make a choice on every issue, thus reducing the likelihood that vocal members will be overly influential. When someone disagrees, he or she must offer specific amendments to the statements offered. But respondents can also choose the "middle ground" of letting a policy be tried for a year. Finally, anonymity reduces the likelihood that those in positions of authority will force consensus from subordinates.

Hartman concludes by warning that this form of Delphi is not a panacea. A great deal of "footwork" is needed to make the process work. Potential areas of compromise must be assessed. Informal meetings with key individuals from both groups must be held to synthesize the initial policy statements. "Statements must be written quite carefully to minimize the possibility that different interpretations of their meaning may occur, possibly resulting in 'false' agreement." Finally, the "mediator" must be perceived as fair and neutral.

Staff Development Preferences

The Delphi technique was recently used in two public school districts in Kentucky to assess inservice needs, according to Kenneth Brooks. Before questionnaires were sent out, each certified employee was given an identification number that "allowed responses to be anonymous while permitting the researcher to categorize responses by participant (teacher, principal, etc.) and by work site (individual school or central office)."

Staff members were asked to fill out questionnaires that asked them to identify five areas in which there was a critical need for inservice and five areas where inservice was thought to be undesirable. A critical area for inservice was defined as "a topical area of professional concern that the individual felt could be improved through staff development."

The responses to the questionnaires were combined into two lists and then returned to the participants for ranking. Staff members rated desirable inservice topics on a seven-point Likert scale, and they indicated whether they agreed or disagreed with topics on the undesired list.

The responses were analyzed "and a measure of central tendency and frequency determined." The ranked topic lists were again returned to the participants, who "were instructed to review the group position and indicate their own position in light of this additional information." Respondents were also given the opportunity to support their views with brief narrative statements.

Although the original design of the Delphi called for three rounds of rankings, after two rounds "sufficient consensus had been achieved to make that unnecessary." Brooks notes that the staffs of different schools had significantly different priorities for inservice. Thus, the district provided each school with a record of how its staff ranked the inservice items.

Ellenstown, Washington, Public Schools

The Delphi technique gives school districts an excellent specialized method of polling their communities about attitudes and preferences concerning school policies. Alfred Rasp, Jr. reports on such a use of Delphi by the public schools in Ellenstown, Washington. Through a survey the district sought to collect "data from which goals for building better programs could be developed." This four-phase Delphi was mailed to a sample of "local students, staff, parents, citizens, and teacher trainers from the state colleges and universities."

The first questionnaire was fairly open-ended. When recording their opinions, respondents were asked to think in terms of the period from 1975 to 1985:

As a result of the experiences provided by the Ellenstown School District, students should:
Know _____
Be Able to _____
Feel _____

Ellenstown School District should:
Increase _____
Maintain _____
Reduce _____

From these first-round questionnaires, a second questionnaire was developed that contained a list of statements. Respondents were asked to circle numbers on a one-to-seven scale. Here are two sample items:

As a result of the experiences provided by the Ellenstown School District, each student should:

low				high			
1	2	3	4	5	6	7	View competition in all things as healthy.
1	2	3	4	5	6	7	Be able to read and understand a newspaper.

A third-round questionnaire was mailed only to those who responded to the second questionnaire. In the third round, the modal answer (the answer cited most frequently) was indicated by a square. The individual's response was indicated by a circle. Respondents were asked to study each item.

If the mode for the item did not represent their thinking at that moment, they were requested to state their reasons in a space following the item. The third questionnaire had this form:

As a result of the experiences provided by the Ellenstown School District, each student should:

low   high
1 [2] 3 4 (5) 6 7   View competition in all things as healthy.

1 2 3 4 (5) [6] 7   Be able to read and understand a newspaper.

The fourth round recalculated the consensus from the third round and also included a minority dissenting report for each item. The respondent was asked to consider this information as well as the group consensus and to make a final judgment. Rasp and his colleagues decided, in retrospect, that the fourth round was not necessary.

The results of this survey, concludes Rasp, provided Ellenstown's superintendent and staff with valuable information from citizens about community values and school priorities. Even in the face of certain limitations, "Delphi does have strength and utility. It collects and organizes judgments in a systematic fashion. It gains input. It establishes priorities. It builds consensus. It organizes dissent. In short, it cannot be overlooked as a useful and reliable decision-making tool."

Dallas-Fort Worth SWEP Survey

The Skyline Wide Educational Plan (SWEP) instituted by the Dallas and Fort Worth Independent School districts is a much larger, more ambitious attempt to survey community values for the school district than we have thus far encountered. Robert Burns reports that the procedures vary slightly from traditional Delphis in that only two questionnaire rounds were used. Also, the number of participants (over 900 persons invited to respond) was quite large in this case. The attrition rate for the two questionnaires was 75 percent; that is, nearly 700 people either did not respond at all or dropped out after the first round. Considering the attrition rate, the decision to have only two rounds may have been wise.

Unlike the Ellenstown Delphi, the first SWEP questionnaire was not open-ended. It consisted of 105 goal statements in the general categories of "basic skills, citizenship, ethics, aesthetics, careers, health and recreation, and life management." In addition, the questionnaire included twenty-nine "process goals statements." For each item, respondents were asked to answer in two ways. A simple yes-no answer was requested to see if the respondent felt that the item represented a "core" skill that "all students should have before completion of their program of studies." A five-point Likert scale was also used so that the respondent could assign a priority to each item. On the second questionnaire, space was allowed for the expression of minority opinions.

Perhaps an even greater difference between this and earlier surveys is the use of a computer to analyze and display the data. The districts have not only analyzed the answers to find the degree of consensus for each item, but have also analyzed the data in terms of "age, sex, patron, ethnicity, occupation, and residence." The use of the computer certainly makes it possible to manipulate the data in more ways for more purposes. Used this way, a Delphi probe can be an extremely complicated procedure.

USING THE DELPHI

Under what conditions should Delphi be used? Carl Moore and James Coke suggest that it is advantageous in the following situations:

- The problem does not lend itself to precise analytical techniques but can benefit from subjective judgments on a collective basis.
- The individuals needed to contribute to the examination of a broad or complex problem have no history of adequate communication and may represent diverse backgrounds with respect to experience or expertise.
- More individuals are needed than can effectively interact in a face-to-face exchange.
- Time and cost make frequent group meetings infeasible.
- The efficiency of face-to-face meetings can be in-

creased by a supplemental group communciation process.
- Disagreements among individuals are so severe or politically unpalatable that the communication process must be refereed and/or anonymity assured.
- The heterogeneity of the participants must be preserved to assure validity of the results, i.e., avoidance of domination by quantity or by strength of personality ("bandwagon effect").

As successful as Delphi may be in these kinds of situations, some precautions for the would-be designer of a probe are offered by almost every writer on the subject. Early in the design stage, a decision must be made about a method of reporting results. Although some Delphis supply verbal rather than numerical data, most rely on a mathematical measure of consensus.

Of the mathematical probes mentioned above, the SWEP survey reported its results in terms of the mean (the average of all responses). The Ellenstown schools' Delphi reported its results in terms of the mode (the response most frequently chosen). Frederick Cyphert and Walter Gant reject the mean because "few of the response scales used in a Delphi instrument assume equal intervals." The mode is generally favored "in efforts to gain opinions about desired future conditions," while the median (the number midway between two extremes) is "often used in surveys focusing on judgments about time or quantity."

Another factor in a Delphi survey is time. Questionnaire results must be read and analyzed, and the new questionnaire compiled and mailed out quickly. Long delays between rounds must be minimized if respondents are to be kept interested. Margaret Skutsch and Diana Hall estimate that three rounds of a mail-out Delphi with thirty respondents would require about 142 hours of work and two months for completion of the project. More complex projects would require correspondingly more time.

A more significant problem concerns the need for objectivity in composing the questionnaire materials. Rasp notes that "almost every study on the Delphi has testified to an uneasiness regarding the development of the second questionnaire." Michael Folk and other writers point out that the translation of raw verbal data into a goal statement or any kind of supposedly objective item is a difficult task. The content is subject to the biases of the compilers.

Carl Moore and James Coke believe that Delphis often fail because the designer imposes "views and perceptions of a problem upon the respondent group by overspecifying the structure of the Delphi and not allowing for the contribution of other perspectives related to the problem." Other reasons for Delphi failure are poor techniques of summarizing and presenting the group's data, and the assumption of some users that Delphi can substitute for all other human communications.

THE CONSENSUS PHENOMENON

The greatest philosophical controversy over Delphi has to do with the consensus phenomenon itself. What causes it? W. Timothy Weaver says the Delphi process assumes that the experts or respondents will make logical, reasoned conclusions. But, he maintains, people may in fact change toward consensus for social or psychological reasons.

Moore and Coke suggest that an artificial consensus may be generated when the designer underestimates the demanding nature of a Delphi. If respondents are not recognized as consultants and properly compensated for their time (assuming the Delphi is not an integral part of their job function), they may more easily agree with the norm.

Cyphert and Gant's study even provides some evidence that the Delphi can be used to manipulate participant response. They inserted a bogus item in their questionnaire results and reported that it had achieved a high degree of consensus. Subsequent responses showed that participants tended to rate it higher when informed that its consensus was high. Richard Weatherman and Karen Swenson, along with many others, warn that this convergence phenomenon needs to be studied more closely. Paradoxically perhaps, the Delphi cannot give reasons why people prefer one idea over another. It only explains, in the minority report, why consensus does *not* occur.

Some critics warn that the Delphi is a conservative,

establishment-oriented instrument. Weatherman and Swenson point out that

> divergent thinkers, who may be under-represented on a Delphi panel, may prove to be the best forecasters. Such persons might find it especially difficult to acquiesce or be committed to a consensus and fail to participate at all. This difficulty may be reflected in item content as well: if experts representing the main currents of thought in a discipline develop items on the initial questionnaire, the error may be compounded.

As the future forecasting tool it was designed to be, the Delphi is not given high marks. However, as a tool to gather information about values and ways the future can be shaped, Delphi can be extremely valuable. Michael Folk offers some final advice for those who are considering their own Delphi. First, you will learn more about the procedure by doing it yourself. Second, acquaint yourself with alternative versions, especially those that deemphasize future forecasting. There is no reason, for example, why Delphi must be restricted to a mailing format. Third, acquaint yourself with the literature so there will be no disappointment about the outcome.

A COMPARISON OF NOMINAL GROUP AND DELPHI

John Crawford and William Cossitt compared three group processes in terms of "their ability to facilitate the quantitative and qualitative productivity of a decision-making group." Forty-five subjects, working in groups of five, were told to use regular face-to-face communication, the nominal group technique, or a three-round, three-day Delphi to prepare a list of recommendations for a job description.

As the researchers had hypothesized, the Delphi groups came up with the largest number of ideas — twenty-seven — compared with the nominal groups' seventeen and the face-to-face groups' ten. The decisions made by the Delphi groups were also adjudged to be of significantly higher quality than decisions made via the other techniques.

The study's findings largely support the idea that "one

can improve the quantity and quality of a group's decision-making productivity by systematically removing the inhibiting effects of face-to-face interaction from the group process." This can be achieved without significantly diminishing participants' senses of socio-emotional satisfaction with the group process, according to the authors' data. Although there was a trend toward less satisfaction as face-to-face contact lessened, the trend was not significant.

Crawford and Cossitt suggest that all three techniques can be used in a situation where it is desirable to maximize the number of ideas generated, their quality, and the satisfaction of participants. For example, following a four-round Delphi, participants could meet in a face-to-face conference that utilizes the more significant elements of the nominal group procedure. Used together in this way, these techniques can generate benefits that can "exceed the general advantages of Delphi alone."

CONCLUSION

The school district is a people-oriented enterprise. For this reason it is important that all school leaders, regardless of their technological literacy, be involved in solving the district's problems and making its policies. If modern management theory has anything at all to say to school districts, it is that all employees have valuable contributions to make, and they are happier in jobs where their opinions are solicited and respected. The models included here have been selected because they offer a nontechnological alternative to problem-solving and because they solicit and respect the opinions of involved workers and clients.

But a model, by its nature, provides only a general outline or working definition. When it comes into contact with a real situation, it can, and should, be changed in many ways. What we have provided here are only broad outlines that are not intended to be inclusive or exhaustive of materials on these models. We hope they furnish a simple place to begin.

BIBLIOGRAPHY

Many of the items in this bibliography are indexed in ERIC's monthly catalogs *Resources in Education (RIE)* and *Current Index to Journals in Education (CIJE)*. Reports in *RIE* are indicated by an "ED" number; journal articles in *CIJE* are indicated by an "EJ" number.

Most items with an ED number are available from the ERIC Document Reproduction Service (EDRS), P.O. Box 190, Arlington, VA 22210. To order from EDRS, specify the ED number, type of reproduction desired — microfiche (MF) or paper copy (PC), and number of copies. Add postage, figured at the current rates, to the cost of all orders and include check or money order payable to EDRS. ED numbers not yet assigned are available from the Clearinghouse.

INTRODUCTION

Austin, Gilbert R. "Exemplary Schools and the Search for Effectiveness." *Educational Leadership,* 37, 1 (October 1979), pp. 10-14. EJ 208 050.

Balderson, James H. "Principal Power Bases: Some Observations." *The Canadian Administrator,* 14, 7 (April 1975), pp. 1-5. EJ 115 902.

Barth, Roland S. "Reflections on the Principalship." *Thrust for Educational Leadership,* 9, 5 (May 1980), pp. 4-6.

Bennis, Warren G. "Leadership Theory and Administrative Behavior: The Problem of Authority." *Administrative Science Quarterly,* 4, 3 (December 1959), pp. 259-60.

Bird, Charles. *Social Psychology.* New York: D. Appleton-Century Company, 1940.

Blumberg, Arthur, and Greenfield, William. *The Effective Principal: Perspectives on School Leadership.* Boston: Allyn and Bacon, 1980.

Burns, James MacGregor. "Two Excerpts from 'Leadership'." *Educational Leadership,* 36, 6 (March 1979), pp. 380-84. EJ 197 875.

Congress of the United States, Senate Select Committee on Equal Educational Opportunity. "Revitalizing the Role of the School Principal," [Part VI, Chapter 24, Section B]. In its *Toward Equal Educational Opportunity* (92nd Congress, 2nd Session. Senate Report No. 92-0000), pp. 305-07. Washington, D.C.: U.S. Government Printing Office, 1972. Complete document, 445 pages, available as ED 072 153 MF $0.91 PC $30.05.

Edmonds, Ronald. *A Discussion of the Literature and Issues Related to Effective Schooling.* [1979]. 49 pages. ED 170 394 MF $0.91 PC not available from EDRS.

Fiedler, Fred E.; Chemers, Martin M.; and Mahar, Linda. *Improving Leadership Effectiveness: The Leader Match Concept.* New York: John Wiley & Sons. 1976.

Goldhammer, Keith; Becker, Gerald; Withycombe, Richard; Doyel, Frank; Miller, Edgar; Morgan, Claude; De Loretto, Louis; and Aldridge, Bill. *Elementary School Principals and Their Schools: Beacons of Brilliance and Potholes of Pestilence.* Eugene, Oregon: Center for the Advanced Study of Educational Administration, University of Oregon, 1971. 209 pages. ED 056 380 MF $0.91 PC $15.20.

Gorton, Richard A., and McIntyre, Kenneth E. *The Senior High School Principalship. Volume II: The Effective Principal.* Reston, Virginia: National Association of Secondary School Principals, 1978. 98 pages. ED 158 440. NASSP, 1904 Association Dr., Reston, VA 22091. $5.00 prepaid.

Hanson, E. Mark. *Educational Administration and Organizational Behavior.* Boston: Allyn & Bacon, 1979.

Lipham, James M. "Leadership: General Theory and Research." In *Leadership: The Science and the Art Today,* edited by Luvern L. Cunningham and William J. Gephart, pp. 1-15. Itaska, Illinios: F.E. Peacock Publishers, 1973.

Lipham, James M. and Daresh, John C., eds. *Administrative and Staff Relationships in Education: Research and Practice in IGE Schools. Wisconsin Research and Development Center for Individualized Schooling Monograph Series.* Madison: Research and Development Center for Individualized Schooling, 1979. 149 pages. ED 186 448. Wisconsin Research and Development Center Document Service, University of Wisconsin, School of Education, 1025 West Johnson St., Madison, WI 53706 ($6.50).

Myers, Donald A. "The Chatauqua Papers: A Dissent." *National Elementary Principal,* 54, 1 (September-October 1974), pp. 18-26. EJ 104 149.

Sergiovanni, Thomas J. "Is Leadership the Next Great Training Robbery?" *Educational Leadership,* 36, 6 (March 1979), pp. 388-94. EJ 197 877.

Terry, George R. *Principles of Management.* 3d ed. Homewood, Illinois: Richard D. Irwin, 1960.

Thomson, Scott D. "Editorial: Effective Leadership." *NASSP Newsletter,* 27, 8 (April 1980), p. 2.

Welte, Carl E. "Management and Leadership: Concepts with an Important Difference." *Personnel Journal,* 57, 11 (November 1978), pp. 630-32, 642. EJ 197 456.

CHAPTER 1: PORTRAIT OF A LEADER

Bass, Bernard M. *Leadership, Psychology, and Organizational Behavior.* New York: Harper & Brothers. 1960.

Bird, Charles. *Social Psychology.* New York: D. Appleton-Century Company, 1940.

Blumberg, Arthur, and Greenfield, William. *The Effective Principal: Perspectives on School Leadership.* Boston: Allyn and Bacon, 1980.

Cartwright, Dorwin, and Zander, Alvin. *Group Dynamics: Research and Theory.* 3d ed. New York: Harper & Row, 1968.

Goldhammer, Keith; Becker, Gerald; Withycombe, Richard; Doyel, Frank; Miller, Edgar; Morgan, Claude; De Loretto, Louis; and Aldridge, Bill. *Elementary School Principals and Their Schools: Beacons of Brilliance and Potholes of Pestilence.* Eugene, Oregon: Center for the Advanced Study of Educational Administration, University of Oregon, 1971. 209 pages. ED 056 380 MF $0.91 PC $15.20.

Gorton, Richard A., and McIntyre, Kenneth E. *The Senior High School Principalship. Volume II: The Effective Principal.* Reston, Virginia: National Association of Secondary School Principals, 1978. 98 pages. ED 158 440. NASSP, 1904 Association Dr., Reston, VA 22091. $5.00 prepaid.

Gouldner, Alvin W. *Studies in Leadership: Leadership and Democratic Action.* New York: Harper & Brothers, 1950.

Hanson, E. Mark. *Educational Administration and Organizational Behavior.* Boston: Allyn and Bacon, 1979.

Hemphill, John K.; Griffiths, Daniel E.; and Frederiksen, Norman. *Administrative Performance and Personality: A Study of the Principal in a Simulated Elementary School.* New York: Teachers College, Columbia University, 1962.

Hurlock, Elizabeth B. *Child Development.* NewYork: McGraw-Hill Book Company, Inc., 1956.

Lipham, James M. "Leadership: General Theory and Research." In *Leadership: The Science and the Art Today,* edited by Luvern L. Cunningham and William J. Gephart, pp. 1-15. Itaska, Illinois: F.E. Peacock Publishers, 1973.

Morphet, Edgar L.; Johns, Roe L.; and Reller, Theodore L. *Educational Organization and Administration: Concepts, Practices, and Issues.* 2d ed. Englewood Cliffs, New Jersey: Prentice-Hall, 1967.

St. Clair, Kenneth, and McIntyre, Kenneth. "The Recruitment, Selection and Preparation of Educational Leaders." In *Leadership: The Science and the Art Today,* edited by Luvern L. Cunningham and William J. Gephart, pp. 271-304. Itaska, Illinois: F.E. Peacock Publishers, 1973.

Speiss, Jack. "Concepts of Leadership." 1975. 15 pages. ED 102 680 MF $0.91 PC $2.00.

Stogdill, Ralph M. *Handbook of Leadership. A Survey of Theory and Research.* New York: The Free Press, Macmillan Publishing Company, 1974.

Wilson, Robert E. "The Anatomy of Success in the Superintendency." *Phi Delta Kappan,* 62, 1 (September 1980), pp. 20-21. EJ 232 032.

Yahraes, Herbert. *What Research Shows About Birth Order, Personality, and IQ.* Rockville, Maryland: Division of Scientific and Public Information, National Institute of Mental Health (DHEW), 1978. 13 pages. ED 178 204 MF $0.91 PC $2.00.

CHAPTER 2: WOMEN AND BLACKS

Adams, Edward F. "A Multivariable Study of Subordinate Perceptions of and Attitudes toward Minority and Majority Managers." *Journal of Applied Psychology,* 63, 3 (June 1978), pp. 277-88. EJ 181 520.

Behavior Today. The Professionals' Newsletter, 5, 2 (January 14, 1974).

Biklen, Sari Knopp. "Introduction: Barriers to Equity—Women, Educational Leadership, and Social Change." In *Women and Educational Leadership,* edited by Sari Knopp Biklen and Marilyn B. Brannigan, pp. 1-23. Lexington, Massachusetts: D.C. Heath and Company, 1980.

Byrne, David R.; Hines, Susan A.; and McCleary, Lloyd E. *The Senior High School Principalship. Volume I: The National Survey.* Reston, Virginia: National Association of Secondary School Principals, 1978. NASSP, 1904 Association Dr., Reston, VA 22091. $3.00.

Chapman, Robert L. "The Role Expectation of the Black Urban Principal As Perceived by Himself, Administrators, Influentials, and Other Active Community Persons." Paper, American Educational Research Association annual meeting, New Orleans, February 1973. 28 pages. ED 075 527 MF $0.91 PC $3.65.

Coffin, Gregory C. "The Black Administrator and How He's Being Pushed to Extinction." *American School Board Journal,* 159, 11 (May 1972), pp. 33-36. EJ 059 518.

Dale, Charlene, T. "Patterns of Discrimination." In *Wanted — More Women: Where Are the Women Superintendents?* by Charlene Dale and others, pp. 1-7. Washington, D.C.: National Council of Administrative Women in Education, 1973. Entire document 29 pages. ED 084 620 MF $0.91. PC not available from EDRS.

322

"The Elusive Black Educator." *School Management,* 13, 3 (March 1969), pp. 54-85.

Ethridge, Samuel B. "Impact of the 1954 Brown vs. Topeka Board of Education Decision on Black Educators." *The Negro Educational Review,* 30, 4 (October 1979), pp. 217-32. EJ 215 279.

Frelow, Robert D. "The Racial Integration Model and Minority Administrators." Paper, American Educational Research Association annual meeting, New Orleans, January 1973. 12 pages. ED 078 119 MF $0.91 PC $2.00.

Friedan, Betty, and West, Anne Grant. "Sex Bias: The Built-in Mentality That Maims the Public Schools." *American School Board Journal,* 159, 4 (October 1971), pp. 16-20. EJ 043 700.

Funderburk, Earl C. "Women: Their Responsibility in Professional Unity." In *Women: A Significant National Resource,* pp. 23-29. Washington, D.C.: American Association of School Administrators; and National Council of Administrative Women in Education, 1971. Entire document 50 pages. ED 082 297 MF $0.91. PC not available from EDRS.

Gross, Neal, and Trask, Anne E. *The Sex Factor and the Management of Schools.* New York: John Wiley & Sons, 1976.

Hines, Vynce A., and Grobman, Hulda. "The Weaker Sex Is Losing Out,"*American School Board Journal,* 132, 3 (March 1956), pp. 100, 102.

Hoyle, John. "Who Shall Be Principal?" *National Elementary Principal,* 48, 3 (January 1969), pp. 23-24.

James, J. C. "The Black Principal: Another Vanishing American." *National Elementary Principal,* 50, 4 (February 1971), pp. 20-25. EJ 035 645.

Johnson, Dorothy. "What Is the Future of Women in School Administration?" In *Women: A Significant National Resource,* pp. 31-45. Washington, D.C.: American Association of School Administrators; and National Council of Administrative Women in Education, 1971. Entire document 50 pages. ED 082 297 MF $0.91 PC not available from EDRS.

Krchniak, Stefan P. "Variables Associated with Low Incidence of Women in School Administration: Towards Empirical Underdings." Paper presented at annual meeting of American Educational Research Association, Toronto, March 1978. 25 pages. ED 150 719 MF $0.91 PC $2.00.

Krohn, Barbara. "The Puzzling Case of the Missing Ms." *Nation's Schools and Colleges,* (November 1974), pp. 32-38.

Lyon, Catherine Dillon, and Saario, Terry N. "Women in Public Education: Sexual Discrimination in Promotions." *Phi Delta Kappan,* 55, 2 (October 1973), pp. 120-23. EJ 085 962.

Meskin, Joan D. "The Performance of Women School Administrators—A Review of the Literature." *Administrator's Notebook*, 23, 1 (1974).

Mickish, Ginny. "Can Women Function as Successfully as Men in the Role of Elementary Principal?" *Research Reports in Educational Administration*, 2, 4 (January 1971). Boulder, Colorado: Bureau of Educational Research, 1971. 20 pages. ED 062 679 MF $0.91 PC $2.00.

Miner, John B. "Motivational Potential for Upgrading among Minority and Female Managers." *Journal of Applied Psychology*, 62, 6 (December 1977), pp. 691-97. EJ 171 503.

Moody, Charles D. "The Black Superintendent." *School Review*, 81, 3 (May 1973), pp. 375-82. EJ 080 138.

Pharis, William L., and Zakariya, Sally Banks. *The Elementary School Principalship in 1978: A Research Study*. Washington, D.C.: National Association of Elementary School Principals, 1979. 132 pages. ED 172 389. NAESP, 1801 North Moore St., Arlington, VA 22209. $15.00.

Pierce, Barbara. "Few at the Head of the Class." *Ms.*, 9, 6 (December 1980), p. 25.

Schmuck, Patricia Ann. "Deterrents to Women's Careers in School Management." Unpublished article. n.d.

Schmuck, Patricia Ann. *Sex Differentiation in Public School Administration*. "Wanted: More Women" Series. Washington, D.C.: National Council of Administrative Women in Education, 1975. 130 pages. ED 126 593 MF $0.91 PC not available from EDRS.

Schmuck, Patricia Ann. "The Sex Dimension: An Overview." In *Educational Policy and Management: Sex Differential*, edited by Patricia Schmuck and W. W. Charters, Jr., pp. 4-9. New York: Academic Press, 1981.

Seawell, William H., and Canady, Robert Lynn. "Where Have All the Women Gone?" *National Elementary Principal*, 43, 4 (May/June 1974), pp. 46-48.

Townsel, Charles W. "The Urban School Administrator: A Black Perspective." n.d. 18 pages. ED 117 254 MF $0.91 PC $2.00.

Truett, Carol, "Women in Educational Administration: Is There a Basic Role Conflict?" Paper presented at conference on Women and Work, Bloomington, Indiana, March 1979. 29 pages. ED 172 440 MF $0.91 PC $3.65.

Weber, Margaret B.; Feldman, Jean R.; and Poling, Eve C. "Why Women Are Underrepresented in Educational Administration." *Educational Leadership*, 38, 4 (January 1981), pp. 320-22. EJ 240 448.

Wilson, Laval S. "Training Minority Men for the Superintendency." *Phi Delta Kappan*, 53, 3 (November 1971), pp. 187-88. EJ 046 052.

CHAPTER 3: LEADERSHIP STYLES

Barrett, Leverne A., and Yoder, Edgar P. "Are You an Administrator or a Leader?" *NASSP Bulletin*, 64, 440 (December 1980), pp. 56-59. EJ 236 618.
Bonoma, Thomas V., and Slevin, Dennis P. *Executive Survival Manual: A Program for Managerial Effectiveness*. Boston; and Belmont, California: CBI Publishing Company; and Wadsworth Publishing Company, 1978.
DeTurk, Phillip H. "Survival in the Principalship." *National Elementary Principal*, 56, 2 (November/December 1976), pp. 33-37. EJ 150 155.
Fiedler, Fred. E. *A Theory of Leadership Effectiveness*. New York: McGraw-Hill Book Company, 1967.
Fiedler, Fred E. "Responses to Sergiovanni." *Educational Leadership*, 36, 6 (March 1979), pp. 394-96. EJ 197 878.
Fiedler, Fred E.; Chemers, Martin M.; and Mahar, Linda. *Improving Leadership Effectiveness: The Leader Match Concept*. New York: John Wiley & Sons. 1976.
Gates, Philip E.; Blanchard, Kenneth H.; and Hersey, Paul. "Diagnosing Educational Leadership Problems: A Situational Approach." *Educational Leadership*, 33, 5 (February 1976), pp. 348-54.
Halpin, Andrew W. "How Leaders Behave." In *Organizations and Human Behavior: Focus on Schools*, edited by Fred D. Carver and Thomas J. Sergiovanni, pp. 287-315. New York: McGraw-Hill Book Company, 1969.
Hanson, E. Mark. *Educational Administration and Organizational Behavior*. Boston: Allyn and Bacon, 1979.
Hencley, Stephen P. "Situational Behavioral Approach to the Study of Educational Leadership." In *Leadership: The Science and the Art Today*, edited by Luvern L. Cunningham and William J. Gephart, pp. 139-64. Itaska, Illinois: F.E. Peacock Publishers, 1973.
Hersey, Paul, and Blanchard, Kenneth. *Management of Organizational Behavior: Utilizing Human Resources*. Englewood Cliffs, New Jersey: Prentice-Hall, 1969.
Holloway, William H., and Niazi, Ghulam A. "A Study of Leadership Style, Situation Favorableness, and the Risk Taking Behavior of Leaders." *Journal of Educational Administration*, 16, 2 (October 1978), pp. 160-68. EJ 199 523.
Lipham, James M. "Leadership: General Theory and Research." In *Leadership: The Science and the Art Today*, edited by Luvern L. Cunningham and William J. Gephart, pp. 1-15. Itaska, Illinois: F.E. Peacock Publishers, 1973.

SCHOOL LEADERSHIP: HANDBOOK FOR SURVIVAL

McGregor, Douglas. *The Human Side of Enterprise.* New York: McGraw-Hill, 1960.

Miskel, Cecil G. "Principals' Attitudes Toward Work and Coworkers, Situational Factors, Perceived Effectiveness, and Innovation Effort." *Educational Administration Quarterly,* 13, 2 (Spring 1977), pp. 51-70. EJ 164 198.

Reddin, William J. *Managerial Effectiveness.* New York: McGraw-Hill Book Company, 1970.

Sergiovanni, Thomas J. "Is Leadership the Next Great Training Robbery?" *Educational Leadership,* 36, 6 (March 1979), pp. 388-94. EJ 197 877.

Sergiovanni, Thomas J., and Elliott, David L. *Educational and Organizational Leadership in Elementary Schools.* Englewood Cliffs, New Jersey: Prentice-Hall, 1975.

Tannenbaum, Robert, and Schmidt, Warren H. "How to Choose a Leadership Pattern." In *Organizational Behavior and the Practice of Management,* edited by David R. Hampton, Charles E. Summer, and Ross A. Webber, pp. 501-09. Glenview, Illinois: Scott, Foresman and Company, 1968.

CHAPTER 4: SCHOOL-BASED MANAGEMENT

Beaubier, Edward W., and Thayer, Arthur N., eds. *Participative Management—Decentralized Decision Making: Working Models. A Monograph.* Burlingame: Association of California School Administrators, [1973]. 87 pages. ED 073 542 MF $0.91 PC $6.95.

Bremer, John. "Power and the Principalship." *National Elementary Principal,* 55, 2 (November-December 1975), pp. 18-21. EJ 127 664.

Caldwell, Brian J. "Resource Allocation at the School Level: An Examination of School-Based Budgeting in Canada and the United States." Paper, Seventh National Conference on Educational Administration, Australian Council for Educational Administration, Adelaide, South Australia, August 31-September 5, 1980. 54 pages. ED 195 044 MF $0.91 PC $5.30.

California State Department of Education. *Establishing School Site Councils. California School Improvement Program.* Sacramento: 1977. 30 pages. ED 150 737 MF $0.91 PC not available from EDRS.

Cunningham, Luvern L. "The Magnificent Pandora of Decentralization." *The School Administrator,* (June 1970), pp. 5-8. Copies not available.

Cunningham, Paul H. "Decentralized Budgeting: Making the Management Team Work." Paper, National School Boards Association annual meeting, Anaheim, April 1978. 16 pages. ED 154 499 MF $0.91 PC $2.00.

Decker, Erwin A., and others. *Site Management. An Analysis of the Concepts and Fundamental Operational Components Associated with the Delegation of Decision-Making Authority and Control of Resources to the School-Site Level in the California Public School System.* Sacramento: California State Department of Education, 1977. 37 pages. ED 150 736. Publications Sales, California State Department of Education, P.O. Box 271, Sacramento, CA 95802. $1.50.

Dickey, William K. "School Site Budgeting—A School Business Administrator's View." *Educational Economics*, (February 1977), pp. 15, 17. No longer published.

Fowler, Charles W. "School-Site Budgeting and Why It Could Be the Answer to Your Problems." *Executive Educator*, Premier Issue, (October 1978), pp. 37-39. EJ 194 000.

Gasson, John. "Autonomy, the Precursor to Change in Elementary Schools." *National Elementary Principal*, 52, 3 (November 1972), pp. 83-85. EJ 067 451.

Gowler, Doug. "A Principal's Open Letter to Stephen Bailey." *National Elementary Principal*, 59, 4 (June 1980), pp. 17-18. EJ 227 828.

Guthrie, James W. "Creating Efficient Schools: The Wonder Is They Work at All." Paper in *The Financing of Quality Education, Proceedings of a Symposium (Rochester, New York, October 27-28, 1977)*, edited by William A. Johnson, Jr. and others. Rochester, New York: Urban League of Rochester; and College of Education, University of Rochester, 1977. 27 pages. ED 177 672. Complete document, 117 pages, ED 177 668 MF $0.91 PC $8.60.

Houts, Paul L. "The Changing Role of the Elementary School Principal: Report of a Conference." *National Elementary Principal*, 55, 2 (November-December 1975), pp. 62-73. EJ 127 671.

"An Interview with Scott Thomson." *NASSP Bulletin*, 64, 432 (January 1980), pp. 76-84. EJ 214 230.

Kirst, Michael W. "The Changing Politics of Education: Actions and Strategies." Paper in *The Changing Politics of Education: Prospects for the 1980's*, edited by Edith K. Mosher and Jennings L. Wagoner, Jr., pp. 145-70. Bloomington, Indiana: Phi Delta Kappa, 1978. 26 pages. ED 166 786. Complete document, 359 pages, ED 166 774. McCutchan Publishing Corp., 2526 Grove St., Berkeley, CA 94704. $14.00.

Longstreth, James. "School Site Management and Budgeting Systems: A Guide for Effective Implementation." Preliminary draft, mimeographed. Washington, D.C.: National Urban Coalition, [1979].

National Urban Coalition. "Four Case Studies of School Site Lump Sum Budgeting." Preliminary draft, mimeographed. Washington, D.C.: National Urban Coalition, [circa 1978].

Parker, Barbara. "School Based Management: Improve Education by Giving Parents, Principals More Control of Your Schools." *American School Board Journal*, 166, 7 (July 1979), pp. 20-21, 24. EJ 204 749.

Pierce, Lawrence C. *School Based Management. OSSC Bulletin Volume 23, Number 10*. Eugene, Oregon: Oregon School Study Council, University of Oregon, June 1980. 56 pages. ED 188 320. Oregon School Study Council, University of Oregon, Eugene, OR 97403. $2.00, $1.50 prepaid.

Schofield, Dee. *Community Involvement in Educational Governance.* School Leadership Digest, Second Series, Number 2. Arlington, Virginia: National Association of Elementary School Principals, 1975. 30 pages. ED 112 455 MF $0.91 PC $3.65.

Shuster, Albert H. "Going It Alone: The Autonomous School." *National Elementary Principal,* 53, 3 (March-April 1974), pp. 52-56. EJ 096 027.

Throop, Frank Allen. "Professional Autonomy in the Lansing Public Schools: A Model for the Decentralization of Administrative Functions in an Urban School System." Ph.D. dissertation, Michigan State University, 1973. 207 pages. University Microfilms, Dissertation Copies, P.O. Box 1764, Ann Arbor, MI 48106. Order No. 74-13, 987. MF $13.00 PC $24.00.

Tucker, Harvey J., and Zeigler, L. Harmon. *The Politics of Educational Governance: An Overview.* State-of-the-Knowledge Series, Number 36. Eugene, Oregon: ERIC Clearinghouse on Educational Management, University of Oregon, 1980. 73 pages. ED 182 799. ERIC Clearinghouse on Educational Management, University of Oregon, Eugene, OR 97403. $3.50.

Wells, Barbara, and Carr, Larry. "With the Pursestrings, Comes the Power." *Thrust for Educational Leadership,* 8, 2 (November 1978), pp. 14-15. EJ 200 705.

Zale, Andrew P. "Toffler: Schools Will Be More Flexible." *American School Board Journal,* 167, 7 (July 1980), p. 4.

CHAPTER 3: LEADERSHIP STYLES

Barrett, Leverne A., and Yoder, Edgar P. "Are You an Administrator or a Leader?" *NASSP Bulletin*, 64, 440 (December 1980), pp. 56-59. EJ 236 618.

Bonoma, Thomas V., and Slevin, Dennis P. *Executive Survival Manual: A Program for Managerial Effectiveness*. Boston; and Belmont, California: CBI Publishing Company; and Wadsworth Publishing Company, 1978.

DeTurk, Phillip H. "Survival in the Principalship." *National Elementary Principal*, 56, 2 (November/December 1976), pp. 33-37. EJ 150 155.

Fiedler, Fred. E. *A Theory of Leadership Effectiveness*. New York: McGraw-Hill Book Company, 1967.

Fiedler, Fred E. "Responses to Sergiovanni." *Educational Leadership*, 36, 6 (March 1979), pp. 394-96. EJ 197 878.

Fiedler, Fred E.; Chemers, Martin M.; and Mahar, Linda. *Improving Leadership Effectiveness: The Leader Match Concept*. New York: John Wiley & Sons. 1976.

Gates, Philip E.; Blanchard, Kenneth H.; and Hersey, Paul. "Diagnosing Educational Leadership Problems: A Situational Approach." *Educational Leadership*, 33, 5 (February 1976), pp. 348-54.

Halpin, Andrew W. "How Leaders Behave." In *Organizations and Human Behavior: Focus on Schools*, edited by Fred D. Carver and Thomas J. Sergiovanni, pp. 287-315. New York: McGraw-Hill Book Company, 1969.

Hanson, E. Mark. *Educational Administration and Organizational Behavior*. Boston: Allyn and Bacon, 1979.

Hencley, Stephen P. "Situational Behavioral Approach to the Study of Educational Leadership." In *Leadership: The Science and the Art Today*, edited by Luvern L. Cunningham and William J. Gephart, pp. 139-64. Itaska, Illinois: F.E. Peacock Publishers, 1973.

Hersey, Paul, and Blanchard, Kenneth. *Management of Organizational Behavior: Utilizing Human Resources*. Englewood Cliffs, New Jersey: Prentice-Hall, 1969.

Holloway, William H., and Niazi, Ghulam A. "A Study of Leadership Style, Situation Favorableness, and the Risk Taking Behavior of Leaders." *Journal of Educational Administration*, 16, 2 (October 1978), pp. 160-68. EJ 199 523.

Lipham, James M. "Leadership: General Theory and Research." In *Leadership: The Science and the Art Today*, edited by Luvern L. Cunningham and William J. Gephart, pp. 1-15. Itaska, Illinois: F.E. Peacock Publishers, 1973.

McGregor, Douglas. *The Human Side of Enterprise.* New York: McGraw-Hill, 1960.

Miskel, Cecil G. "Principals' Attitudes Toward Work and Coworkers, Situational Factors, Perceived Effectiveness, and Innovation Effort." *Educational Administration Quarterly,* 13, 2 (Spring 1977), pp. 51-70. EJ 164 198.

Reddin, William J. *Managerial Effectiveness.* New York: McGraw-Hill Book Company, 1970.

Sergiovanni, Thomas J. "Is Leadership the Next Great Training Robbery?" *Educational Leadership,* 36, 6 (March 1979), pp. 388-94. EJ 197 877.

Sergiovanni, Thomas J., and Elliott, David L. *Educational and Organizational Leadership in Elementary Schools.* Englewood Cliffs, New Jersey: Prentice-Hall, 1975.

Tannenbaum, Robert, and Schmidt, Warren H. "How to Choose a Leadership Pattern." In *Organizational Behavior and the Practice of Management,* edited by David R. Hampton, Charles E. Summer, and Ross A. Webber, pp. 501-09. Glenview, Illinois: Scott, Foresman and Company, 1968.

CHAPTER 4: SCHOOL-BASED MANAGEMENT

Beaubier, Edward W., and Thayer, Arthur N., eds. *Participative Management—Decentralized Decision Making: Working Models. A Monograph.* Burlingame: Association of California School Administrators, [1973]. 87 pages. ED 073 542 MF $0.91 PC $6.95.

Bremer, John. "Power and the Principalship." *National Elementary Principal,* 55, 2 (November-December 1975), pp. 18-21. EJ 127 664.

Caldwell, Brian J. "Resource Allocation at the School Level: An Examination of School-Based Budgeting in Canada and the United States." Paper, Seventh National Conference on Educational Administration, Australian Council for Educational Administration, Adelaide, South Australia, August 31-September 5, 1980. 54 pages. ED 195 044 MF $0.91 PC $5.30.

California State Department of Education. *Establishing School Site Councils. California School Improvement Program.* Sacramento: 1977. 30 pages. ED 150 737 MF $0.91 PC not available from EDRS.

Cunningham, Luvern L. "The Magnificent Pandora of Decentralization." *The School Administrator,* (June 1970), pp. 5-8. Copies not available.

Cunningham, Paul H. "Decentralized Budgeting: Making the Management Team Work." Paper, National School Boards Association annual meeting, Anaheim, April 1978. 16 pages. ED 154 499 MF $0.91 PC $2.00.

Decker, Erwin A., and others. *Site Management. An Analysis of the Concepts and Fundamental Operational Components Associated with the Delegation of Decision-Making Authority and Control of Resources to the School-Site Level in the California Public School System.* Sacramento: California State Department of Education, 1977. 37 pages. ED 150 736. Publications Sales, California State Department of Education, P.O. Box 271, Sacramento, CA 95802. $1.50.

Dickey, William K. "School Site Budgeting—A School Business Administrator's View." *Educational Economics,* (February 1977), pp. 15, 17. No longer published.

Fowler, Charles W. "School-Site Budgeting and Why It Could Be the Answer to Your Problems." *Executive Educator,* Premier Issue, (October 1978), pp. 37-39. EJ 194 000.

Gasson, John. "Autonomy, the Precursor to Change in Elementary Schools." *National Elementary Principal,* 52, 3 (November 1972), pp. 83-85. EJ 067 451.

Gowler, Doug. "A Principal's Open Letter to Stephen Bailey." *National Elementary Principal,* 59, 4 (June 1980), pp. 17-18. EJ 227 828.

Guthrie, James W. "Creating Efficient Schools: The Wonder Is They Work at All." Paper in *The Financing of Quality Education, Proceedings of a Symposium (Rochester, New York, October 27-28, 1977),* edited by William A. Johnson, Jr. and others. Rochester, New York: Urban League of Rochester; and College of Education, University of Rochester, 1977. 27 pages. ED 177 672. Complete document, 117 pages, ED 177 668 MF $0.91 PC $8.60.

Houts, Paul L. "The Changing Role of the Elementary School Principal: Report of a Conference." *National Elementary Principal,* 55, 2 (November-December 1975), pp. 62-73. EJ 127 671.

"An Interview with Scott Thomson." *NASSP Bulletin,* 64, 432 (January 1980), pp. 76-84. EJ 214 230.

Kirst, Michael W. "The Changing Politics of Education: Actions and Strategies." Paper in *The Changing Politics of Education: Prospects for the 1980's,* edited by Edith K. Mosher and Jennings L. Wagoner, Jr., pp. 145-70. Bloomington, Indiana: Phi Delta Kappa, 1978. 26 pages. ED 166 786. Complete document, 359 pages, ED 166 774. McCutchan Publishing Corp., 2526 Grove St., Berkeley, CA 94704. $14.00.

Longstreth, James. "School Site Management and Budgeting Systems: A Guide for Effective Implementation." Preliminary draft, mimeographed. Washington, D.C.: National Urban Coalition, [1979].

National Urban Coalition. "Four Case Studies of School Site Lump Sum Budgeting." Preliminary draft, mimeographed. Washington, D.C.: National Urban Coalition, [circa 1978].

Parker, Barbara. "School Based Management: Improve Education by Giving Parents, Principals More Control of Your Schools." *American School Board Journal*, 166, 7 (July 1979), pp. 20-21, 24. EJ 204 749.

Pierce, Lawrence C. *School Based Management. OSSC Bulletin Volume 23, Number 10*. Eugene, Oregon: Oregon School Study Council, University of Oregon, June 1980. 56 pages. ED 188 320. Oregon School Study Council, University of Oregon, Eugene, OR 97403. $2.00, $1.50 prepaid.

Schofield, Dee. *Community Involvement in Educational Governance*. School Leadership Digest, Second Series, Number 2. Arlington, Virginia: National Association of Elementary School Principals, 1975. 30 pages. ED 112 455 MF $0.91 PC $3.65.

Shuster, Albert H. "Going It Alone: The Autonomous School." *National Elementary Principal*, 53, 3 (March-April 1974), pp. 52-56. EJ 096 027.

Throop, Frank Allen. "Professional Autonomy in the Lansing Public Schools: A Model for the Decentralization of Administrative Functions in an Urban School System." Ph.D. dissertation, Michigan State University, 1973. 207 pages. University Microfilms, Dissertation Copies, P.O. Box 1764, Ann Arbor, MI 48106. Order No. 74-13, 987. MF $13.00 PC $24.00.

Tucker, Harvey J., and Zeigler, L. Harmon. *The Politics of Educational Governance: An Overview*. State-of-the-Knowledge Series, Number 36. Eugene, Oregon: ERIC Clearinghouse on Educational Management, University of Oregon, 1980. 73 pages. ED 182 799. ERIC Clearinghouse on Educational Management, University of Oregon, Eugene, OR 97403. $3.50.

Wells, Barbara, and Carr, Larry. "With the Pursestrings, Comes the Power." *Thrust for Educational Leadership*, 8, 2 (November 1978), pp. 14-15. EJ 200 705.

Zale, Andrew P. "Toffler: Schools Will Be More Flexible." *American School Board Journal*, 167, 7 (July 1980), p. 4.

CHAPTER 5: TEAM MANAGEMENT

American Association of School Administrators. *The Administrative Leadership Team.* Arlington, Virginia: 1979. AASA, 1801 North Moore St., Arlington, VA 22209. $3.50.

Anderson, Lester W. "Management Team Versus Collective Bargaining for Principals." *NASSP Bulletin,* 54, 346 (May 1970), pp. 169-76. EJ 020 959.

"The Brewing—and, Perhaps, Still Preventable—Revolt of the School Principals." *American School Board Journal,* 163, 1 (January 1976), pp. 25-27. EJ 130 919.

Coelho, Robert J. "Administrative Team Approach—Development and Implementation." Paper, American Association of School Administrators annual meeting, Dallas, February 1975. 21 pages. ED 106 947 MF $0.91 PC $2.00.

Cross, Ray. "The Administrative Team or Decentralization?" *National Elementary Principal,* 54, 2 (November-December 1974), pp. 80-82. EJ 107 277.

Duncan, Robert C. "New Wine in New Bottles: The Administrative Team Revisited." *Planning and Changing,* 7, 2 (Summer 1976), pp. 35-44. EJ 150 202.

Erickson, Kenneth A., and Gmelch, Walter H. *School Management Teams: Their Structure, Function, and Operation. ERS Monograph.* Arlington, Virginia: Educational Research Service, Inc., 1977. 66 pages, ED 144 230. ERS, Inc. 1800 N. Kent St., Arlington, VA 22209. $9.00.

Floratos, Nick; Murchison, William R.; Baumgartner, Jay; Long, John; Guest, Bill; and Walker, Don. "The Management Team and Survival."*Thrust for Educational Leadership,* 8, 2 (November 1978), pp. 5-8. EJ 200 701.

McNally, Harold J. "A Matter of Trust: The Administrative Team." *National Elementary Principal,* 53, 1 (November-December 1973), pp. 20-25. EJ 085 992.

National Association of Secondary School Principals. *Management Crisis: A Solution.* Washington, D.C.: 1971. 33 pages. ED 056 399 MF $0.91 PC not available from EDRS.

Salmon, Paul B. "Are the Administrative Team and Collective Bargaining Compatible?" *Compact,* 6, 3 (June 1972), pp. 3-5. EJ 061 340.

Schmuck, Richard A. "Development of Management Teamwork: National Overview." Paper, Educational Managers Annual Academy, Wemme, Oregon, July 1974. ED 094 456 MF $0.91 PC $2.00.

Starr, Warren D. "Forging the Administrative Team." *NASSP Bulletin,* 62, 414 (January 1978), pp. 16-20. EJ 171 506.

Wynn, Richard. *Theory and Practice of the Administrative Team.* Washington, D.C.: National Association of Elementary School Principals. 52 pages. ED 082 367 MF $0.91 PC not available from EDRS.

CHAPTER 6: PARTICIPATIVE DECISION-MAKING

Alutto, Joseph A., and Belasco, James A. "Patterns of Teacher Participation in School System Decision Making." *Educational Administration Quarterly,* 9, 1 (Winter 1973), pp. 27-41. EJ 070 763.

Anthony, Margaret, "An Inside View of Shared Leadership." *Educational Leadership,* 38, 6 (March 1981), pp. 487-88. EJ number not yet assigned.

Crockenberg, Vincent, and Clark, Woodrow W., Jr. "Teacher Participation in School Decision Making: The San Jose Teacher Involvement Project." *Phi Delta Kappan,* 61, 2 (October 1979), pp. 115-18. EJ 208 030.

Keef, James L. "Teacher 'Restlessness' and Decision Making." *ClearingHouse,* 52, 9 (May 1979), pp. 410-12. EJ 202 531.

Knoop, Robert, and O'Reilly, Robert. *Participative Decision Making in Curriculum.* [1975]. 10 pages. ED 102 684 MF $0.91 PC $2.00.

Likert, Jane Gibson, and Likert, Rensis. "New Resources for Improving School Administration." *NASSP Bulletin,* 64, 435 (April 1980), pp. 49-58. EJ 219 600.

Lipham, James M. *Effective Principal, Effective School.* Reston, Virginia: National Association of Secondary School Principals, 1981. 26 pages. ED number not yet available. NASSP, 1904 Association Dr., Reston, VA 22091. $3.00, payment must accompany order.

Longstreth, James. "School Site Management and Budgeting Systems: A Guide for Effective Implementation." Preliminary draft, mimeographed. Washington, D.C.: National Urban Coalition, [1979].

Lowell, Carl Duane. "The Distribution of Power, Group-Decision, and Behavioral Outcomes." Ph.D. dissertation, University of Oregon, 1972. 296 pages. University Microfilms International, P.O. Box 1764, Ann Arbor, MI 48106. Order No. 73-13746 MF $7.50 HC $15.00.

McNally, Harold J. "A Matter of Trust. The Administrative Team." *National Elementary Principal,* 53, 1 (November-December 1973), pp. 20-25, EJ 085 992.

Mohrman, Allan M., Jr.; Cooke, Robert A.; and Mohrman, Susan Albers. "Participation in Decision Making: A Multidimensional Perspective." *Educational Administration Quarterly,* 14, 1 (Winter 1978), pp. 13-29. EJ 183 277.

Mt. Diablo Unified School District. *The Mt. Diablo Individual School Management "ISMS."* Concord, California: 1978. 105 pages. ED 163 618. MF $0.91 PC not available.

Muccigrosso, Robert M. "Leadership through Shared Problem Solving." *Momentum,* 11, 1 (February 1980), pp. 28-31. EJ 226 873.

Piper, Donald L. "Decisionmaking: Decisions Made by Individuals vs. Those Made by Group Concensus or Group Participation." *Educational Administration Quarterly,* 10, 2 (Spring 1974), pp. 82-95. EJ 100 938.

Schmuck, Richard A.; Runkel, Philip J.; Arends, Jane H.; and Arends, Richard I. *The Second Handbook of Organizational Development in Schools.* Palo Alto, California: Mayfield Publishing Company, 1977. Mayfield Publishing Co., 285 Hamilton Ave., Palo Alto, CA 94301. $16.95.

Speed, Noel Eric. *Decision Participation and Staff Satisfaction in Middle and Junior High Schools That Individualize Instruction.* Madison, Wisconsin: Research and Development Center for Individualized Schooling, University of Wisconsin, 1979. 228 pages. ED 182 849 MF $0.91 PC not available from EDRS.

Wadia, Maneck S. "Participative Management: Three Common Problems." *Personnel Journal,* 59, 11 (November 1980), pp. 927-28. EJ 235 787.

Weingast, David. "Shared Leadership—'The Damn Thing Works.'" *Educational Leadership,* 37, 6 (March 1980), pp. 502-4, 506. EJ 217 753.

CHAPTER 7: SCHOOL CLIMATE

Brookover, Wilbur; Beady, Charles; Flood, Patricia; Schweitzer, John; and Wisenbaker, Joe. *School Social Systems and Student Achievement. Schools Can Make a Difference.* New York: Praeger Publishers, 1979. 237 pages.

Chamberlin, L. J. *Effective Instruction through Dynamic Discipline.* Columbus, Ohio: Charles E. Merrill, 1971.

Clark, Frank J. *Improving the School Climate. Operations Notebook 19.* Burlingame, California: Association of California School Administrators, 1977. 43 pages. ED 145 567. ACSA, 1575 Old Bayshore Hwy., Burlingame, CA 94010. $2.00, members; $4.00, nonmembers.

Coleman, James S., and others. *Equality of Educational Opportunity.* Washington, D.C.: Department of Health, Education and Welfare; U.S. Government Printing Office, 1966. 235 pages. ED 012 275. MF $0.91 PC $16.85.

Halpin, Andrew W. "The Organizational Climate of Schools." Chapter 4 in *Theory and Research in Administration,* pp. 121-249. New York: The Macmillan Co., 1966. Out of print.

Halpin, Andrew W., and Croft, Don B. *The Organizational Climate of Schools.* St. Louis: Washington University, 1962. 199 pages. ED 002 897 MF $0.91 PC $13.55.

Howard, Eugene R. "School Climate Improvement." *Thrust for Education Leadership,* 3, 3 (January 1974), pp. 12-14. EJ 092 195.

Jencks, Christopher, and others. *Inequality: A Reassessment of the Effect of Family and Schooling in America.* New York: Basic Books, 1972. 399 pages. ED 077 551. Basic Books, Inc., 404 Park Ave. S., New York, NY 10016. $12.50.

Lindstrom, Robert J. "Between Cliff-Hanger and Climax." *Thrust for Educational Leadership,* 7, 2 (November 1977), pp. 6-7, 14.

Lipham, James M. *Effective Principal, Effective School.* Reston, Virginia: National Association of Secondary School Principals, 1981. 26 pages. EA 013 836. NASSP, 1904 Association Dr., Reston, VA 22091. $3.00.

Litwin, George H., and Stringer, Robert A., Jr. *Motivation and Organizational Climate.* Boston: Division of Research, Graduate School of Business Administration, Harvard University, 1968. 214 pages.

Maynard, William. "A Case Study: The Impact of a Humanistic School Climate." *NASSP Bulletin,* 60, 399 (April 1976), pp. 16-20. EJ 149 642.

Ogilvie, Doug, and Sadler, D. Royce. "Perceptions of School Effectiveness and Its Relationship to Organizational Climate." *Journal of Educational Administration,* 17, 2 (October 1979), pp. 139-47. EJ 225 433.

"On School Effectiveness: A Conversation with Peter Mortimore." *Educational Leadership,* 38, 3 (May 1981), pp. 642-45. EJ number not yet assigned.

Phi Delta Kappa. *School Climate Improvement: A Challenge to the School Administrator. An Occasional Paper.* Bloomington, Indiana: 1974. 149 pages. ED 102 665. Phi Delta Kappa, Eighth St. & Union Ave., Bloomington, IN 47401. $3.00.

Ravitch, Diane. "The Meaning of the New Coleman Report." *Phi Delta Kappan,* 62, 10 (June 1981), pp. 718-20. EJ number not yet assigned.

Rutter, Michael; Maughan, Barbara; Mortimore, Peter; Ouston, Janet; and Smith, Alan. *Fifteen Thousand Hours. Secondary*

Schools and Their Effects on Children. Cambridge, Massachusetts: Harvard University Press, 1979. 285 pages.

Schmuck, Richard A.; Runkel, Philip J.; Arends, Jane H.; and Arends, Richard I. *The Second Handbook of Organization Development in Schools.* Palo Alto, California: Mayfield Publishing Company, 1977. 590 pages. Mayfield Publishing Co., 285 Hamilton Ave., Palo Alto, CA 94301. $16.95.

Shaheen, Thomas A., and Pedrick, W. Roberts. *School District Climate Improvement: A Challenge to the School Superintendent.* Denver: CFK Ltd., 1974. 154 pages. ED 105 605. Nueva Day Care and Learning Center, CFK, Ltd. Publications, 6565 Skyline Blvd., Hillsborough, CA 94010. $4.00.

Steele, Fritz, and Jenks, Stephen. *The Feel of the Work Place: Understanding and Improving Organization Climate.* Reading, Massachusetts: Addison-Wesley, 1977. 194 pages.

Warrick, D. D. "Managing the Stress of Organizational Development." *Training and Development Journal,* 35, 4 (April 1981), pp. 36-41. EJ 241 908.

Wynne, Edward A. "Looking at Good Schools." *Phi Delta Kappan,* 62, 5 (January 1981), pp. 377-81. EJ 238 632.

Zigarmi, Drea, and Sinclair, Ron. "The Effect of a Strike on Perceived Organizational Climate: A Study of a Middle School." *Education,* 99, 3 (Spring 1979), pp. 270-78. EJ 203 589.

CHAPTER 8: COMMUNICATING

Armistead, Lew. *An Organic Guide to School Public Relations: ACSA Operations Notebook 5.* Burlingame, California: Association of California School Administrators, 1977. 55 pages. ED 151 943. ASCA, 1575 Old Bayshore Highway, Burlingame, CA 94012. $2.00 members; $4.00, nonmembers.

Bagin, Don; Grazian, Frank; Harrison, Charles. *PR for School Board Members. A Guide for Members of Boards of Education and School Administrators to Improve and Strengthen School Information Programs.* Volume 8: AASA Executive Handbook Series. ERIC/CEM State-of-the-Knowledge Series, Number 33. Washington, D.C. and Eugene, Oregon: American Association of School Administrators; and ERIC Clearinghouse on Educational Management, University of Oregon, 1976. 74 pages. ED 127 656. AASA, 1801 N. Moore St., Arlington, VA 22209. Stock No. 021-00458. $2.50 prepaid.

Carpenter, C. C. "Principal Leadership and Parent Advisory Groups." *Phi Delta Kappan,* 56, 6 (February 1975), pp. 426-27. EJ 110 933.

Gemmet, Richard. *A Monograph on Interpersonal Communications.* Redwood City, California: San Mateo County Superintendent of Schools, 1977. 48 pages. ED 153 323. San Mateo County Office of Education, 333 Main St., Redwood Clity, CA 94063. $2.00, checks payable to County School Service Fund.

Hofstrand, Richard K., and Phipps, Lloyd J. *Advisory Councils for Education: A Handbook.* Urbana: Department of Vocational and Technical Education, University of Illinois, 1971. 49 pages. ED 057 213 MF $0.91 PC $3.65.

Ingari, Sandro. "A Case Study in Human Relations." *NASSP Bulletin,* 60, 401 (September 1976), pp. 103-6. EJ 153 064.

Jung, Charles; Howard, Rosalie; Emory, Ruth; and Pino, Rene. *Interpersonal Communications: Participant Materials and Leader's Manual.* Portland, Oregon: Northwest Regional Educational Laboratory, 1973. 935 pages. ED 095 127. Xicom, Inc., Production Management, RFD 1, Sterling Forest, Tuxedo, NY 10987. Participant manual, $14.50; leader's manual, $22.50.

Price, Nelson C. *School Community Councils and Advisory Boards: A Notebook for Administrators. Why? Who? What? When? How? Operations Notebook 18.* Burlingame, California: Association of California School Administrators, 1977. 49 pages. ED 145 583. ACSA, 1575 Old Bayshore Highway, Burlingame, CA 94010. $2.50.

Pulley, Jerry L. "The Principal and Communication: Some Points of Interference." *NASSP Bulletin,* 59, 387 (January 1975), pp. 50-54. EJ 110 325.

Sayers, Susan. *Effective Groups: Guidelines for Participants. Keys to Community Involvement Series: 9.* Arlington, Virginia; and Portland, Oregon: National School Public Relations Association, and Northwest Regional Educational Laboratory, 1973. 23 pages. ED 161 125. NSPRA, 1801 N. Moore St., Arlington, VA 22209. $2.00; set of 15 keys, $24.00.

Schmuck, Richard A.; Runkel, Philip J.; Arends, Jane H.; and Arends, Richard I. *The Second Handbook of Organization Development in Schools.* Palo Alto, California: Mayfield Publishing Company, 1977. 590 pages. ED 163 664. Mayfield Publishing Company, 285 Hamilton Ave., Palo Alto, CA 94301. $16.95.

Schutz, William. "The Ego FIRO Theory and the Leader as Completer." In *Leadership and Interpersonal Behavior,* edited by Luigi Petrullo and Bernard M. Bass, pp. 48-65. New York: Holt, Rinehart and Winston, 1961.

Stanton, Jim; Whittaker, Bobbi; and Zerchykov, Ross. *Resource Guide and Bibliography on School Councils.* Boston, Massachusetts: Institute for Responsive Education, 1978. 104 pages. ED 157 142 MF $0.91 PC not available from EDRS.

Valentine, Jerry W.; Tate, Bradford L.; Seagren, Alan T.; and Lammel, John A. "Administrative Verbal Behavior: What You Say Does Make a Difference." *NASSP Bulletin,* 59, 395 (December 1975), pp. 67-74. EJ 135 571.

CHAPTER 9: LEADING MEETINGS

Auger, B. Y. *How to Run Better Business Meetings: A Businessman's Guide to Meetings That Get Things Done.* St. Paul: Visual Products Division, Minnesota Mining and Manufacturing Co., 1972. 191 pages. Visual Products Div., Minnesota Mining & Manufacturing Co., 3M Center, Building 220-10W, St. Paul, MN 55101. $11.95.

Bormann, Ernest G., and Bormann, Nancy C. *Effective Small Group Communication.* Minneapolis: Burgess Publishing Co., 1972. 102 pages. Burgess Publishing Co., 7108 Ohms Lane, Minneapolis, MN 55435. $5.25.

Bormann, Ernest G.; Howell, William S.; Nichols, Ralph G.; and Shapiro, George L. *Interpersonal Communication in the Modern Organization.* 1969. 315 pages. Prentice-Hall, Englewood Cliffs, NJ 07632. $12.95.

Bradford, Leland P. *Making Meetings Work: A Guide for Leaders and Group Members.* 1976. 121 pages. University Associates, 7596 Eads Ave., La Jolla, CA 92037. $10.00 paper.

Burgoon, Michael; Heston, Judee K.; and McCroskey, James. *Small Group Communication: A Functional Approach.* New York: Holt, Rinehart and Winston, 1974. 217 pages. Holt, Rinehart and Winston, 383 Madison Ave., New York, NY 10017. $8.95.

"Burnt-Out Principals." *Newsweek,* 91, 11, March 13, 1978, pp. 76-77.

Doyle, Michael, and Straus, David. *How to Make Meetings Work: The New Interaction Method.* New York: Wyden Books, 1976. 301 pages. Wyden Books, 747 Third Ave., New York, NY 10017. $2.50.

Dunsing, Richard J. *You and I Have Simply Got to Stop Meeting This Way.* New York: AMACOM, American Management Associations, 1978. 164 pages. AMACOM, 135 West 50th St., New York, NY 10020. $9.95.

Fordyce, Jack K., and Weil, Raymond, *Managing WITH People: A Manager's Handbook of Organization Development Methods.* Reading, Massachusetts: Addison-Wesley Publishing Co., 1971. 192 pages. Addison-Wesley Publishing Co., Jacob Way, Reading, MA 01867. $7.95.

Halverson, Don E. *Effective Meeting Management.* Redwood City, California: San Mateo County Office of Education, 1977. 46 pages. ED 173 941. San Mateo County Office of Education, 333 Main St., Redwood City, CA 94063. $2.00.

Jay, Antony, "How to Run a Meeting." *Harvard Business Review,* 54, 2 (March-April 1976), pp. 43-57. EJ 134 472.

Jones, John E., and Pfeiffer, J. William, eds. *The 1979 Annual Handbook for Group Facilitators.* La Jolla, California: University Associates, 1972-1979. University Associates, 7596 Eads Ave., La Jolla, CA 92037. Paper $14.50 each annual; looseleaf $36.50 each.

Lowell, Carl Duane. "The Distribution of Power, Group-Decision, and Behavioral Outcomes," Ph.D. dissertation, University of Oregon, 1972. 296 pages.

Maude, Barry. *Managing Meetings.* London: Business Books Limited, 1975. 70 pages. Business Books Ltd., Mercury House, Waterloo Rd., London SE 1. £5.95.

Parker, Jack T. *The Collier Quick and Easy Guide to Running a Meeting.* New York: Collier Books, 1963. 93 pages. Out of print.

Schindler-Rainman, Eva; Lippitt, Ronald; and Cole, Jack. *Taking Your Meetings Out of the Doldrums.* La Jolla, California: University Associates, 1977. 100 pages. University Associates, Inc., 7596 Eads Ave., La Jolla, CA 92037. $7.50.

Schmuck, Richard A.; Runkel, Philip J.; Arends, Jane H.; and Arends, Richard I. *The Second Handbook of Organization Development in Schools.* Palo Alto, California: Mayfield Publishing Co., 1977. 590 pages. Mayfield Publishing Co., 258 Hamilton Ave., Palo Alto, CA 94301. $16.95.

Snell, Frank. *How to Hold a Better Meeting.* New York: Harper & Brothers, 1958. 148 pages. Out-of-print.

Spaulding, William E. "Undiscovered Values in Meetings." *Journal of Systems Management,* 29, 6 (June 1978), pp. 24-27.

Tannenbaum, Robert, and Schmidt, Warren H. "How to Choose a Leadership Pattern." *Harvard Business Review,* 36, 2 (March-April 1958), pp. 95-101. Also reprinted in *Harvard Business Review,* 51, 3 (May-June 1973), pp. 162-64, *passim.*

This, Leslie E. *The Small Meeting Planner.* Houston, Texas: Gulf Publishing Co., 1972. 234 pages. Gulf Publishing Co., P.O. Box 2608, ATTN: Book Division, Houston, TX 77001. $12.95.

Toffler, Alvin. *Future Shock.* New York: Bantam Books, 1970. 561 pages. Bantam Books, Inc., 666 Fifth Ave., New York, NY 10019. $2.75.

CHAPTER 10: MANAGING TIME AND STRESS

Association of California School Administrators. *An Update on Time Management. ACSA Operations Notebook 8.* Burlingame, California: 1979. 65 pages. ED 172 426. ACSA, 1575 Old Bayshore Highway, Burlingame, CA 94010. $3.50.

Block, Arthur. *Murphy's Law and Other Reasons Why Things Go Wrong!* Los Angeles: Price/Stern/Sloan, 1980. 94 pages.

Born, W. Michael. "Time Management for the Harried Campus Administrator." *Educational Record,* 60, 3 (Summer 1979), pp. 227-33. EJ 211 312.

Colorado State Department of Education. *A School Improvement-Accountability Process Kit. PAK No. 4.6—Managing Time.* Denver: District Planning and Accountability Services, 1975. 35 pages. ED 141 924 MF $0.91 PC $3.65.

Cross, Ray. "How to Beat the Clock: Tips on Time Management." *National Elementary Principal,* 59, 3 (March 1980), pp. 27-30. EJ 219 611.

Douglass, Donna Niksch, and Douglass, Merrill E. "Timely Techniques for Paperwork Mania." *Personnel Administrator,* 24, 9 (September 1979), pp. 19-22. EJ 206 368.

Drucker, Peter F. *The Effective Executive.* New York: Harper & Row, 1966. 178 pages.

Dudley, Donald L., M.D., and Welke, Elton. *How to Survive Being Alive.* Garden City, New York: Doubleday & Co., 1977. 179 pages.

Duignan, Patrick. "Administration Behavior of School Superintendents: A Descriptive Study." *Journal of Educational Administration,* 18, 1 (July 1980), pp. 5-26. EJ 236 676.

Giammatteo, Michael C., and Giammatteo, Dolores M. *Executive Well-Being: Stress and Administrators.* Reston, Virginia: National Association of Secondary School Principals, 1980. 67 pages. ED 180 134. NASSP, 1904 Association Dr., Reston, VA 22091. $4.00.

Giesecke, Carol, and others. *Self-Instructional Module on Time Utilization. D-1 Revising Existing Structures, Document No. 10g, Revised. Independent Study Training Material for Professional Supervisory Competencies.* Austin, Texas: Texas Education Agency; and Department of Educational Administration, University of Texas, 1975. 54 pages. ED 120 989 MF $0.91 PC $5.30.

Gmelch, Walter H. "Release From Stress." Oregon School Study Council. *OSSC Bulletin,* 24, 9, 10 (May/June 1981), pp. 1-75. OSSC, College of Education, University of Oregon, Eugene, OR 97403. $6.50.

Gmelch, Walter H. "The Principal's Next Challenge: The Twentieth

Century Art of Managing Stress." *NASSP Bulletin,* 62, 415 (February 1978), pp. 5-12. EJ 173 486.

Ivancevich, John M., and Matteson, Michael T. "Optimizing Human Resources: A Case for Preventive Health and Stress Management." *Organizational Dynamics,* 9, 2 (Autumn 1980), pp. 4-25.

Kiev, Ari, M.D. *A Strategy for Handling Executive Stress.* Chicago: Nelson-Hall, 1974. 178 pages.

Koff, Robert; Laffey, James; Olson, George; and Cichon, Donald. "Stress and the School Administrator." *Administrator's Notebook,* 28, 9 (1979-80). pp. 1-4. EJ 242 356.

Lakein, Alan. *How to Get Control of Your Time and Your Life.* New York: Signet, The New American Library, 1974. 160 pages.

Lewis, Darrell R., and Dahl, Tor. "Time Management in Higher Education Administration: A Case Study." Paper, American Educational Research Association annual meeting, Washington, D.C., January 1975. 25 pages. ED 104 239 MF $0.91 PC $2.00.

Mambert, W. A. "Busy, Busy, Busy—and Promises to Keep." *Credit,* 6, 6 (November/December 1980), pp. 25-27.

Manuso, James S. "Executive Stress Management." *Personnel Administrator,* 24, 11 (November 1979), pp. 23-26. EJ 210 942.

Quick, James C., and Quick, Jonathan D. "Reducing Stress through Preventive Management." *Human Resource Management,* 18, 3 (Fall 1979), pp. 15-22. EJ 211 009.

Reynolds, Helen, and Tramel, Mary E. *Executive Time Management: Getting 12 Hours' Work out of an 8-Hour Day.* Englewood Cliffs, New Jersey: Prentice-Hall, 1979. 174 pages.

Sexton, Michael J., and Switzer, Karen Dawn Dill. "The Time Management Ladder." *Educational Leadership,* 35, 6 (March 1978), pp. 482-83, 485-86. EJ 175 684.

Smith, Lee H. "A Systematic Approach to Self/Unit/Organization Time Management." In *Defining Leadership. AAUSCU Studies—1980—No. 3,* edited by Hollis Moore and others, pp. 33-49. Washington, D.C.: American Association of State Colleges and Universities, 1980. 49 pages. Complete document ED 192 702. American Association of State Colleges and Universities, Suite 700, One Dupont Circle, Washington, D.C. 20036. $2.50.

Washington, Kenneth R. "Urban Principals and Job Stress." *Phi Delta Kappan,* 61, 9 (May 1980), p. 646.

Weldy, Gilbert R. *TIME: A Resource for the School Administrator.* Washington, D.C.: National Association of Secondary School Principals, 1974. 63 pages. ED 094 475. NASSP, 1904 Association Dr., Reston, VA 22091. $3.00

CHAPTER 11: MANAGING CONFLICT

Bailey, Stephen K. "Preparing Administrators for Conflict Resolution." *Educational Record*, 52, 3 (Summer 1971), pp. 223-39. EJ 045 040.
Frey, Diane, and Young, Joseph A. "Managing Conflict in Educational Settings." *NASSP Bulletin*, 62, 415 (February 1978), pp. 18-21. EJ 173 488.
Kelley, Edgar A. "Principles of Conflict Resolution." *NASSP Bulletin*, 63, 426 (April 1979), pp. 11-17. EJ 197 922.
Lipham, James M., and Hoeh, James A., Jr. *The Principalship: Foundations and Functions*. New York: Harper and Row, 1974.
Nebgen, Mary K. "Conflict Management in Schools." *Administrator's Notebook*, 26, 6 (1978), pp. 1-4. EJ 183 246.
Robbins, Stephen P. *Managing Organizational Conflict. A Nontraditional Approach*. Englewood Cliffs, New Jersey: Prentice-Hall, 1974. 156 pages.
Schmidt, Warren H., and Tannenbaum, Robert. "Management of Differences." In *The Social Technology of Organization Development*, compiled by W. Warner Burke and Harvey A. Hornstein. pp. 127-40. La Jolla, California: University Associates, 1972. 340 pages.
Schmuck, Richard A.; Runkel, Philip J.; Arends, Jane H.; and Arends, Richard I. *The Second Handbook of Organization Development in Schools*. Palo Alto, California: Mayfield Publishing Company, 1977. 590 pages. Mayfield Publishing Co., 285 Hamilton Ave., Palo Alto, CA 94301. $16.95.

CHAPTER 12: SOLVING PROBLEMS

Brooks, Kenneth W. "Delphi Technique: Expanding Applications." *North Central Association Quarterly*, 53, 3 (Winter 1979), pp. 377-85. EJ 206 895.
Burns, Robert J. *Skyline Wide Educational Plan (SWEP) Product Evaluation Report: Educational Goals for the Future (1980's)*. SWEP Evaluation Report No. 2. Dallas: Department of Research and Evaluation, Dallas Independent School District, 1974. 120 pages. ED 109 760 MF $0.91 PC $8.60.
Collison, Brooke B., and Dunlap, Suzanne Fitzgerald. "Nominal Group Technique: A Process for In-Service and Staff Work." *School Counselor*, 26, 1 (September 1978), pp. 18-25. EJ 188 503.
Crawford, John E., and Cossitt, William B. "Effective Decision Making within the Organization: A Comparison of Regular,

NGT, and Delphi Group Processes." Paper, Western Speech Communication Association annual meeting, Portland, Oregon, February 1980. 40 pages. ED 182 786 MF $0.91 PC $3.65.

Cyphert, Frederick R., and Gant, Walter L. "the Delphi Technique: A Case Study." *Phi Delta Kappan,* 52, 5 (January 1971), pp. 272-73. EJ 031 660.

Dalkey, Norman, and Helmer, Olaf. "An Experimental Application of the Delphi Method to the Use of Experts." *Management Science,* 9, 3 (April 1963), pp. 458-67.

Delbecq, Andre L., and Van de Ven, Andrew H. "A Group Process Model for Problem Identification and Program Planning." *Journal of Applied Behavioral Science,* 7, 4 (Summer 1971), pp. 466-92. EJ 048 000.

Folk, Michael. "A Critique of Some Future Prediction Techniques and Their Implications for Educational Planners." *Educational Planning,* 2, 3 (January 1976), pp. 35-52. EJ 144 690.

Gaskell, William G. *The Development of a Leadership Training Process for Principals. Final Report.* Ellensburg, Washington: Central Washington State College, 1973. 59 pages. ED 074 615 MF $0.91 PC $5.30.

Hartman, Arlene. "Reaching Consensus Using the Delphi Technique." *Educational Leadership,* 38, 6 (March 1981), pp. 495-97. EJ 243 844.

Massachusetts State Department of Education. *Force Field Analysis.* Boston: 1976. 17 pages. ED 153 190 MF $0.91 PC $2.00.

Moore, Carl M., and Coke, James G. "Delphi: An Overview, An Application, Some Lessons." Paper, Speech Communication Association annual meeting, Washington, D.C., December 1977. 32 pages. ED 149 403 MF $0.91 PC $3.65.

Mosley, Donald C., and Green, Thad B. "Nominal Grouping As an Organization Development Intervention Technique." *Training and Development Journal,* 28, 3 (March 1974). pp. 30-36.

Rasp, Alfred, Jr. "Delphi: A Decision-Maker's Dream." *Nation's Schools,* 92, 1 (July 1973), pp. 29-32. EJ 079 292.

Sanders, Stanley G. "Force-Field Analysis: A Functional Management System." *Planning and Changing,* 7, 4 (Winter 1977), pp. 143-47. EJ 157 006.

Skutsch, Margaret, and Hall, Diana. *Delphi: Potential Uses in Educational Planning. Project Simu-School: Chicago Component.* Chicago: Department of Facilities Planning, Chicago Board of Education, 1973. 30 pages. ED 084 659 MF $0.91 PC $3.65.

Thomas, Lewis. "What Is Delphi?" *Educational Leadership,* 38, 6 (March 1981), p. 497. Reprinted with permission from Lewis Thomas, *The Medusa and the Snail.* New York: Bantam Books, 1980.

Van de Ven, Andrew H., and Delbecq, Andre L. "Nominal versus Interacting Group Processes for Committee Decision-Making Effectiveness." *Academy of Management Journal,* 14, 2 (June 1971), pp. 203-12.

Vroman, H. William. "An Application of the Nominal Group Technique in Educational Systems Analysis." *Educational Technology,* 15, 6, (June 1975), pp. 51-53. EJ 139 679.

Weatherman, Richard, and Swenson, Karen. "Delphi Technique." Chapter 5 in *Futurism in Education: Methodologies,* edited by Stephen P. Hencley and James R. Yates, pp. 97-114. Berkeley, California: McCutchan Publishing Corporation, 1974. Entire document 510 pages. ED 113 795. McCutchan Publishing Corporation, 2526 Grove Street, Berkeley, CA 94704. $15.20 plus $0.75 handling.

Weaver, W. Timothy. "The Delphi Forecasting Method." *Phi Delta Kappan,* 52, 5 (January 1971), pp. 267-72. EJ 031 659.

Welty, Gordon. "Some Problems of Selecting Delphi Experts for Educational Planning and Forecasting Exercises." *California Journal of Educational Research,* 24, 3 (May 1973), pp. 129-34.

Zastrow, Charles, and Navarre, Ralphe. "The Nominal Group: A New Tool for Making Social Work Education Relevant." *Journal of Education for Social Work,* 13, 1 (Winter 1977), pp. 112-18. EJ 155 404.

INTERVIEWS

CHAPTER 4: SCHOOL-BASED MANAGEMENT

Brown, Larry, educational specialist, Office of District Management, Division of Public Schools, Department of Education, Tallahassee, Florida. Telephone interview, 22 October 1980.
Corey, A. Stanley, superintendent, Irvine Unified School District, Irvine, California. Telephone interview, 27 October 1980.
Gowler, Doug, principal, Sagebrush Elementary School, Cherry Creek School District, suburban-metropolitan Denver, Colorado. Telephone interview, 28 October 1980.
Guthrie, James, professor of education, University of California, Berkeley. Telephone interview, 23 October 1980.
Henriquez, Armando, superintendent, Monroe County School District, Key West, Florida. Telephone interview, 23 October 1980.
Lindstrom, Robert, superintendent, Oak Grove School District, San Jose, California. Telephone interview, 29 October 1980.
Longstreth, James, former superintendent, Alachua County School District, Gainesville, Florida, now professor of education, University of Florida, Gainesville. Telephone interview, 23 October 1980.
Moretti, Ernest, assistant superintendent for instruction, Fairfield-Suisun Unified School District, Fairfield, California. Telephone interview, 28 October 1980.
Pierce, Lawrence C., professor and department head, Department of Political Science, University of Oregon, Eugene. Interview, 22 October 1980.
Prophet, Matthew, superintendent, Lansing School District, Lansing, Michigan. Telephone interview, 22 October 1980.

CHAPTER 5: TEAM MANAGEMENT

Baumgartner, Jay, principal, Madison Elementary School, Rio Linda Elementary School District, Rio Linda, California. Telephone interview, February 1981.
Bontrager, Mark, administrative assistant to the superintendent and former principal, Yakima Public School District, Yakima, Washington. Telephone interview, February 1981.

Coelho, Robert J., superintendent, Attleboro School District, Attleboro, Massachusetts. Telephone interviews, February, June 1981.

Sayler, Dale, principal, Yakima Public School District, Yakima, Washington. Telephone interview, February 1981.

CHAPTER 8: COMMUNICATING

King, Jodie, principal, Vejas Elementary School, Walnut Valley, California. 8 February 1980.